The Second World War was a turning point in Jean-Paul Sartre's intellectual life. Before it, he was an apolitical philosopher and novelist whose work on the nature of human freedom led to *Being and nothingness* and the philosophy of existentialism. The subsequent experience of war and imprisonment led him ever closer to the politics of Marxism and a profound rethinking of the human condition. In *Jean-Paul Sartre and the politics of reason*, Andrew Dobson argues that to think of Sartre's philosophy in isolation from his social and political development is to misunderstand the nature of his general project. He examines Sartre's major post-war writings in detail, in particular both volumes of the *Critique of dialectical reason*. His reading of Sartre suggests that the biographies of Baudelaire, Genet, and Flaubert – so often regarded as tangential to his main work – are in fact central to Sartre's self-appointed task of demonstrating the intellectual and political superiority of Marxism and Marxist method. Dr Dobson makes use of posthumously published works, such as the *War diaries* and volume 2 of the *Critique*, to show that Sartre's *oeuvre* can be read as a developing theory of history, which culminates in the gigantic, unfinished biography of Gustave Flaubert. *Jean-Paul Sartre and the politics of reason* thus provides a clear and readable description of some of Sartre's less familiar works, as well as an interpretation stressing that they are part of a consistent and enduring political project.

Jean-Paul Sartre and the politics of reason

# Jean-Paul Sartre and the politics of reason

## A theory of history

Andrew Dobson

*Department of Politics, Keele University*

CAMBRIDGE
UNIVERSITY PRESS

Published by the Press Syndicate of the University of Cambridge
The Pitt Building, Trumpington Street, Cambridge CB2 1RP
40 West 20th Street, New York, NY 10011, USA
10 Stamford Road, Oakleigh, Melbourne 3166, Australia

First published 1993

Printed in Great Britain at the University Press, Cambridge

*A catalogue record for this book is available from the British Library*

*Library of Congress cataloguing in publication data*

Dobson, Andrew.
    Jean-Paul Sartre and the politics of reason: a theory of history
    / Andrew Dobson.
        p.    cm.
    Includes bibliographical references and index.
    ISBN 0 521 43449 1
    1. Sartre, Jean-Paul, 1905–1980   2. History – Philosophy.
3. Existentialism.   4. Dialectical materialism.   I. Title.
B2430.S34D63   1993
194 – dc20   92-42301 CIP

ISBN 0 521 43449 1 hardback

UP

For my friends in Oxford – then and now

To understand the causal sequence of events and to find somewhere in the sequence one's own place – that is the first duty of a revolutionary.
Leon Trotsky, *My Life: An Attempt at an Autobiography*

Must not think too much about the value of History. You run the risk of getting disgusted with it.
Jean-Paul Sartre, *Nausea*

# Contents

# Acknowledgements

This book was written over a number of years, and more people have contributed to it than can possibly be recorded here. Some, though, were indispensable. Mary Warnock supervised the doctoral thesis from which it is adapted. She will not recognise much of it, but without her calm, encouraging, and authoritative presence the project would not even have got off the ground, let alone see the light of day. Christina Howells provided me with help at a crucial moment during this period, and her work on Sartre since has been an important influence on my own development. My doctoral examiners Steven Lukes and István Mészáros managed to make a daunting experience positively pleasant, and many of their thoughtful suggestions for improvement have been incorporated in this final version.

More recently my Keele University reading-group colleagues Jonathan Dancy, Richard Godden, and John Goode helped reveal aspects of the *Critique of Dialectical Reason* whose existence I had barely suspected, and their readings of chapters 4–7 of this book enabled me to clarify further in print what I had only grasped vaguely round the table. I am most grateful to them for their persistence. I owe a similar debt of thanks to various publishers' referees – all anonymous except for Sean Sayers – who both pointed out shortcomings and made a number of suggestions for changes. I have tried to act appropriately on their wise advice. Quintin Hoare was kind enough to provide me with a proof copy of his translation of volume two of the *Critique* well before publication; this kind of generosity is rare in academic life, and his gesture was enormously helpful to me.

I am indebted to the Leverhulme Trust for providing me with a grant for secretarial help to prepare the typescript, and to Pauline Weston for so quickly and effectively transferring my original script to disc. Without the assistance of either or both, this book would have been much longer in the making. During the latter stages of preparation, Keele University has kindly granted me both study leave and a research fellowship, parts of which I have used to complete this project. I am profoundly grateful for these opportunities. I want, finally, to thank departmental colleagues for their willingness to cover my teaching during my sabbatical term.

Andrew Dobson
Keele University
1993

# Introduction

Intellectual trends in France succeed one another with bewildering rapidity, and nothing seems better guaranteed to secure the death of a French intellectual than to locate her or him in a trend whose time has come – and gone. From this point of view it is customary to report the death of Jean-Paul Sartre three times over: laid to rest first by structuralism, then by post-structuralism and postmodernism, and finally, on 19 April 1980, by the grave-diggers of the Montparnasse cemetery in Paris.

Since this last interment (the only one, incidentally, with any real air of finality about it) Sartre commentators have organised themselves into two camps: those, like structuralists and postmodernists, who decry his 'humanistic optimism', and those who (often nostalgically) defend it. Structuralists argued that Sartre's stress on the subject as a creator of history and of meaning failed to take account of the way in which the subject is itself constituted by various structural relations in, for example, language and the unconscious. Postmodern theory follows much structuralist analysis in focusing on the way in which the subject is constructed, but denies structuralist claims concerning the possibility of objectivity, truth, and the unmasking of 'reality'. In favouring the instability of meaning and unsettled notions of reality postmodernists seem about as far from Sartre as it is possible to get.

Sartre and his supporters, on the other hand, have found all this deeply disabling. The subject, they say, far from being decentered, is in evidence every time it is confronted by a situation, and goes beyond it while preserving it. To believe, as structuralists do, that the subject is 'spoken' by structures is to forget that, while structures do indeed condition, structures are themselves made and remade by the intentional acts of subjects. Further, because the subject lies at the heart of creation, everything human is capable of being understood – in contrast to the vertiginous sense of continually deferred meaning favoured by postmodern theory.

Again, for Sartre, the decentering, or even the disappearance, of the subject is fatally linked to the disappearance of history. Trotsky's affirmation recorded at the beginning of this book confirms that historical

1

understanding is a condition of historical progress. Sartre will claim that, once the subject is erased, the historical process is rendered unintelligible, precisely because it is the *praxis* of subjects that both creates the process and raises the possibility of its intelligibility.

Sartre's optimistic humanism, then, lies in his belief that what human beings make of what they are made to do is more fundamental than what is done to them, and reaction to Sartre since his death has been organised around support or opposition to this point of view. Whatever their differences, though, both camps seem to agree that Sartre was indeed an optimistic humanist. Part of my intention in what follows is to call this interpretation into question by suggesting that Sartre's encounter with Marxism severely dented both his humanism and his optimism. Human intention is undermined by various forms of alienation, and, while Sartre remains optimistic as to the intelligibility of the human condition, he is far less sanguine about the possibility of authentic political progress in the sense of reducing the sum of human suffering.

Sartre begins by famously claiming that we are the possessors of a terrible freedom to create the world. As I show in the first three chapters, however, these intoxicating revelations could not survive his encounter with the dead weight of history in the guise of the Second World War. Sartre discovered his early philosophy of freedom to be inadequate – both internally inconsistent and at odds with the world he found around him. Flung into a maelstrom of events which seemed beyond his control, he determined to develop a practical analysis of the individual's relationship with history – a philosophy of history. In these three chapters I unfashionably stress the political circumstances that motivated Sartre's philosophical development, so that his philosophy is interpreted as a coming to terms with politics rather than – as is customary – simply driven by internally motivated considerations.

The historical narrative in these three chapters takes us up to about 1960, thereby providing the context for the great majority of Sartre's works discussed in subsequent chapters. There are evidently many competing accounts of post-war French history, and I cannot hope to have satisfied everyone in this respect. My intention is only to provide a background, and I hope that the sketches I have made do the job required of them without raising too many questions.

Neither here nor elsewhere have I made use of Sartre's explicitly fictional work. This may seem odd, given that his fiction was motivated by his general intellectual concerns and can hardly be divorced from them. There are, for example, reflections on the nature of history and the difficulties involved in writing it in *Nausea* (Sartre, 1966, pp. 20, 25–6, 63, 88, 104, 138 and 252). I decided against referring in detail to Sartre's fiction, though, because it is not always clear how far the views of his fictional characters are the views of Sartre himself. It would be unwise to jump to the conclusion, for example, that *Nausea*'s Antoine de Roquentin speaks uncomplicatedly for Sartre; such a conclusion would need to be corroborated by careful analysis. Even then, of course, doubts would remain, and there seemed no point in further muddying already turbid waters with exegetical doubts of this sort.

For reasons that will become clear, Sartre's early philosophy of freedom allowed him no possibility of a theory of history, and he needed a platform from which to work. For over a century, left-wing politics had been dominated by the shadow of Marx, and this, together with Sartre's association with the PCF (*Parti Communiste Française*) as the major representative of the radical left in France, made Sartre's encounter with Marxism almost inevitable.

What he encountered horrified him. He found a Marxism defiled by the PCF, locked in a sterile debate revolving around mechanicism, crude materialism, and economism. This, from Sartre's point of view, was a 'revolutionary' philosophy which displaced human beings from the centre stage of history. He was convinced of the importance of Marxist thought, but believed that it had sclerosed into inert dogma. His theory of history developed as he attempted, as he put it, to reintroduce Marxism to humanity.

Through many infuriating dark patches, Sartre provides us with flashes of brilliant illumination. The theme of his dialogue with Marxism is that of historical materialism: the notion that we make history as it makes us. The development of this theory in Sartre, and his attempt to make it intelligible, is my primary focus. Its most formal exposition is to be found in the two volumes of the *Critique of Dialectical Reason*, and chapters 4–7 are devoted to a description of, and commentary on, these two large books.

Once these chapters have been digested it will be clear that Sartre's view of the human condition, and the circumstances that mould it, was markedly more sophisticated in 1962 than it was in 1943. His views on the historical process are not confined to works written in a philosophical vocabulary however. It is part of my argument that his biographies of Baudelaire, Genet, and Flaubert need to be seen as constitutive of his developing theory of history, rather than tangential to it. This is my argument in chapter 8.

Chapters 9–13 rework this development – but this time exclusively from the point of view of his biographical method and its exemplars. Just as the *Critique of Dialectical Reason* is more sophisticated in respect of the circumstances surrounding the historical process that *Being and Nothingness*, so the biography of Flaubert pushes his biographical method towards complexities only very dimly apparent in the Baudelaire and Genet. In chapter 9, then, I describe Sartre's early thoughts on writing biography, derived from *Being and Nothingness*, and go on in chapters 10 and 11 to show how these are played out in the cases of Baudelaire and Genet. In chapter 12 I show how the method is made more complex by themes and categories introduced in the *Critique*, and chapter 13 is devoted to illustrating how this works in Sartre's gigantic (but unfinished) biography of Flaubert.

I hope that the whole book – and especially chapters 4–13 – will be useful to readers unfamiliar with some of Sartre's lesser-known and later texts. I have written these chapters deliberately descriptively with this end in mind, and I have quoted as often as possible from English-language translations with accessibility for the general reader as a principal criterion.

More than with perhaps any other thinker apart from Karl Marx, Sartre's work has been subject to endless debate as to its continuity. A standard argument is that his move from *Being and Nothingness* to the *Critique* represents a radical break, with Marxism replacing existentialism as the vehicle for enquiry (for example, Warnock, 1965). The counter-argument is that themes apparent in his early work (for example, freedom and commitment) resurface later and are merely treated in a more sophisticated fashion (for example, Barnes, 1974).

It will be clear from what I have said already that I side with those who argue for a radical shift in trajectory, but for different reasons. I do not believe that the shift took place solely for internal intellectual reasons, but because his own context and circumstance forced him to re-examine the very basis of his philosophical position (see also, for example, Aronson, 1980). This is not to say that themes present in his early work disappear later on, but that these themes are most fruitfully read against the background of a change in trajectory occasioned by political interest.

At the same time, Sartre's work clearly carries with it reflections on both the nature and the writing of history, and to this extent he makes a contribution to the philosophy of history itself. It is standard practice to divide the philosophy of history into two branches, one concerned with an analytical study of the work of historians (and questions of objectivity, truth, and so on) and the other with the nature of the historical process itself. The first is more common in the Anglo-Saxon tradition, with the second being developed primarily on the continent through the work of philosophers like Hegel, Marx, and Spengler. This second branch – sometimes referred to as the 'speculative' branch – is usually cast as a nineteenth-century phenomenon which has increasingly come into disrepute as it has shown itself ever more incapable of standing up to the kind of scrutiny demanded by the first branch.

In the sense that Sartre seeks to reveal the mechanisms of the historical process, he is clearly in the speculative tradition, but his work is so eclectic and so varied that it defies simple definition. His interest in the general historical process does not preclude an interest in the particular historical event (indeed, it entails it); he is a historian as well as a philosopher of history (as his biographies demonstrate); and he is a teller of stories as well as a teller of (what he would have us believe are) true stories. In these respects Sartre bridges the divide between 'analytic' and 'speculative' traditions in the philosophy of history: he would persuade us of the truth of his system by asking us to test the success of his historical (chiefly biographical) reconstructions. I conclude that in this context Sartre's enterprise falls short of total success, but that his failure (such as it is) is a necessary, and even a heroic, one in that it reveals the tensions inherent in writing specific histories according to a general method – however complex.

So Sartre cannot be easily appropriated as either the last bastion of a discredited humanism or the harbinger of post-humanist trends. Nor, as a philosopher of history, is he comfortably assimilated in either of the two main traditions of the nineteenth and twentieth centuries. But these perplexities are offset by the certainties that give rise to them. Sartre said in 1964, just months before refusing the Nobel Prize for Literature, that his book *Nausea* meant nothing alongside a child dying of hunger. In a new phase of French intellectualism Jean Baudrillard recently affirmed that the 100,000 deaths in the Gulf war were a hyperreal fiction.

It is, of course, invidious to make people representative of epochs, but, as inequality deepens around the world, and relations of subordination show as little sign as ever of being undone, nobody does the sufferers any favours by claiming that they are only as real as their images on the television screen, or that the meaning of their deaths is continually deferred in a self-referential discourse of image or text. Sartre's stubborn affirmation of the human origin of history and its intelligibility and materiality are a guarantee that his death – so often announced as final – will only ever be provisional.

*Part One*

# 1    Marxism in pre-war France

Oh sure, I knew what Marxism was, as I've said many times before, I had
read and re-read Marx, but that is nothing: you really begin to understand
something in context with the world. To understand Marxism meant
above all understanding the class struggle – and that I only understood
after 1945.

(Sartre, 1980b, pp. 77–8)

In respect of the principal concern of this book – Sartre's theory of history
– his relationship with Marxism is important for two reasons. In the first
place, his development of a theory of history is a political project, and only
became possible in its most fully worked-out form once he took an interest
in politics – specifically, Marxist politics. Second, his contact with Marxist
theory provided him with the framework – historical materialism – for his
mature theory of history. These developments will be detailed as the book
proceeds, but it is important to be clear at the outset about the genesis of
his interest in Marxism and, thereby, of his attempts to work out a theory
of history. In this respect Ronald Hayman strikes the right note when he
writes that, 'The philosophical concern with history is less academic than
political' (1986, p. 309).

Sartre once admitted, as indicated by the quotation at the head of this
chapter, that he did not begin to understand Marx until after the Second
World War. It has been suggested that 1945 represented a turning-point in
the reading of Marx in France because, until then, the majority of Marx's
texts had not been translated into French (Poster, 1975, p. 42). It is true
that much of Marx's early work, in particular, remained untranslated in
France even as late as the 1950s, but it is also true that many people there
read Marx and Hegel before the Second World War, and Sartre's reasons
for not doing so cannot be easily explained away by the unavailability of
certain texts. Sartre himself notes that Marx was read at universities in the
mid 1920s, but only 'in order to refute him'. At the same time, 'Communist
students were very careful not to appeal to Marxism or even to mention it
in their examinations; had they done so, they would have failed' (Sartre,
1968, p. 34). The intention of the following few pages is to show that Marx

and Hegel *were* available to interested readers in France before the Second World War (even if only in truncated form or idiosyncratic interpretation) and that Sartre did not read (in the sense of understand) them because his preoccupations precluded such an interest.

Certainly, up until the early 1930s, the influence of Hegel on French thought was negligible, and to the extent that modern France came to Marx in the 1920s through an imported Leninism, much of what early French Marxists knew of Marxism was a Leninist version of his work. Ronald Hayman notes that it was around this time (1925) that Sartre 'was...reading Marx, without taking much in' (1986, p. 55). Sartre himself, in conversation with de Beauvoir in 1974, put the contact with Marx rather later. In response to the question, 'When did you first read Marx?', he replied, 'In my third year at the Ecole Normale. The third and fourth years...I thought I had understood it and in fact I understood nothing' (de Beauvoir, 1985, p. 381). This would have been around 1927–8. Apart from André Breton's surrealists, and a group of young Marxists in the 1920s, no one outside an increasingly Stalinist French Communist Party took a great interest in either Marx or Hegel until Jean Wahl, Lucien Herr, Alexandre Koyré, and Alexandre Kojève, each in different ways, began to incorporate Hegel into the French intellectual tradition. Herr wrote a favourable article on Hegel in the *Grande Encyclopédie* before the First World War, and Jean Wahl wrote on Hegel's 'unhappy consciousness' in 1929 (Hyppolite, 1971, p. 233). In 1931, Koyré began a series of lectures on Hegel's religious thought at the Ecole Pratique des Hautes Etudes. From now on, the Cartesian tradition was under fire and the attempt to rehabilitate Hegel, cut short by the First World War, continued apace.

In 1933, Alexandre Kojève, a Russian emigré scholar, took over Koyré's course at the Ecole Pratique and countered the religious bent of both Wahl's and Koyré's work with a radically naturalistic interpretation of Hegel – particularly the *Phenomenology of Spirit*. For Kojève, Hegel's Absolute Spirit represents humanity – the transcendent God of Christianity is dead and the 'deity' is immanent. To this extent, fulfilment will be this-worldly, and so the entire human enterprise is brought back to earth. Until this Hegel renaissance, French philosophy had hardly even pondered the relationship between reason and history, and social theory, as it had arrived in France through Pareto, Durkheim, and Weber, tended to stress a gloomy irrationality in which the circularisation of elites, *anomie*, and a depressingly routinised social world seemed unsurpassable. But, with the Hegelian discerning of reason in history, the apparently irrational becomes rational, and contradictions become the motive force of history striving for perfection, rather than the conditions for everlasting conflict.

Kojève makes this explicit in his concentration on Hegel's dialectic of the master and slave. The master/slave relationship involves a struggle for recognition, and Kojève stresses that the relation of recognition is such that each depends on the other for his/her existence. From this perspective, the first moment of humanity is necessarily *social* – there can never be a society of isolated individuals because the struggle for recognition must involve interdependence. But the relationship is unstable. Although masters are dependent upon slaves for their status as masters, they are aware that their authority is bestowed by one whom they regard as sub-human, and so this authority is never entirely satisfactory.

Further, according to Kojève's reading of Hegel, the slave pushes humanity towards full self-realisation in seeking to overcome oppression. The master, whose status lends him/her a modicum of prestige, is transcended by the slave who seeks to go beyond the master towards a fuller humanity. The way is now open for Kojève to present a full-blown picture of a revolutionary Hegel, and that is what he does, colouring his interpretation with his own Marxism: 'If idle Mastery is an impasse, laborious slavery, in contrast, is the source of all human, social, historical progress. History is the history of the working slave' (quoted in Poster, 1975, pp. 13–14). To this extent, Hegel was never a reactionary philosopher to the French. They came to him at about the same time as the early Marx was beginning to be widely read, and the two read in conjunction made for a powerful social critique to graft onto the importance granted to subjectivity by the existentialists. However, the full force of the confluence of Hegel, Marx, and existentialism was not to come until the Second World War had broken down much of the established political and intellectual order and left France in ferment.

Kojève's lectures continued uninterrupted from 1933 to 1939 at the Ecole Pratique, and were attended by a number of French intellectuals, among whom were Raymond Aron, Georges Bataille, Jean Desanti, Raymond Queneau, Maurice Merleau-Ponty and Jacques Lacan. It appears that Sartre, although enrolled on the lecture list, (p. 8) never attended: 'So far as I know, Jean-Paul Sartre never attended the lectures of Alexandre Kojève at the Ecole Pratique de Hautes Etudes that so profoundly influenced Maurice Merleau-Ponty or Jacques Lacan' (Aron, 1973, p. xii). Simone de Beauvoir does not mention Kojève's lectures anywhere in her memoirs, and would only seem to have begun reading Hegel herself in 1940 (de Beauvoir, 1965, p. 456). It is important to establish Sartre's relationship with Hegel at this time, because some commentators have overstressed the influence of the Hegelian tradition on existentialism. Wilfrid Desan, for example, claims that Sartre *did* attend Kojève's lectures, and comes to the unwarranted conclusion that, 'the study of Hegel was inspirational in the launching of three separate, singularly powerful movements', one of which he says was the existentialist movement (Desan, 1974, p. 24). However, this is not to say that Hegel had no influence on Sartre's earliest writings, and we shall see shortly that some of his terminology is remarkably similar to that of Kojève's Hegel. Rabil, though, is probably right to suggest that, 'it is difficult to say whether or not there was a direct influence of Kojève on Sartre' (Rabil, 1967, p. 79).

Just as Alexandre Kojève's years of lecturing at the Ecole Pratique were coming to an end, Jean Hyppolite took up the task of presenting Hegel to the French public. Hyppolite taught himself German by reading the *Phenomenology*, and began to produce articles on Hegel while still a professor at the Sorbonne, before publishing the first complete French translation of the *Phenomenology* between 1939 and 1941. Most of Hyppolite's work on Hegel was done after 1945, and so does not concern us here, but even before the Second World War he was keen to redress the balance, believing Kojève's interpretation of Hegel to be 'too uniquely anthropological' (Hyppolite, 1971, quoted in Archard, 1980, p. 6). Yet, despite these disagreements, and bearing in mind Hyppolite's attempt to let Hegel's *Phenomenology* speak for itself, it is plain that both Kojève and Hyppolite were intent on giving France a humanist Hegel, a radical philosopher who asserted the intelligible relationship between reason and history rather than their divorce. This reading of Hegel had a significant influence on the re-reading of Marx that took place in the 1940s and 1950s, and it contributed greatly to the conflict between the dogma of French Communist ideology and the attempt undertaken by various French intellectuals to free Marxism from its determinist shackles. Certainly, Kojève and Hyppolite made the post-war reading of Hegel easier for the French by being steeped in current French philosophical concerns – subjectivity, human freedom – and colouring their Hegel interpretations accordingly. Kojève had read Heidegger's *Being and Time* and Hyppolite was affected by Sartre's *Being and Nothingness*, borrowing its terminology to explain many Hegelian terms. In this way, links between the German and French traditions were forged, paving the way for an exciting reassessment of Marxist theory.

But what of Marx himself in pre-war France? Contrary to Poster's assertion already noted, it seems that a large proportion of Marx's work was available in translation as early as the beginning of this century (Zévaès, 1947, pp. 185–91).[1] Even though Zévaès notes that Joseph Ray's

---

[1] Zévaès notes the following major translations: *Capital*, Joseph Roy 1872–5; *Capital* (abridged), Gabriel Deville 1883. *Communist Manifesto* Laura Lafargue 1882. *The Civil War in France*, published by *le Socialiste* 1886; Amédée Dunois 1925; Bureau d'Editions

first translation of *Capital* in 1883 went 'almost unnoticed' (p. 185) and Gabriel Deville says in his preface to an abridged version of *Capital* in 1883 that this 'masterly' work had been 'sadly, up until now either ignored or distorted in France' (p. 187), the fact remains that the works were there to be read if anyone was so inclined. In an interesting footnote, Rabil reveals that the all-important *Economic and Philosophical Manuscripts of 1844* were translated into French as early as 1927 from a Russian manuscript even before they appeared in German. However, Rabil says that the *Manuscripts* are not mentioned in any of the major Marx bibliographies in France, and concludes that 'this early translation was not widely read, or at least that the milieu was not yet prepared for Marx' (Rabil, 1967, p. 275). It is difficult to have complete confidence in George Lichtheim's generalised assertion that Marx's early writings 'became known in France from 1933 onwards' (Lichtheim, 1966, p. 84), but it is hard to deny that translations were available and that people read them. For instance, Lichtheim himself notes that Henri Lefebvre, an original member of the *Philosophies* group, was already questioning the rigid line of the French Communist Party in 1939, having been deeply affected by the *1844 Manuscripts* (p. 88).

The *Philosophies* group itself is of importance here as probably 'the first Marxist–Leninist group in France' (p. 86). Its members, originally Pierre Morhange, George Politzer (de Beauvoir, 1965, pp. 20–1), Henri Lefebvre, Norbert Guterman, Georges Friedmann and Paul Nizan, founded the journal *Philosophies* in 1924 and, although it lasted for only six issues, the journal represented a positive attempt to interpret Marxism in a humanist light. It might be claimed that the group's approach was so odd that it had little to do with Marxism – certainly its expressed aim to defend 'the spirit, mysticism and liberty' (Fauvet and Duhamel, 1977, p. 117) found little favour with the nascent French Communist Party. Lefebvre himself, when called upon to criticise Sartre's *Being and Nothingness* in 1946, reflected that the *Philosophies* group's steps towards Marxism 'began with an unhealthy, adolescent "existentialism"' (Poster, 1975, p. 115), and de Beauvoir's recollection of the group, whom she met at the Sorbonne, shows how far they were from following a dogmatic Communist Party line:

1933. *Eighteenth Brumaire of Louis Bonaparte*, published by *le Socialiste* 1891; Léon Rémy (published with *Class Struggle in France* in one volume) 1900; Marcel Olivier 1928. *Critique of the Philosophy of Right*, Edouard Fortin 1895. *Poverty of Philosophy* (with a preface by Engels) 1896. *Critique of Political Economy*, Léon Rémy 1899. *Capital* (volumes 2 and 3) Julien Borchardt and Hyppolite Vanderrydt 1900–2. *Contribution to Political Economy*, Laura Lafargue 1909. *Gotha Programme*, published by *l'Humanité* 1922. *Letters to Kugelmann*, Rosa Michel (preface by Lenin) 1930.

According to them, philosophy could not be distinguished from revolution, in which lay humanity's final hope... they were interested above all in manifestations of the Spirit; economy and politics to their mind could only play subordinate roles. They condemned capitalism because it had destroyed the 'sense of being' in man. (Archard, 1980, p. 6)

Small wonder that Lefebvre saw fit to indulge in self-criticism after the Second World War when he came to believe that the Party was the only truly revolutionary force in French politics. To be sure, most of the *Philosophies* group eventually succumbed to the embrace of the Communist Party, and Marxist scholarship deteriorated accordingly. Nevertheless, these people, brought up in the ferment of the introduction of Marx and Hegel to France, never completely forgot 'that assertions and dogmas are poor substitutes for argument' (Caute, 1964, p. 270), and they continued to provide a healthy form of opposition to post-war Party dogmatists such as Roger Garaudy, Jean-Toussaint Desanti, and Jean Kanapa. In contrast to the *Philosophies* group, a number of scientists – members of the Communist Party – were trying to reduce Marxism to 'a method of research' (Poster, 1975, p. 36) through their journal *La Pensée, revue du rationalisme moderne*. Their position accorded well with the Communist Party dogma of the time, ignoring the knotty questions of subjectivity and alienation, and it was precisely *La Pensée*'s approach to Marxism that Sartre was keen to refute after 1945.

Nor was it the case that Sartre himself never came into contact with people interested in, or knowledgeable about, Marxism. He had links with the Trotskyists in the 1930s through Colette Audry, a friend of Simone de Beauvoir, and he was a close friend of Paul Nizan right up until the latter's death at the front in 1940, having first met him at the age of 11 at the Lycée Henri IV (Contat and Rybalka, 1974, I, p. 4). They continued their association at the Ecole Normale Supérieure (which had already begun to develop a politically radical reputation) from 1924 onwards (p. 5 and Cohen-Solal, 1987, pp. 57ff.). Later, Sartre recalled that his concerns for the notions of freedom and determinism went right back to schoolyard conversations with Nizan at La Rochelle, when Nizan told him that any defence of free-will was a 'hopeless position' (Sartre, 1980b, p. 20). So the seeds of friendship were sown early, but, as Nizan's interest in Marxism flowered, he moved closer to the Communist Party and Sartre refused to follow. As has been noted, it is clear that Sartre did read some Marx at this point – probably as much for personal reasons as anything else, since he felt that 'Marxism was challenging me because it was the thinking of a friend and it was cutting across our friendship' (Sartre, 1978d, p. 59), but his commitment did not extend to a full assimilation of Marxism and the action it would entail: 'In any case, he [Nizan] was sure of one thing: the established order must be destroyed. For my part, I was pleased that this order existed so I could take pot-shots at it with words' (Sartre, in foreword to Nizan, 1968, p. 22).

Finally, it does not appear that Sartre had anything to do with the *Cercle de la Russe Neuve*, which in 1936 became the *Association pour l'étude de la culture soviétique*, and with which Nizan was also connected. It would seem reasonable to assume that anyone of Sartre's intellectual status, and with friends moving in Marxist circles, might want to contribute to such a loosely knit organisation of people from the natural and social sciences. Yet so small was the extent of Sartre's political awareness and interest at this time that his nods in the direction of Marxism were limited to a few slighting references and ill-understood applications of theory.

The following exchange demonstrates how retarded was Sartre's appreciation of Marx and Hegel – and even Husserl – in the early 1930s:

POUILLON: Was the real discovery, in terms of importance to you, Husserl?

SARTRE: Yes, but much later. I entered the Ecole Normale in 1924, we passed
   our *agrégation* in 1929, and it was somewhere in the neighbourhood of
   1933...

POUILLON: As late as that?

SARTRE: Yes, no earlier than 1933. I didn't know who Husserl was; he wasn't
   part of the French cultural tradition...

DE BEAUVOIR: We didn't even know who Hegel was!

SARTRE: That's right, we didn't. It was Lachelier who used to say: 'There won't
   be any Hegel as long as I'm around!' And Brunschvig, in his *La Conscience
   Occidentale*, devoted no more than a few pages to Hegel, and not a word
   about Marx! The result, as I have often said, is that I was behind, behind
   in relation to all my fellow students for whom Freud, Marx and surrealism
   represented experiments that they might well argue over and dispute but
   which they nonetheless shared to some degree, experiments which were of
   their own time. (Sartre, 1980b, p. 20)[1]

Of course, it is worth noting here that Sartre would have acquired the ability to read German as a result of his stay in Berlin in 1933 and 1934 when he discovered Husserl. Although spoken German 'was a struggle' for him and apparently prevented him 'from experiencing the love of German women' (Sartre, in Cohen-Solal, 1987, pp. 97 and 99), he could have read Hegel and Marx after this time without even needing to resort to French translations, unavailable or not.

---

[1] At various points in the book I use Sartre's (and de Beauvoir's) own testimony as evidence. Some will argue that there is a risk attached to this, but my view is that even testimony designed to justify the past in terms of the present says something important about the career and development of its source. In this case it is clear that Sartre wishes he had encountered Hegel and Marx earlier than he did, and this serves to underline how important they were to him later on.

Sartre's early perspective was one of individual consciousness transcending situations towards freedom and responsibility. The stress that he laid on such responsibility made him extremely averse to any form of philosophy that might hint at determinism, and, at this stage, Sartre saw such a philosophy in Marx's historical materialism. Although he calls this theory 'fruitful' (Sartre, *Transcendence of the Ego*, quoted in Mészáros, 1979, p. 137), he is concerned that it is based on a 'metaphysical materialism' (p. 138). With half an eye on forthcoming chapters, we should note that Sartre is not rejecting materialism *tout court*, but only a dogmatic and unfounded variety.

At this point, in 1937, Sartre's belief that the 'subject–object duality ... is purely logical' (p. 138) precluded any understanding of a philosophy such as historical materialism, which asserts much more than a merely logical relationship between subject and object. These misunderstandings of Marxism were to continue at least as far as *Materialism and Revolution* in 1946 which, as we shall see, turned Marx's materialism into mechanicism, and his *Anti-Semite and Jew* of late 1944 showed how unprepared Sartre was to accept the role of history in the production of social phenomena. Nevertheless, all these references show that he had read some Marx and Hegel, and Sartre's existential concept of human reality as *negating* a given situation to give rise to something new, based in turn upon a distinction between the in-itself and the for-itself, provides a close parallel with Hegel's ascending dialectic, founded on the nihilating effect of human action: 'I found in about 1939 that I had assimilated many things from Hegel, though I didn't know his work well. I did not really come into contact with Hegel until after the war, with Hyppolite's translation and commentary' (Sartre, 1978b, p. 127). The point now is to try and understand why Sartre never made any great attempt to assimilate Marxism, even though he was, as we have seen, in the sort of social and intellectual milieu which would have made this possible.

Certainly his philosophical preoccupations in the early 1930s had much to do with his by-passing Marxism, for a time at least. In his search for something beyond the dichotomy of reason and history presented by traditional French philosophy, Sartre came across Husserl who gave him a philosophy of *situation*, if not a philosophy of *history*. Simone de Beauvoir famously recalls the force of this discovery when Raymond Aron said to Sartre, 'You see my dear fellow, if you are phenomenologist, you can talk about this cocktail and make a philosophy out of it! Sartre turned pale with emotion at this. Here was just the thing he had been longing to achieve for years' (de Beauvoir, 1965, p. 134).

This 'thing' was a philosophy of realism, a philosophy of the concrete, and it allowed Sartre to preserve the radical freedom of consciousness while placing it in a context, in 'situation'. Sartre was deeply concerned with freedom and imagination, and the flight – as freedom – from the real which the imagination seemed to represent.

At this time, both Marx and Freud were crudely interpreted by Sartre as offering variations on a deterministic theme, Freud's being driven by the unconscious mind, and Marx's by the dead weight of history and circumstance – and there was something about imagination which he felt could not be explained in causal terms: 'There is a disconnection of thought which cannot be explained by determinism. Determinism cannot move on the plane of the imaginary. If it's a fact it will create a fact' (p. 26). So Sartre's philosophy, barely concerned with history and focused almost exclusively on the individual, precluded any great interest in the historical and social philosophy of Marx.

But the point that has never been sufficiently stressed is that Sartre did not take *politics* seriously enough to find anything of more than passing interest in Marx. Marx's work does not constitute simply a body of philosophy, it is also a call to action – political action. Certainly those people interested in Marxism before the Second World War, and known to Sartre, were generally political activists – witness the names in the *Philosophies* group. But Sartre was an 'apolitical litterateur' (Poster, 1975, p. 75). Admiring the Popular Front 'from afar', he did not vote in the 1936 elections, although 'it forced us to emerge from our complete indifference' (Sartre, 1978d, p. 46). He attended few marches (de Beauvoir, 1965, p. 26) and the Communist Party was an organisation to stand by and watch, not one with which to get involved: 'We were Communist sympathisers without a shadow of doubt, but we weren't members. The idea never entered our heads' (Sartre, 1980b, p. 31).

During his stay in Berlin, Sartre seemed blissfully unaware of the Nazi threat, even though Hitler had already come to power. His itinerary was that of the diligent, disengaged student of philosophy: he would read Husserl in the morning and then take a walk through the city, lunching on the way before returning home in the early evening 'usually after all sorts of interesting incidents' (p. 30). Sartre continued to take a detached view of political events right up until the Second World War and revelled in the role of the disinterested observer.

Of course, the whole question of what one has to do to be called a political activist is moot, and Sartre himself has referred to his 'incompetence' at the level of 'technical political action' (p. 308), but he was not even using his pen as a political weapon. He has said that at this time he was an 'anarchist', at least of a 'very special kind' (Sartre, 1978d, p. 45), and evidently intends us to understand by this that political activity was alien to him. Brought up in the magical, lonely world of books, imagination, and security, Sartre could not conceive of solidarity in the name of social change, and his jealously guarded independence was to shadow all his relations with political organisations – the Communist Party in particular. On the occasion of his seventieth birthday, Sartre recalled that he lived like a 'man alone' before 1939: 'That was the evidence on which I based everything I believed, everything I wrote and everything I did in my life before 1939' (p. 46).

The 1938 Munich crisis went some way towards shaking him out of his torpor, as he fought an internal battle between his individualist pacifism and his anti-Nazism. At this point, writes Annie Cohen-Solal, 'Sartre started looking at the world as though he were an actor in it' (1987, p. 125). He began to realise that he did not exist only as an individual, but also as a member of the French community, and as such was threatened by the Nazis along with everyone else in France: 'And that feeling came on top of an experience which, though I had not yet realised it, was not simply an individual experience but a social one: my impressions when I had lived in Nazi Germany for a year in 1933' (Sartre, 1978d, p. 46). Nevertheless, one remarkable interview in the summer of 1939 about the Jewish question catches Sartre's equanimity in the face of coming hostilities:

As far as Germany is concerned, I think that antisemitism among the masses has reached its high point there, and I would not be surprised to see a split between the leaders and the populace developing out of it. Generally speaking, I refuse to see anything lasting in Nazism. It's a temporary outbreak. I don't believe in the advent of the 'Nazi man'. (Contat and Rybalka, 1974, I, p. 175)

Sociality is a vital explanatory theme in Sartre's life-work and I shall have more to say about its practical aspects when I come to consider the Second World War and its effects on Sartre. Suffice it to say at present that the tension between commitment and purity was to pursue him for the rest of his life, but that he was convinced by 1977 that his bourgeois individualism had had too tight a grip on him in the pre-war years: 'I was completely wrong – yes, it's true – not to have become more closely involved in political matters, I mean involved on a practical level, but it was difficult' (Sartre, 1980b, p. 33).

All this by way of showing that scarcity of texts or differences of philosophical preoccupation are not sufficient to explain Sartre's lack of interest in Marxism before the Second World War. Sartre's political concerns are so obviously and closely connected with what he wrote, and why he wrote it, that a full understanding of the move from his pre-1945 position to the work he took on after the war must take into account – at some level – his later political preoccupations. Before the war, history and sociality had no meaning for him, and it took the cataclysmic events of invasion, imprisonment, and resistance to cause him to look beyond himself towards other people, towards the fight for social change and Marxism as a weapon to be used.

This is not to say that the years spent on imagination, individualism, and freedom were wasted. On the contrary, these concerns were essential for the spark with which he infused Marxism after 1945 – without them, his whole project of creating a haven of subjectivity and specificity in the corpus of Marxism would never have begun. It is simply that he found his pre-war concepts – in themselves – to be inadequate with relation to the tasks he wanted to accomplish after the war. At the same time, he discovered the PCF's Marxism to be inadequate as a theory of social revolution, but believed he could revive it by fusing it with the insights he had gained in developing his pre-war philosophy. It is this transfusion that I intend to chart.

# 2 The failure of absolute freedom

Sartre had not determined the freedom/situation relation and was even more vacillating about history. (de Beauvoir, 1978, p. 53)

Sartre's pre-war concerns of the imagination, individualism, and freedom – mentioned at the end of the previous chapter – comprise the principal focus of the present one. I aim to describe these concerns, and then to show how, while amounting to an intoxicating theory of freedom, they fall some way short of providing the foundation for a satisfactory theory of political emancipation.

I shall also show, towards the end of this chapter and in the next, how a complete account of Sartre's shift from freedom to emancipation needs to move beyond an uncovering of the internal momentum in his philosophy (Sartre's famous 'thinking against himself'), towards the needs generated by his nascent political sensibilities. This is not reductively to suggest that his philosophical development was 'caused' by his political development, but rather that his burgeoning concern with history, 'reciprocity', and emancipation was politically motivated, and that the best way to read the theory of history which emerges from these concerns is as a political project.

All three of Sartre's major pre-war works, *The Imagination*, *Sketch for a Theory of the Emotions*, and *Psychology of the Imagination* derive their inspiration from the phenomenology of Husserl. In *The Imagination*, for example, the critical theme of Sartre's survey of the history of psychology is the haphazard way in which the study of the mind and the imagination has been carried out. Sartre asserts that a framework for study must be developed *before* the search for facts takes place, and that this categorisation must be done self-consciously.

He makes a similar point in *Sketch for a Theory of the Emotions*, and says of Husserl that he was 'first of all struck by this truth: that there is an incommensurability between essences and facts, and that whoever begins his researches with facts will never attain to essences' (Sartre, 1962, p. 21). With specific regard to emotion he says, 'If we did not have implicit

20

recourse to the essence of emotion it would be impossible for us to distinguish, among the multitude of psychic facts, this particular group of the facts of emotivity' (pp. 21–2). In other words Sartre believes that our recourse to the essence of emotion proves that we have an intuitive sense of that essence, and says of phenomenology that it 'prescribes that we make our recourse explicit – that we should fix, once and for all by concepts, the content of this essence' (p. 22). At this point, Sartre believed that the phenomenological act of reflection could provide us with absolutely certain knowledge.

Reacting to the criticism that the phenomenological 'bracketing-off' of the world is merely a form of idealism which renders us incapable of understanding the world of our real experience, Sartre writes as follows:

The theorists of the extreme Left have sometimes reproached phenomenology for being an idealism and for drowning reality in a stream of ideas. But if idealism is the philosophy without *evil* of Brunschvig, if it is a philosophy in which the effort of spiritual assimilation never meets external resistances, in which *suffering*, *hunger*, and *war* are diluted in the slow process of the unification of ideas, nothing is more unjust than to call phenomenologists 'idealists'. On the contrary, for centuries we have not felt in philosophy so *realistic* a current. The phenomenologists have plunged man back into the world; they have given full meaning to man's agonies and sufferings, and also to his rebellions. (Sartre, in Mészáros, 1979, p. 142)

Sartre makes the same point in *The Psychology of Imagination* when he stresses that 'consciousness must "be-in-the-world". It is essential that consciousness be viewed as "situated in the world" because if it were not, it would never be able to imagine for it is on the foundation of the world that the image is produced' (Sartre, 1948, p. 208).

It is certainly true that phenomenology is a philosophy of the world, yet the radical separation that Sartre introduces between for-itself (roughly, the subject) and in-itself (roughly, the object) provides for no understanding of the interacting, simultaneous nature of their relationship – there is no interworld, there is only nothingness. Similarly, having designated the in-itself as passive, Sartre stresses the creativity of consciousness. Strictly speaking, the in-itself has no meaning beyond that given to it by the for-itself: '" *Being in itself*". This means that it is neither passivity nor activity. Both of these notions are human and designate human conduct or the instruments of human conduct' (Aronson, 1980, p. 72). But, as soon as human consciousness arises in the world, the in-itself is released from full massivity and takes its meaning from the projects which the for-itself creates. At this point it is important to note, first, the radical distinction between the in-itself and the for-itself; and second, the creative, meaning–giving function of the for-itself. On these two pillars Sartre constructs his theory of absolute freedom.

To begin with, we must be quite clear as to what kind of freedom Sartre is concerned with:

The empirical and popular concept of 'freedom' which has been produced by historical, political and moral circumstances, is equivalent to 'the ability to obtain ends chosen'. The technical and philosophical concept of freedom, the only one which we are considering here, means only the autonomy of choice. (Sartre, 1977, p. 483)[1]

The initial task, then, is to seek the roots of this 'autonomy of choice', and for this we must refer to the importance of imagination in Sartre.

From Husserl's phenomenology, Sartre borrowed the notion that consciousness is *intentional* – it aims at objects beyond itself; indeed, if it did not do so, there would be no thought, for consciousness itself is empty. Now, for Sartre, consciousness performs two entirely different functions in *perceiving*, on the one hand, and *imagining*, on the other. Perception is a passive process whereby consciousness waits to encounter objects in the world, and because it is passive it never encounters these objects as they actually are. For instance, when my consciousness perceives a cube, it may see one, two, or three sides of that cube, but never any more – certainly it can never see all six sides at once. The object of perception has the character of 'overflowing' – there is an infinity of relationships involved in perceiving the cube which I would need an infinitely long time to assess. The object of perception is not graspable in its entirety (Sartre, 1948, p. 24).

However, if I am to *think* about that cube, reflection demands that I see it in an entirety, and the only way to do that is to employ an active consciousness – to use the imagination. However, to the extent that the object itself is constituted by an infinity of relationships, the imagination must ignore many of its characteristics in order to present a clear, well-defined cube – the image has 'only a finite number of determinations' (p. 24). From this perspective, imagination is negative in character – it 'can posit the object as non-existent, or as absent, or as existing elsewhere; it can also neutralise itself, that is not posit its object as existing' (p. 16).

Sartre then asks himself, what must consciousness be in order to imagine?, and it is the answer to this question which provides him with the basis for his theory of freedom as it appears in *Being and Nothingness*. The essence of his conclusion is that consciousness is not simply 'in-the-midst-of-the-world', for then it would be too 'engulfed' to be capable of imagination (*BN*, p. 206). So he writes that, 'For a consciousness to be able to imagine it must be able to escape from the world by its very nature, it must be able by its own efforts to withdraw from the world. In a word it must be free' (p. 207).

[1] *Being and Nothingness*, hereafter referred to as *BN*. A full-length discussion in English of *Being and Nothingness* can be found in Catalano, 1974.

In a sense, then, the imagining consciousness is a powerful source of change – it can create and destroy at will, and nor are the implications of this change necessarily confined to the intentions of consciousness. In the *The Psychology of Imagination*, Sartre makes it clear that he considers the imagination to be an integral aspect of changing the 'real' world. He says that 'in the imagination, which has become a psychological and empirical function, is the necessary condition for the freedom of empirical man in the midst of the world' (Sartre, 1948, p. 209). The implication is that imagination conjures up alternative states of existence, one of which we may then try to establish. The possession of a consciousness capable of imagination comprises our guarantee of a measure of freedom with respect to the material world.

The theme of Sartre's pre-war reflections on the state of the study of psychology, then, is the rescue of consciousness from being just another thing in the world. He reserves for consciousness a high-profile, even transcendent, role in our behaviour with respect to the world. This is made particularly clear in his *Sketch for a Theory of the Emotions*. Sartre's essential criticism of what he calls the 'classic' theory of emotion – best represented by William James – is that consciousness plays no part beyond that of a receptacle through which I am made aware of various physiological manifestations. Consciousness, on this reading, merely responds to stimuli – it has no part to play in initiating or organising the emotion. Sartre congratulates Janet, on the other hand, for attempting to include the psychic element of emotion which he felt that James had relegated to a secondary position.

Sartre, however, is still concerned that Janet's theory is overly mechanistic. The latter refers to a case in which a patient came to see him to unburden herself of a problem, said nothing, and began crying. Janet's interpretation is that the woman cried because she could not say anything, while Sartre hints that she cried precisely in order not to say anything (Sartre, 1962, p. 40). The central point of Sartre's theory of emotions, then, is that emotional behaviour is 'an organised pattern of means directed to an end' (p. 41) and that 'emotion is a specific manner of apprehending the world' (p. 57). For instance, if the world appears to present a 'difficulty' (p. 63), then emotion will try to transform the world, and in doing so we transcend the causality which lends the world its 'difficulty':

So then we try to change the world; that is, to live it as though the relations between things and their potentialities were not governed by deterministic processes but by magic. (p. 63)

So all change wrought by emotion is magical, founded on imagination, and fleeing from the horrific massivity of the world as presented by perception. Needs are not satisfied, rather they are altered to fit in with the demands of the world. Even pain is subject to nihilation:

Once when Sartre had renal colic he caused the doctor some embarrassment by asserting that he was not really suffering. Though the pain was such that it kept him pinned to his bed, he regarded it as a "porous", almost intangible entity. (de Beauvoir, 1965, p. 128).

We must be clear, incidentally, that the organised behaviour which is emotion does not take place on the reflective plane of consciousness. For Sartre, 'the emotional consciousness is at first non-reflective, and upon that plane it cannot be consciousness of itself' (Sartre, 1962, p. 56). In support of this position, he asserts that 'an operation *upon* the universe is generally executed without our having to leave the non-reflective plane. For example, at this moment I am writing, but I am not conscious of writing' (p. 59). Naturally enough, Sartre rejects any equivalence between the non-reflective consciousness and the unconscious: 'unreflective conduct is not unconscious conduct' (p. 61).

Sartre's claim that the majority of our 'operations' upon the universe is accomplished on the non-reflective plane is problematic in that it is hard to square with our experience. Such experience as we have tells us that we absorb the world, reflect on it, and then act, thus moving from the non-reflective to the reflective plane and back again. Sartre indicates that this view is mistaken: 'We tend too easily to believe that action involves a constant passing from the non-reflective to the reflective, from the world to oneself' (p. 58). However that may be, the problems of the relationship between thought and action upon which I have touched constitute a central theme of this chapter in their relevance to Sartre's *Being and Nothingness* theory of freedom.

Sartre begins by asserting that we stand before the world in 'an attitude of interrogation' (*BN*, p. 4). Furthermore, as was the case with the imagination, 'There exists for the questioner the permanent objective possibility of a negative reply' (p. 5). In other words, questioning oneself towards the heart of being reveals the possibility of nothingness, founded on the gap between consciousness and its object, and on the nothingness which is consciousness itself. To this extent, there is an element of *fragility* in being, and this despite the fact that Sartre claims the *totality* of being to be 'beyond all possible destruction' (p. 8). Sartre seeks a way out of this impasse by noting that '*one* being is fragile and not all being' (p. 8), and, as we might expect from an active consciousness, it is the for-itself which brings fragility into the world by opening up the possibility of non-being.

More particularly, Sartre demonstrates in his famous café example that there is a *double* nihilation. If I am looking for Pierre, then all the objects in the café serve as the ground on which I hope to see him – undifferentiated because they are not the objects on which I wish to focus my attention. Each object rises up momentarily, appears as peripheral, and then disappears in the original nihilation which is the whole café. Secondly, Pierre himself is revealed as a 'continual disappearance' which 'slips constantly between my look and the solid, real objects of the cafe' (p. 10).

Finally, I conclude that Pierre is not in the café – this judgement being based on a process of double nihilation. So Sartre claims to have wrenched us away from the causal series which is undifferentiated being, on the basis that the ability to, or rather the necessity of, asking questions presupposes the possibility of a 'nihilating withdrawal' from the world. Nothingness cannot come from the in-itself because it is full massivity, rather it comes into the world through consciousness – and this is the basis for human freedom. Nor is this a mere aspect of human-reality, subject to change in time and place – rather to be human is to be free, necessarily, and with harrowing consequences.

The process of nihilation involves a perpetual separation of effect from cause in that its source is internal. The negations by which I define an existent do not exist. It is true that my desire to find Pierre in the café might be motivated by external factors – for example, I want to give him a letter, or I owe him a drink – but the double nihilation I perform in establishing his absence involves consciousness constituting itself as a negation, and the possibility of negation is (necessarily) always open. Sartre puts it this way:

Inasmuch as my present state would be a prolongation of my prior state, every opening by which negation could slip through would be completely blocked. Every psychic process of nihilation implies then a cleavage between the immediate psychic past and present. (p. 10)

And yet the present becomes the past at the moment I conceive of it – in fact that moment is indefinable – and my life slips towards the future. With the permanent possibility of nihilation, and my engagement in the world, the future is *continually* up for review; and, moreover, I am responsible for it. With this permanent rupture in determinations I am forced to make and remake decisions, no matter how often I have made them before. The gambler must every moment 'rediscover the fear of financial ruin or of disappointing his family' (p. 33) in order to quit gambling. The barrier erected yesterday has fled into the past; I must rebuild it today – only to see it disappear once more at the moment of construction. The gambler, says Sartre, 'is as alone and naked before temptation as he was the day before' (p. 33). So the nothingness which is at the heart of human-reality causes possibilities to be constantly reaffirmed:

Human-reality is free because it is not enough. It is free because it is perpetually wrenched away from itself and because it has been separated by a nothingness from what it is and what it will be. (p. 440)

Thus we can never 'be' – a being which 'is' cannot be free. Our freedom lies in making ourselves and our future: in our projection towards the future we are what we are not, and are not what we are. From this perspective Sartre opposes theorists such as Freud, for instance, who seek to explain an act or a neurosis by reference to the subject's past. Sartre wants to locate it in a global structure which has its locus in the future – as a part of the possibilities towards which I project myself. By 1960, Simone de Beauvoir regarded this refusal to recognise childhood experiences as formative with some disquiet:

Freud's pansexualism struck me as having an element of madness about it, besides offending our puritanical instincts. Above all, the importance it attached to the unconscious, and the rigidity of its mechanistic theories, meant that Freudianism, as we conceived it, was bound to eradicate free-will ... in a clear-minded individual, we thought, freedom would win out over complexes, memories, influences or any traumatic experience. It was a long time before we realised that our emotional detachment from, and indifference to, our respective childhoods was to be explained by what we had experienced as children. (de Beauvoir, 1965, pp. 21–2)

As we shall see, Sartre was eventually to place great stress on early experiences as the genesis of the adult human being.

It is clear from all this that Sartre will have no truck with a philosophy which claims that social change is somehow 'written in history', and will inevitably come about when the contradiction between capital and labour has reached breaking-point. A social situation *by itself* cannot determine my actions. I can only project myself towards action by recognising a *lack* in the world, and I can only recognise a lack by *questioning*: 'In a word, the world only gives counsel if one questions it, and one can question it only for a well-determined end' (*BN*, p. 448). This sentence also contains the politically progressive possibilities implied by the existentialist imperative. In emphasising the active, questioning role of the for-itself, Sartre is in a position to encourage a *participatory* role in the world.

To the extent that Sartre holds that we give meaning to the world by withdrawing from it and approaching non-being through nihilation, he comes close to the idealist position which he wants to avoid:

It would be in vain to imagine that consciousness can exist without a given; in that case it would be consciousness (of) itself as consciousness of nothing. But if consciousness exists in terms of the given, this does not mean that the given determines consciousness; consciousness is a pure and simple negation of the given, and it exists as the disengagement from the certain existing given and as an engagement towards a certain not yet existing end. (p. 478)

It is this relationship between freedom and the given – freedom's 'facticity' – to which we must now turn, for here we see Sartre defining freedom as 'autonomy of choice' rather than 'ability to obtain ends chosen' in order to preserve his position. As early as April 1941, de Beauvoir had doubts about this as she discussed Sartre's philosophy with him while he was on leave:

During the days that followed we discussed certain specific problems, in particular the relation between 'situation' and freedom. I maintained that from the angle of freedom as Sartre defined it – that is, an active transcendence of some given context rather than mere stoic resignation – not every situation was equally valid: what sort of transcendence could a woman shut up in a harem achieve? Sartre replied that even such a cloistered existence could be lived in several quite different ways. I stuck to my point for a long time, and in the end made only a token submission. Basically I was right. But to defend my attitude I should have had to abandon the plane of the individual, and therefore idealistic, morality on which we had set ourselves. (1965, p. 434)

Sartre deals with the problem of facticity, first in general terms under the heading 'The Situation', and then by relating these general remarks to specific instances of the situation – my place, my past, my environment, my fellow human being, my death. He begins by agreeing that brute things can limit my freedom of action, but that my freedom in the first instance must posit the ends and framework alongside which these brute things *appear* as limits. In other words, these things will only seem to be limits if our technique reveals them as such – the important fact is that we have control over the ends posited, our framework and our technique. From this perspective, freedom could not exist without a resisting, brute existent world:

the resistance which freedom reveals in the existent, far from being a danger to freedom, results only in enabling it to arise as freedom. There can be a free *pour-soi* only as engaged in a resisting world. Outside of this engagement the notions of freedom, of determinism, of necessity lose all meaning. (*BN*, p. 483)

Sartre himself admits that by this stage we seem to be asserting an 'ontological primacy of the *en-soi* over the *pour-soi*' (p. 484). Yet he goes on to say that the whole question of ontological primacy only arises once freedom has made its surge into the world. The conclusion is that 'freedom is originally a *relation* to the given' (p. 486) – the in-itself is never seen as a pure given; it is always seen in terms of the ends posited by freedom, and is inseparable from it.

In this context a rock will only appear unclimbable if my project is to climb it. Because that project is freely constituted, I can reassert my freedom by changing the project and, for instance, seeing the rock as a beautiful piece of scenery. Common sense tells us that our freedom has been limited by the sheer brute scale of the rock, yet, as we saw, Sartre is not concerned with freedom as success, but only with freedom as autonomy of choice – we can change the rock from mountain into scenery so as to preserve our freedom. Writing in 1948, Herbert Marcuse noted that, 'The treatise on human freedom has here reached the point of self-abdication. The persecution of the Jews, and "les tenailles du bourreau" [the executioner's pincers] are the terror which is the world today, they are the brute reality of unfreedom. To the existentialist philosopher, however, they appear as examples of the existence of human freedom' (Marcuse, 1948, p. 322). Just one year later, in his *Anti-Semite and Jew*, Sartre himself was to criticise the bourgeois humanism which claims that all people are free.

Similar arguments are used for all the remaining instances of facticity. Sartre asserts that the *place* in which I live (in all its geographical and climatic particulars) has no meaning without reference to the individual subject who lives there. There is no such thing as a place 'in isolation' – the place cannot be seen as limiting unless it is related to the end which the subject has freely posited: 'It is the accessibility or inaccessibility of this end which defines place. It is therefore in the light of non-being and of the future that my position can actually be understood' (*BN*, p. 493).

In relation to my past as facticity, Sartre agrees that it is a backdrop, unchosen, against which I must make my future: 'Every action designed to wrench me away from my past must first be conceived in terms of my particular past; that is, the action must before all recognise that it is born out of the particular past which it wishes to destroy' (p. 496). Freedom thus becomes the choice of an end in terms of the past; and yet although the past is ossified as brute, unchangeable fact, how I choose to interpret that past in relation to the total project which is my being, is my decision – I *create* the past. I only lose my past once I am dead, and its creating is taken over by other people. A corollary of this is that no particular event can take on a definitive meaning until human history has ended – for Sartre, Hegel's 'owl of Minerva' hoots at the end of human endeavour, not at the end of a historical epoch.

As for the third specific, Sartre makes a distinction between environment and place: 'My "environment" must not be confused with the place I occupy and which we have already discussed. My environment is made up of the instrumental-things which surround me' (p. 504). But the argument against certain instruments being a hindrance to my freedom remains the same – their 'coefficient of adversity' must be defined in terms of my project. If my bicycle tyre is punctured and this is to cause a modification of my project, then it must do so subject to two reservations. First, that the change in environment cannot *of itself* occasion a change of project; and second, that I must apprehend the puncture as a *lack* in the situation. Sartre concludes that, 'This does not mean that it is always *possible* to get around the difficulty, to repair the damage, but simply that the very impossibility of continuing in a certain direction must be freely constituted' (p. 506).

For the Sartre of 1943, then, freedom lies in the ability to redefine projects – providing for successful conclusions to these projects is irrelevant. As a theory of political freedom this is clearly inadequate, and its shortcomings are brilliantly exposed in an article by Herbert Marcuse to which I have already made reference (Marcuse, 1948). Factory workers may decide that their initial project involves the demand for ownership of the factory, yet as that project becomes unrealistic in the face of management intransigence, they redefine the project and demand a reduction in working hours instead. Yet still the management represents a 'difficult' world, and the workers' project is again reduced – this time, perhaps, to the demand for a small wage rise. Throughout this confrontation, the workers retain their freedom in Sartre's terms, but *political* freedom lies elsewhere; in this case with management.

Looking back at his work in 1977, with 30 years experience of politics grafted onto the heady flights of pre-war imagination, Sartre said that,

There are things I approve of and others I look upon with a feeling of shame. Among the latter – and I've already gone on record on this point – is what I wrote in 1945 or thereabouts to the effect that, no matter what the situation might be, one is always free. And as examples I noted that a worker is always free to join a union or not, as he is free to choose the kind of battle he wants to join, or not to join. And all that strikes me as absurd today. There's no question that there is some basic change in the concept of freedom. I still remain faithful to the basic notion of freedom, but I can see what can modify its results in any given person. (Sartre, 1980b, p. 58)

Besides an inadequate theory of freedom, Sartre's 1943 philosophy contained another major stumbling-block in the path of effective political action – having derived an individualist ontology, he pushed it to such an extreme that the notion of *sociality* could have no place in it. For Sartre, the existence of others is no problem – it cannot be proven, but by their look they 'let themselves be seen' (*BN*, p. 512). In fact, at the root of the question of other people, there is the fundamental assumption that there *is* another – another which is not-me. Once the other is revealed to me, I am aware of a consciousness which organises the world in spite of me, and as such constitutes a threat to my supremacy. This person's intentional consciousness takes my world from me and towards her/him and I become an object for that consciousness: 'My freedom is alienated in the presence of the other's pure subjectivity which founds my objectivity' (p. 375).

The upshot is that the fact of the other's existence results in the 'collective ownership of techniques' (p. 512), and I am of necessity thrown in the midst of others and in the midst of these collective techniques – organisation, road signs, and instructions appear before me, pre-ordained. Sartre can only confirm what we might expect of freedom in this situation – i.e. that, 'the only positive way which I have to exist my factual belonging to these collectives is the use which I constantly make of my techniques which arise from them' (p. 512).

In other words, my ends and choices have to be constructed on top of a world that is *already* constructed, and Sartre seems unsure as to whether this constitutes a limit to freedom or not. On the one hand he says that, 'we have shown that the existence of meanings which do not emanate from the *pour-soi* cannot constitute an external limit of its freedom' (p. 519), and yet then, having established that the other confers meaning on me – making me a given rather than a giver – he asserts:

In short, by the fact of the other's existence, I exist in a situation which has an outside and which, due to this very fact, has a dimension of alienation which I can in no way remove from the situation any more than I can act directly upon it. This limit to my freedom is, as we shall see, posited by the other's pure and simple existence – that is, by the fact that my transcendence exists for another transcendence. (p. 525)

The conflict engendered is founded on the other's transcendence, and this freedom makes subject–subject relationships fraught with difficulty. Sartre preserves the basic character of these relationships in the *Critique of Dialectical Reason*, but there he gives them a material basis. Here, in *Being and Nothingness*, to begin with, communication will be inadequate. The words I write or speak are taken from me as soon as they are written or uttered, and are taken up by another freedom to be interpreted as s/he wishes: 'I cannot even conceive what effect my gestures and attitudes will have since they will always be taken up and founded by a freedom which will surpass them and since they can have a meaning only if this freedom confers one upon them' (p. 373). To this extent, I will never know if I am communicating what I want to, and likewise I never know if I am understanding correctly what the other says to me.

Given this conflict of transcendent freedoms, Sartre concludes that there are two attitudes I can take towards the other. Either I recognise that through the other's look I am objectified and then try to transcend that objectification by making the other an object for me; or I can try to appropriate that freedom without it losing its transcendent character.

These attitudes are doomed to infinite circularity as I switch from free subject to imprisoned object, or 'sadism' to 'masochism' (pp. 364–410). In attempting to objectify the other, I seek to turn him/her into an instrument, to assert my transcendence by making the other pure in-itself: 'The sadist has reapprehended his body as a synthetic totality and centre of action; he has resumed the perpetual flight from his own facticity. He experiences himself in the face of the other as pure transcendence' (p. 399).

However, this attempt to objectify is bound to fail, for, in order to treat the other as object, I must first recognise it as subject, and as requiring objectification. Sartre is to carry this notion over to his analysis of the relationship between native and colonialist. The colonialist treats the native like a dog, but can only do so while he realises that, at bottom, the native is human, pure subjectivity. Hence the unstable nature of colonialist regimes, and hence the possibility of liberation from colonialism.

Now, once I have recognised that the other is a subject (as I must do in order to objectify him/her), I am flung back to the other pole in my relationship with the other, that of masochism. As the other's subjectivity bears down on me, I retreat into myself as an object for the other, 'I refuse to be anything more than an object' (p. 378). Yet this attempt, too, must fail. It is necessarily impossible for me to see myself as an object, for it is through my own transcendence that I try to be transcended. Thus with every attempt I make to objectify myself, my 'objectness' slips away from me and 'this effort is accompanied by the exhausting and delicious consciousness of failure' (p. 379) as I realise my subjectivity and slip back towards sadism: 'Even the masochist who pays a woman to whip him is treating her as an instrument and by this very fact posits himself as a transcendence in relation to her' (p. 379). In this way, we are tossed back and forth between the two reefs of sadism and masochism, or subjectivity and objectivity. Nor is this a dialectical relationship, but rather a circular one as 'the failure of one [attitude] motivates the adoption of the other' (p. 363).

As we become resigned to this situation, we lapse into *hate* (p. 410). Realising that no union with the other is possible, we demand a world in which our freedom remains supreme, as it did before the look of the other reduced us to objectivity. This is tantamount to wishing a world without others; to hate is to wish the death of the other. Nor is this simply the death of one another, but of *all* others; in hate I demand that mine be the only transcendence in the world. But again even hate is doomed to failure, for in order for it to come about I implicitly recognise that others do exist and that 'conflict is the original meaning of being-for-others' (p. 364). Again, this view is preserved in the *Critique* but given a material basis – in this case the embeddedness of human relationships in an apparently untrans-cendable condition of scarcity.

But here Sartre has just one more notion of community to dispose of before he can claim to have founded a philosophy based on unresolvable conflict, and this he discusses under the two headings 'us-object' and 'we-subject' (pp. 415–30). Essentially, the us-object corresponds to the subject who is looked at by another subject and thus becomes an object for the other. If I am with a person, or even walking behind him/her in the street, and we are looked at by another, we become a community in the sense of community-as-object. In other words, we are dependent upon the look of the other for our community – plainly this is not the kind of community that political unity envisages. Yet such is Sartre's explanation of class-consciousness (p. 420). The class is constituted, not by objective or historical conditions, but by the subjective awareness that the collectivity is considered to be so by a consciousness which transcends it; i.e. a 'third', be it a 'master', 'feudal lord', a 'bourgeois or a capitalist' (p. 421).

To the extent that I 'experience myself existing for the other outside any individual experience of a look' (p. 42), it is also possible to experience the community of the us-object without the look of the third – there is always the permanent objective possibility of this happening. This we-subject is constructed in a rather more complicated fashion, and presents greater problems for Sartre. As he rightly says, the we-subject experience comes to us from the world, but he dismisses it as being of no ontological importance – rather it is a 'psychological' phenomenon stemming, for instance, from 'the fact that I am engaged with others in a common rhythm which I contribute to creating' (p. 424). It is true that through my transcendence I freely realise this project, but this amounts to a modification of consciousness; unstable because it is subject to the appearance and disappearance of organisations, secondary because its experience is subordinate to the ontological fact of conflict. It in no way corresponds to 'a real unification of the for-itselfs under consideration' (p. 424). The we-subject is provisional.

In summary, Sartre has disposed of the notion of community with two deft strokes. First, he has defined an ontology such that the only basic truth is the transcendence of the for-itself. Having made it transcendent, and thus having asserted its absolute freedom, it is inevitable that conflict will be the original meaning of intersubjectivity. The ontological fact of the solitary for-itself means that the master–slave relationship can never be transcended: a universal consciousness can never be derived from the existence of separate consciousnesses, for each consciousness is a universal. And second, as soon as Sartre catches a glimpse of historicity he ducks his head and lets it fly by. Near the end of his discussion of the we-subject, he describes it as: 'a psychological experience realised by an historic man immersed in a working universe and in a society of a definite economic type. It reveals nothing particular; it is a purely subjective *Erlebnis* [experience]' (p. 429).

The fact is that the we-subjects of the kind Sartre describes do exist, and they should not be rejected as peripheral for the sole reason that they do not accord with his ontology. Yet in 1943, Sartre did not have the equipment to make any more than a sweeping rejection of such solidarity as the we-subject represents – the 'historic man immersed in a working universe' was a totally alien concept. Furthermore, he had no interest in it – he was concerned with the activities of transcendent consciousness, not with the activities of rooted human beings.

For the same reason, Sartre at this stage appears unconcerned that he is unable to found a morality on the ontology he has developed in *Being and Nothingness*. Political action requires a set of values, a standard by which to judge the world, a goal to be attained. Sartre runs through the catalogue of failures of sadism and masochism, indifference and desire, and concludes that 'l'homme est une passion inutile' (Sartre, 1943, p. 678) – usually translated as 'Man is a useless passion' (*BN*, p. 615) – contingent and existing without reason. Sartre's last word on the issue in *Being and Nothingness* is an oft-quoted footnote at the end of his discussion on hate: 'These considerations do not exclude the possibility of an ethics of deliverance and salvation. But this can be achieved only after a radical conversion which cannot be discussed here' (*BN*, p. 412).

The 'radical conversion' is left undefined, but it would seem to have something to do with historicising humanity and rejecting the analytic distinction between the for-itself and the in-itself. Sartre himself: 'That's it. I have always thought that morality did exist. But it can only exist in concrete situations, therefore it pre-supposes man actually involved in a world, and one sees what happens to freedom in it. In other words, *Critique de la Raison Dialectique* is the sequel to *Being and Nothingness*, and morality can only come afterward' (Sartre, 1980b, p. 77).

This reflection, made with considerable hindsight, finds support among the enormous quantity of pages which Sartre wrote immediately after the Second World War, collected posthumously under the title *Cahiers pour une morale*. Indeed, the title is misleading as the topics covered in Sartre's two notebooks vary enormously. He deals, among other things, with violence, Christianity, the roots of oppression, and the nature of prayer, and he deals with them all within the ontology developed in *Being and Nothingness*.

As far as morality is concerned, Sartre is clearly opposed to any notion which seeks to abstract it from a context. He takes, for example, the rule 'one must not lie' and observes that this means 'in each case and whatever the situation' (Sartre, 1983, p. 248). His complaint about such a rule is that 'the end is posited outside of any consideration of the situation or of the world' (p. 248). The problem with such an approach, says Sartre, is not only that recommendations for a decision should take into account the situation surrounding that decision, but that failure to do so implies a misunderstanding of the position of the human being in a resisting world. Sartre comments that such an attitude treats the freedom of the human being as if it were the same as the freedom of God – 'the absolutely free creativity' (p. 249).

One cannot make an abstract universal of morality, says Sartre, because the concrete social situation changes with time. Near the beginning of the first notebook, he refers to the problem of collaboration or resistance, clearly with his war experience still in mind. He says that in 1940 he demanded of each French citizen that s/he refuse to collaborate, but goes on to say that in the event of a war between Russia and America, and another invasion of France, the answer would not necessarily be the same.

'A Platonic Good', says Sartre, 'which would exist in and for itself would have no meaning' (p. 573). Good cannot be divorced from the subjectivity which decides what it is to be – my relationship with Good is defined by the fact that it is something in my future towards which I move by transcending myself: 'Good cannot be conceived of outside of an active subjectivity' (pp. 573–4). Good is constantly to be made, and is constantly in question – it is essentially fragile. Anyone who would see in Sartre a definition of morality of the type 'Good is such-and-such', misreads the Sartrean version of the individual's relationship with the world. The individual is the creator of morality: 'Man must be considered as the being through which Good comes into the world' (p. 574).

The *Cahiers* takes us no nearer, concretely, to the 'ethics of deliverance and salvation' to which Sartre refers in *Being and Nothingness*. In his notebooks he treats morality as a feature of the human condition entirely within the framework of the ontology developed in *Being and Nothingness*. While being internally consistent, this treatment does not satisfy the desire to know how to behave morally, and many were led to criticise this lack of concrete advice – a criticism to which we shall see Sartre replying in *Existentialism and Humanism*.

It seems that the conversion to which Sartre refers in his *Being and Nothingness* footnote, and which he deems necessary for his ethics, would indeed have to be radical. Our contingence and absurdity are founded on our freedom, which in turn is founded on the absolute separation between subject and object – the basis of Sartre's ontology. How could any 'radical conversion' on my part *within* that ontology *affect* the ontology? Sartre must reject the separation between subject and object and instead look to the relations between them, both internal and external, in order to see their reciprocal interdependence.

In this context, then, *Being and Nothingness* is notable for its lack of a sense of history. Sartre has so constructed his ontology that the *situation* in which consciousness finds itself means very little, and the interactions *between* consciousness and situation mean even less. As Sartre sums up the book: 'I tried to offer a certain number of generalities about man's existence, without taking into account the fact that that existence is always situated historically, and that it is defined by that situation' (Sartre, 1980b, p. 76). However, by the time *Being and Nothingness* was published, Sartre had discovered history in the form of the German invasion of France, an event that transformed his life and provided for an increasingly complex world-view.

# 3 Force of circumstance – World War Two and beyond

> The war really divided my life in two...I abandoned my pre-war individualism and the idea of the pure individual and adopted the social individual and socialism. That was the turning point in my life: before and after. Before, I was led to write works like *Nausea*, where the relation to society was metaphysical. After, I was gradually led to write the *Critique of Dialectical Reason*.
>
> (Sartre, 1978d, p. 48)

> In 1944, Sartre thought that any situation could be transcended by subjective effort; in 1951, he knew that circumstances can sometimes steal our transcendence from us, no individual salvation is possible, only a collective struggle.
>
> (de Beauvoir, 1978, p. 254)

There can be no doubt that the war years effected a decisive change in Sartre. 'On his way into the tunnel, he is a high-school philosophy teacher with two published books, an isolated person, an individualist hardly involved in the affairs of this world, totally apolitical. On his way out, he is a writer who spreads his talents over different genres, politically active and intentionally so', writes Annie Cohen-Solal (1987, p. 131). The Second World War was a watershed in his life during which he tempered his individualism with an awareness of solidarity, gained a new respect for history and its effects on an individual life, plunged into the arena of political action, and began to understand the value of Marxism as a guide to such action.

The experience of war mobilisation itself was intensely social for Sartre:

One day in 1939, I received a mobilisation slip and had to go to the barracks in Nancy to join other men I didn't know who had been mobilised as I had been. This was what made the social aspect enter my mind. I suddenly understood that I was a social being when I saw myself torn from where I was, taken away from the people who mattered to me, and put on a train going some place I didn't want to go, with other fellows who didn't want to go any more than I did, who were still in civilian clothes like me, and who like me were asking how they had ended up there. When I looked at these fellows as I passed them in the barracks where I was pacing up and down not knowing what to do, I saw something they had in common despite their differences, something I shared. They were no longer simply like the people I had known in my *lycée* some months before, when I did not suspect that they and I were social individuals. Until then, I had thought that I was above everyone else. Through this mobilisation I had to encounter the negation of my freedom in order to become aware of the weight of the world and my ties with all the others and their ties with me. (Sartre, 1978d, pp. 47–8)

Sartre's life as a weather observer at Brumath was hardly trying, yet, despite the lack of action, changes were being wrought in his attitudes. In early February 1940, he managed to get a week's leave to visit de Beauvoir in Paris. She wrote that,

Sartre was thinking a good deal about the post-war period; he had firmly made up his mind not to hold aloof from politics any longer. His new morality was based on the notion of 'genuineness', and he was determined to make a practical application of it to himself. It required every man to shoulder the responsibility of his situation in life and the only way to do that was to transcend that situation by engaging upon some course of action ... It will be clear that a radical change had taken place in him – and in me too, since I rallied to his point of view immediately; for not so long ago our first concern had been to keep our situation at arm's length by means of fantasy, deception and plain lies. (de Beauvoir, 1965, pp. 428–9)

Having described the 'magical' changes of the world effected by consciousness in his study on the emotions, Sartre now began to conceive of change in a different way. In the face of history, freedom is compromised, 'magic' is powerless, and change must stem from action, soiled and vulgar, in the world.

And still the crowds pressed in. De Beauvoir's account of Sartre's return to duty is heavy with people: 'Crowds of soldiers and their womenfolk making for the underground passage ... this departure as part of a collective mood ... all these men and women ... two crowded trains ... a long line of women ... closeness and solidarity ... violent feeling of collective tension in the air' (p. 430).

As it turned out, this experience of intimacy was a preparation for what was to come, for, on 21 June 1940, Sartre was captured by the Germans without having fired a shot, and in September he was transferred to Stalag XII at Trèves. Once again he experienced a physical closeness to which he was wholly unaccustomed, suggesting that his new-found sense of solidarity was not born so much of a sharing of the 'shame of defeat', as David Archard would seem to indicate (Archard, 1980, p. 28), but had far more to do with the intense physical intimacy which prison life demanded. Sartre himself:

There were, as you doubtless know, open toilets. Well, let me tell you there's nothing quite like going to the toilet in the open, surrounded by your fellow-prisoners, for breaking down elitism in whatever form it might exist. There you have a beautiful example of where idealism disappears. The point I'm trying to make, then, is that this constant physical intimacy, with its constant communication around the clock, was a sign of the kind of communication that existed. (Sartre, 1980b, pp. 49–50)

Moreover, Sartre was to miss this intimacy on his return to Paris from imprisonment. In a cafe, the drinkers 'seemed more distant than the stars', each one 'shimmering comfortably in their tubes of rarefied gas'. 'I had rejoined bourgeois society', he says, 'where I would have to learn to live once again at a "respectful distance". This sudden agoraphobia betrayed my vague feeling of regret for the collective life from which I had been severed for ever' (Sartre, 1955, p. 178). At this point Sartre decided to become involved in political resistance work. With varying degrees of success he worked with a close group of friends (Marxist and non-Marxist) in a group called *Socialisme et Liberté* (Socialism and Liberty) and then, in 1943, he joined the Communist-dominated *Comité National des Ecrivains* (National Committee of Writers).

Once discovered, he never forgot the notion of sociality, and the issue of the means and occasions by and in which it could be engendered was to occupy him from then on. His burgeoning attempt to understand its mechanisms received its fullest treatment in the *Critique of Dialectical Reason*. The stark contrast between the community of Sartre's war life and the isolated, conflicting consciousnesses of *Being and Nothingness* needs no stressing, and his experience of the former was buttressed by the 1944 Paris uprisings.

At that time Albert Camus was editor of the clandestine newspaper *Combat*, and he asked Sartre to do a series of articles on the summer uprising. As he walked round the streets, Sartre saw people becoming rebels before his eyes – 'The street has once again become – as it did in 1789 and 1848 – the theatre for great collective movements and social life', and 'In this time of drunkenness and joy everybody feels the need to plunge back into the collective life' (Contat and Rybalka, 1974, I, p. 101). In 1945, writing about the liberation of Paris, Sartre drew a direct comparison between the storming of the Bastille and the events of August 1945, holding that both had the characteristics of 'festival' and 'apocalypse' (p. 126). This 'spontaneous organisation of revolutionary forces', this 'explosion of freedom, the disruption of the established order, and the invention of a spontaneous and effective order' (Contat and Rybalka, 1974, II, p. 163) proved seductive for Sartre, and the events at the Bastille in 1789 were to become a central issue in the anthropology of the *Critique*. There can be no doubt that his concern for sociality was forged during the war years of collective action, and it is of some significance that the same man who wrote that 'hell is other people' could also revel in this spontaneous Parisian triumph of revolution over 'seriality'.

A second burgeoning concern emerges from a study of his *War Diaries*: how to write good history. Even at this very early stage Sartre is searching for a historical method, and as time went by this search became more and more the focus of his intellectual attention, culminating in the gigantic assault on Flaubert in *The Family Idiot*.

In his *Diaries* Sartre claims that he had already discovered historicity through Heidegger before he collided with it at the beginning of the war: 'it [Heidegger's influence on Sartre] supervened to teach me authenticity and history just at the very moment when the war was about to make these notions indispensable to me' (1984, p. 182). But it seems that the principal reason for these reflections on history and historiography was a reading of Raymond Aron's *Introduction à la philosophie de l'histoire* (Sartre, 1984, p. 296).

In the first place he is concerned at Aron's suggestion that 'any effort to grasp a historical event *as it was* (and not as it appeared through layers of technical or cultural significations, through prejudices themselves historical, or through postulates of an individual philosophy) appears [to be] a recourse to God. The event itself is the event as it would appear to God' (p. 204). Sartre sees some sense in this, particularly in view of the fact that 'the historian is historical', but he cannot agree that 'a fact can be absolutely only "for" an absolute being' because he refuses what he calls 'this reduction of the in-itself to being-for'. On the contrary he writes that, 'I think I have shown in the course of these notebooks [which in many respects amount to a dress-rehearsal for *Being and Nothingness*] that being-for can only appear against a background of in-itself of which it is the nihilation' (pp. 204–5).

This amounts to an assertion of the 'bruteness' of facts, but once Sartre has shown that brute facts exist ('The fact *is*, quite simply. Not in God's eyes – in itself' [p. 206]) he then has to show that they can be known. In this particular passage in the *War Diaries* Sartre gives no indication of how he is to deal with the problems associated with the situated historian. How is the historian, always already immersed in history, to get a purchase on the flow of events of which s/he is a part? On the face of it, it seems that in knowing, the historian will irremediably change the known. This is neatly expressed in *Le Sursis* in 1942 where the war is described as 'the totality of all my thoughts, all Hitler's words, all Gomez's actions, but nobody is there to do the adding up' (quoted in Hayman, 1986, p. 308).

A little over two weeks later in his notebooks Sartre returns to the question of history-writing, this time in the context of a reading of Emil Ludwig's *Kaiser Wilhlem II*, and comes to the conclusion that 'the event is strictly indescribable' (Sartre, 1984, p. 300). The reasons for this are complex, but can be summarised as follows. In the first place, Sartre approvingly quotes Marx's dictum that men are 'both the authors and actors of their own drama' (p. 298). He takes the example of a particular play being performed at a particular place in a particular year, and writes that this situation is a human one inasmuch as 'it's an object *for* consciousnesses which converge *towards* it, and it exists only in relation to consciousnesses'.

But then, he continues, 'what's much less human and rational – what recaptures author, spectators and players in the indistinction of an existence *in-itself* – is the *fact* that all these consciousnesses have converged towards a single play, on 6 May 1680, at the Hotel de Bourgogne' (p. 299). This, then, is the 'event' – 'a certain synthetic unity of consciousnesses [existing] in the mode of the *in-itself*'. The *content* of this event, says Sartre, is 'entirely human', but 'the unity itself – *qua* existence *in itself* – is radically inhuman' p. 299).

Moreover it is this 'inhuman' quality of the event which makes it 'indescribable', as we saw Sartre pointing out above. In this respect the historian is engaged in an impossible task if, as Sartre asserts, 'it's this event – in its absolute existence – that the historian aims for' p. 299). At this point it is worth recalling Sartre's refusal, noted earlier, to accept that, 'If I ask what a fact is absolutely, I receive the answer back that a fact can be absolutely only "for" an absolute being – so I'm referred back to God' (p. 204). In the light of his characterisation of events as partially 'inhuman', it now seems clear that the best Sartre can do is to assert the 'factness' of facts while believing them to be nevertheless indescribable – and this for reasons which he earlier rejected as being 'idealist', i.e. that a fact can be absolutely only for an absolute being. Now we see that the indescribable nature of events is due to the 'inhuman' aspect of the event being inaccessible to the human historian. This question of intelligibility is raised in great and continuing detail in the *Critique of Dialectical Reason*. There, Sartre has at his disposal a tool – dialectical reason – which he lacks here, and which he feels can, if properly used, lead to intelligibility.

In these reflections on Ludwig's *Kaiser Wilhelm II* Sartre raises another historiographical problem which he expresses as follows:

I recognize, with Aron, that in the explanation of the historical event as in its comprehension, various layers of signification may be found. And these layers of signification – each at its appropriate level – allow one to describe the evolution of the historical process in an adequate manner. But these significations are parallel, and it's not possible to move from one to another. (p. 294)

The fact is that Sartre *wants* to be able to move from one to another, and in large part the development of his historical method consists in him showing how it is possible – indeed essential – to do this. Here he cursorily rejects the strategy of lumping all the layers of explanation together and expecting a unity to emerge:

A common error of historians is to put these explanations on the same level, linking them by an 'and' – as if their juxtaposition ought to give rise to an organized totality, with ordered structures, which would be the phenomenon itself enfolding its causes and various processes. In fact, the significations remain separate. (p. 295)

At this point Sartre puts forward a notion which is to be a guiding theme of his historical – and particularly biographical – writing. He announces that the various levels of signification can be tied together because 'these different layers of meaning are *human*, and as such produced by a human reality that historializes itself' (p. 297). More graphically he writes: 'Couldn't one try to show *not* the situation acting on man – which leads to the disjunction of the signifying layers – but man throwing himself through situations and living them in the unity of human reality?' (p. 301). So in the same way that the inhumanity of the event prevented its description by the human historian, so the human project of the human being, which lends signification to the indescribable event, provides the thread which ties up, and binds together, the layers of the event's meaning.

There follows an attempt, in the *War Diaries*, to sketch the history of William II from this point of view. The details of this sketch are not important, but Sartre's conclusion is. It runs as follows:

All I've sought to show is that it's the historical method – and the psychological prejudices governing it – rather than the actual structure of things which produces this division of the factors of History into parallel signifying layers. This parallelism disappears if one deals with the historical personage in terms of the unity of his historialization. (p. 318)

Here, in a nutshell, is the historiographical strategy which Sartre is to employ in his biographies of Baudelaire, Mallarmé, and Genet, and which is to play such an important part in his unfinished treatment of Gustave Flaubert.

Not only is his early historical method outlined here, but so are his thoughts on history itself. Sartre appears to believe that History (the capital 'H' in the quotation above is significant) has a single and unified meaning, at least in respect of the history of any given individual. It is, of course, one thing to say this, and quite another to claim that the history of a *multiplicity* of individuals has a unified meaning, and this problem (which Sartre does raise in the *War Diaries*, p. 298) does not receive sustained treatment until volume two of the *Critique of Dialectical Reason*.

Beyond his concern for history, Sartre's increasing willingness to grasp the political nettle is reflected in a book he wrote around this time entitled *Anti-Semite and Jew*. This work is, with half an eye on his future intellectual development, methodologically interesting. Besides comprising evidence of Sartre's growing concern for political problems and an admission that the Jewish problem warrants more attention than the cursory dismissal given in 1939 (see p. 18), a number of themes are struck here which were to become permanent features of his work – one of the most important being his criticism of analysis.

The analytic spirit allows one to split up an individual's opinions and treat them all as equally weighty – the kind of liberal humanism in which 'all opinions are permitted' (Sartre, 1965a, p. 7). This approach, says Sartre, means that, 'A man may be a good father and a good husband, a conscientious citizen, highly cultivated, philanthropic, *and* in addition, an anti-Semite' (p. 8). But anti-Semitism is more than an opinion – it is a *passion*, a synthesis which involves the wholly personality of the anti-Semite. Analysis is also at fault to the extent that it involves abstractions – the world becomes a machine in which history is made by identical atoms going about their business, automatically reacting to circumstance. From this perspective, the democrat is wrong to recognise 'neither Jew, nor Arab, nor bourgeois, nor worker, but only man – man always the same in all times and all places' (p. 55). The collectivity is not merely a collection of individual elements, or a collection of molecules, says Sartre, rather it comprises specific individuals in a state of active synthesis, and to the extent that the liberal-democrat saves the Jew as human being, but destroys him/her as Jew, s/he exhibits a tinge of anti-Semitism for 'he is hostile to the Jew to the extent that the latter thinks of himself as a Jew' (p. 57). Sartre demands that the Jew should confirm his/her Jewishness and live it to the full, authentically. The inauthentic Jew lives in bad faith and is,

like the worker who wished to deny his condition as worker by acting like a bourgeois instead of demanding to be liberated as a *worker*, that is, instead of going beyond his situation through a revolutionary attitude which involves recognition of this situation. (Contat and Rybalka, 1974, I, p. 145)

So, for Sartre, we are defined by our situation, and we form a synthetic whole with it, deciding our possibilities within the limits defined by that situation and giving it meaning by choosing. But the synthetic whole which we form with our situation is not the same as History. The Jew is an *invention*, a creation in the mind of the anti-Semite: the Jew has no historical existence – 'The essential thing here is not an historical fact but the idea that the agents of history formed for themselves of the Jew' (Sartre, 1965, p. 13).

The lack of history in this analysis prevents Sartre from asking the question 'Why the Jew?' – 'Why are the Jews, of all possible pretexts, of all possible scapegoats, selected as the sacrificial objects of Western culture?' (Hook, 1949, pp. 469). De Beauvoir eventually became aware of the essay's deficiencies (de Beauvoir, 1978, p. 52), and Sartre said in an interview in 1966 that,

Its shortcomings leap out at me. I had to deal with the problem from a twin point of view, historical and economic. I kept myself to a phenomenological description. If I were to redo my essay today ... I would try to deepen it in the two directions I mentioned. (Contat and Rybalka, 1974, I, p. 143)

There are, then, essentially three themes developed in *Anti-Semite and Jew* which engender much discussion in Sartre's work after the war. First, there is the rejection of the analytic approach in favour of the view that human-reality is best understood as a synthesis. Sartre does not yet have a grasp of the temporal and *dialectical* nature of this synthesis, but the first steps towards a comprehension of historical materialism have been taken. Second, Sartre notes that we must see the freedom of the Jew in order to hate him/her – we do not hate natural phenomena 'like earthquakes and plagues of locusts' (Sartre, 1965, p. 39). This idea recurs again and again in Sartre's work, but particularly in relation to his analysis of colonialism: the colonialist must recognise the humanity of the native in order to treat him/her as non-human – hence the instability of colonial regimes. Finally, Sartre notes that the passion of the anti-Semite generates the community of the 'lynch-mob', the sort of collectivity which might also come from an 'uprising' (p. 28). He dismisses these phenomena here as 'ephemeral formations which soon vanish without leaving any trace' (p. 30), but much of the *Critique of Dialectical Reason* is taken up with discussing just such formations.

Also at this time Marxism was coming to seem more and more important to Sartre (Sartre, 1978, pp. 59–60), and his work in the Resistance pulled him further to the left. Annie Cohen-Solal notes that he wrote a text for *Socialism and Freedom* in which, 'Among other things, influenced by his recent reading of Marx, he proposed creating a currency that would be based on labor and would establish the value of an object according to the time it took to produce it' (1987, p. 169). He began to attempt to relate his existentialism to Marxist theory and was invited to write an article on that theme in 1944. In reply to Communist attacks, Sartre claimed that existentialism is not a philosophy of quietism – how could it be, since 'existentialism defines man by action' (Sartre, 1944, p. 157)? This remark anticipates a theme to be developed in the 1946 lecture *Existentialism and Humanism*, and allows Sartre to claim kinship with Marx because,

Existentialism isn't too far from the conception of man to be found in Marx. For is it not a fact that Marx would accept this motto of ours for man: make, and in making make yourself, and be nothing but what you have made of yourself. (p. 157)

On the contrary, he asserts, *materialism* is the philosophy of quietism for it encourages the idea that we have no control over our own destiny, and then he points out the inconsistency of explaining human-reality by its social situation, while simultaneously holding people responsible for their actions. Indeed, was Sartre himself the 'social traitor' that the Communists said he was if his actions are materially determined? The materialism he attacks in this essay is of a very crude variety but, nevertheless, its concerns are a signpost for his future and intellectual development.

During the post-war period much of Sartre's output was determined by his relationship with the French Communist Party and the stagnation of Marxist theory which he believed it to represent. From Henri Lefebvre's description of *Being and Nothingness* as an 'excremental philosophy' to the Communists' branding of existentialism as the 'ideological enemy number one' at a post-war conference, the Party was determined to head off the challenge that Sartre seemed to represent.

In the face of such condemnation Sartre began to organise his defence, beginning with a lecture entitled 'Existentialism is a Humanism', given at the Club Maintenant on 28 October 1945.[1] This is an important piece of work which has attracted more criticism than it deserves – certainly the pages concerned with *action* are crucial to an understanding of Sartre's reappraisal of Marx's historical materialism, as well as to an understanding of Sartre's own project of conceiving a philosophy of revolution.

The lecture revolves around the defence of existentialism against four major criticisms – that it is sordid, amoral, quietistic, and that it precludes the possibility of solidarity. Contrary to the claim that existentialism is a base philosophy, Sartre affirms that it confers the greatest dignity on humanity by distinguishing it sharply from the world of objects and showing that choice is its essence. Better still, humanity *has* no essence for, familiarly for Sartre, 'existence comes before essence' (Sartre, 1980a, p. 26).

From this perspective, it is obvious that there is no such thing as human nature – the only thing that does not vary is our condition: 'the necessities of being in the world, of having to labour and die there' (p. 46), and Sartre is to build his notion of solidarity on this element of commonality. The upshot of the choice we have is that we must accept total responsibility – most crucially, we must accept total responsibility for our morals. Sartre

---

[1] The lecture was announced in the papers as 'Existentialism is a Humanism', but is referred to as 'Is Existentialism a Humanism?' by both Sartre and de Beauvoir; see Contat and Rybalka, 1974, I, p. 133.

notes Dostoevsky's observation that, 'If God did not exist, everything would be permitted' (p. 33) – with the death of God, there can be no such thing as *a priori* values, the only values which exist are those we make for ourselves. As we have seen, this is a theme developed in *Cahiers pour une morale* (see pp. 33–4). Here Sartre attempts to extricate himself from a world in which there might be as many value-systems as there are people, by falling back on a version of the Kantian Categorical Imperative. We cannot take a particular course of action unless we would wish that course of action for everyone else: 'When we say that man chooses himself, we do mean that every one of us must choose himself; but by that we also mean that in choosing for himself he chooses for all men' (Sartre, 1980a, p. 29).

The third criticism to which Sartre responds is that existentialism 'is reproached as an invitation to the people to dwell in the quietism of despair' (p. 23). There are, apparently, no moral values, existentialism concentrates on all that is sordid in human affairs, and it offers no solution to daily problems – all that is left is to retire into contemplation. On the contrary, says Sartre, existentialism is the philosophy of action *par excellence*; action is the locus of reality and, 'Man is nothing else but what he purposes, he exists only in so far as he realises himself, he is therefore nothing else but the sum of his actions, nothing else but what his life is' (p. 41).

There are no excuses. We are defined by choice and by action, and circumstances are there to be overcome, not to be used as scapegoats for our misery. This is the positive aspect of existentialism with which Sartre hopes to infuse Marxism. Bogged down in materialism (as Sartre sees it), Marxism is the philosophy of quietism; existentialism is a philosophy of the sternest optimism, critical of the fear of freedom; a call to action and to revolution.

But how can an effective revolutionary theory be based on subjectivity? ask the Marxists. In this respect Sartre confirms the thesis of *Being and Nothingness* in arguing, as we have seen, that human-reality experiences a universality of condition in living on this particular planet, within the limits defined by our mortality. To this extent, our purposes may be diverse, but they are never wholly alien: 'since every human purpose presents itself either as an attempt to surpass these limitations, or to widen them, or else to deny or to accommodate oneself to them' (p. 46).

This degree of common purpose helps us to understand the motives of other people and engenders solidarity. Indeed, in struggling to accommodate the notion of community into his basic subjectivism, Sartre affirms that different *races* are accessible to each other, whereas in *Being and Nothingness* even individuals were opaque mysteries to each other: 'every purpose, however individual it may be, is of universal value. Every purpose, even that of a Chinese, an Indian or a Negro, can be understood by a European' (p. 46).

At the same time as we discover the congruence of purposes, we learn that the freedom of others depends on our own freedom, and suddenly freedom has become a thing to be *willed* (pp. 51–2). In *Being and Nothingness*, freedom was an ontological truth, a fact of human-reality; now it has become a moral imperative, a political exercise. Perceptibly, Sartre has moved onto the plane of politics. The freedom of the transcendent imagination is no longer sufficient; freedom is something to be demanded:

the moment I feel myself a pure freedom I cannot bear to identify myself with a race of oppressors. Thus, I require of all freedoms that they demand the liberation of coloured people against the white race and against myself in so far as I am a part of it, but nobody can suppose for a moment it is possible to write a good novel in praise of anti-semitism. For, the moment I feel my freedom is indissolubly linked to that of all other men, it cannot be demanded of me that I use it to approve the enslavement of a part of these men. (Sartre, 1978e, p. 46)

So the communists, in accusing Sartre of purveying a philosophy of sordidness, amorality, quietism, and bourgeois individualism, forced him to dwell on the relationship between existentialism and Marxism, and convinced him that he had a useful contribution to make to Marxist theory.

The attempt to carve out an alternative to dogmatic Marxism continued in his essay *Materialism and Revolution*, published by *Les Temps Modernes* in June 1946. By now, Sartre was labouring under the conflict between his sympathy for the politics of the PCF and his belief that its ideology was a travesty of the real Marx. For this reason, he conceived of *Materialism and Revolution* as a 'courteous' attack on the Party's philosophical and ideological problems, and not on the Party itself' (Sartre, 1949a, p. 74). This is an extremely important essay in our context, prefiguring, as it does, a maturing of his concern for the dialectic as both an intellectual and a political weapon.

In the essay Sartre says we must ask, 'whether materialism and the myth of objectivity are really required by the cause of the revolution and if there is not a discrepancy between the revolutionary's action and his ideology' (Sartre, 1946, pp. 186–7). He seeks to show that materialism is internally inconsistent, that it stifles the revolutionary impulse; he says what is required by a truly revolutionary philosophy, and attempts to show how we might discover that philosophy.

Materialism has three characteristics, according to Sartre. First, it denies the existence of a 'transcendent finality' (i.e. God); second, it reduces the action of the mind to matter; and third, it eliminates subjectivity because the world is conceived of as a system of objects. Traditionally, materialists accuse idealists of being metaphysicians, but Sartre turns this on its head by asserting that it is the materialists who indulge in metaphysics by the fact of merely asserting, rather than proving, the truth of their materialism. To the extent that, according to the materialist, my reason is governed 'from without' (p. 189), I can have no trust in its operation – it would be sheer coincidence if my mind, as a product of circumstances, happened upon the Truth – 'What stroke of chance enables the raw products of circumstances to constitute the keys to Nature as well?' (p. 189). The challenge of 'proving' the dialectic is one which Sartre takes up at the beginning of the *Critique of Dialectical Reason*. Here, in *Materialism and Revolution*, he writes that materialism reverts to idealism in order to prove itself; it stands outside the totality in order to pontificate upon it, and as such, is a materialism no longer:

When materialism dogmatically asserts that the universe produces thought, it immediately passes into idealist scepticism. It lays down the inalienable rights of Reason on the one hand and takes them away with the other. It destroys positivism with a dogmatic rationalism. It destroys both of them with the metaphysical affirmation that man is a material object, and it destroys this affirmation by the radical negation of all metaphysics. (p. 190)

Sartre then asks whether he has been attending to a 'naive' materialism – what about dialectical materialism? (p. 190) In reply, he asserts that the notion of dialectical materialism is itself inconsistent, in that matter is inert and is 'incapable of producing any thing by itself' (p. 191), and is therefore incapable of the self-sustaining ascension that the dialectic demands. This is the matter of *science*, and science deals with the external relations between objects, while 'Dialectical progress is, on the contrary, cumulative; at each new stage it turns back to the ensemble of positions transcended and embraces them all' (p. 195). In this sense, there is no such thing as natural history, there is only human history, for only human beings, with their ability to interiorise their experiences of the world and then re-exteriorise them in action, can provide for such dialectic accumulation. These are all early intimations of themes vigorously developed in the *Critique*.

Sartre ends the section on materialism by claiming that it has destroyed thought, and has killed the revolutionary impulse, even though it might previously have provided for unity under one ideological banner. More importantly, materialism relieves everyone of responsibility. Caught as we are in the web of cause and effect, how can we ever be responsible for our actions? He further argues that, as well as making the revolution inevitable, materialism also makes it possible for the master to claim no responsibility for his mastery, for his actions are dictated by circumstance. Sartre, on the other hand, wants to show that mastery is a conscious, positive activity – as are colonialism and racism.

Materialism is inappropriate as a revolutionary philosophy because it is 'conditioned thinking' and conceives of 'determined action' (p. 213). The revolutionary wants to go beyond his/her situation and is thus oriented towards the future – materialism can never hope to explain this future projection, this transcendence. A revolutionary philosophy would be one which has humanity in situation, which expresses our reciprocal action on the world, and one which shows that it constitutes an *action* in itself:

What is needed is, in a word, a philosophical theory which shows that human reality is action and that action upon the universe is identical with the understanding of that universe as it is, or, in other words, that action is the unmasking of reality, and, at the same time, a modification of that reality. (pp. 213–14)

This passage sums up the self-appointed task that was to culminate in the *Critique of Dialectical Reason*.

How are we to develop this philosophy of action? Reaffirming the inadequacy of his notion of freedom in *Being and Nothingness*, Sartre realises that 'inner freedom of thought' (p. 222) is next to useless for the employee of the Ford Motor Company who wants political change – in *Materialism and Revolution* it is his work which 'offers the beginning of concrete liberation' (p. 223). For, in working, we recognise that we can have mastery over things, that we can utilise them according to our needs, that we are something over and above the things we are using: 'Thus the worker really learns of his freedom through things; but precisely because he does learn of it through things, he is anything but a thing' (p. 227). The fact that we are not enmeshed in the world, as materialism would demand, is learned from our engagement in the world. We learn that we have an ability that cannot be explained by materialism – the ability to transcend the world of material objects, in making plans, and organising the world so as to fulfil those plans. Nor do we need any metaphysical leap of faith to arrive at this truth – it is a truth which *emerges* once we reflect on our engagement in the world. Once again, Sartre is to resurrect this notion of the 'emergence' of truth in his attempt to 'found' historical materialism in the *Critique of Dialectical Reason*.

In conclusion, this essay reveals itself as a powerful demand for a new revolutionary philosophy, independent of the redundant materialism of Marxism. Yet it is not entirely clear which Marxism Sartre is attacking. Lukács rightly says that Sartre's criticism is useful in opposition to 'mechanistic materialism', but that it is too simplistic for dialectical materialism (Lukács, 1961, pp. 137–8). It seems that by 1946 Sartre had read Stalin's *Dialectical and Historical Materialism* and was criticising materialism on that basis. In 1949, Sartre added five footnotes to the essay for republication in *Situations III*, four of which indicate 'further reading of Marx' (Aronson, 1980, p. 120). The first footnote of the essay suggests that Sartre was not intending to criticise Marx's materialism – at least not directly – but rather the Marxist materialism appropriated by the PCF: 'As I have been unfairly reproached with not quoting Marx in this article, I should like to point out that my criticisms are not directed against him, but against the Marxist scholasticism of 1949' (Sartre, 1946, p. 185). Certainly the materialism in this essay would seem to be of the type that Marx criticised in Feuerbach because it did not take the activity of the human subject into account.

It is apparent, then, that in the years after the Second World War, Sartre was developing a twofold attack on received Marxist theory. First, he saw a need to reintroduce subjectivity; and second, he was concerned for the passivity which a dogmatic materialism might engender. Both of these criticisms revolve around the desire for action. If there is no subjectivity, there is no human action; and if there is materialism, human action is reduced to reaction, to knee-jerk responses. No revolutionary theory can be built on concepts which deny the possibility of politically purposive human activity.

After *Materialism and Revolution*, and with the possible exception of an essay on Yugoslav socialism (Sartre, 1950) in which Sartre wrote that Tito's great achievement was to have put subjectivity back on the revolutionary political agenda, according to local and specific demands, he made little headway with his professed project of reviving Marxism as a revolutionary ideology until about 1957. He was by now convinced that subjectivity must be reintroduced if Marxism is not to degenerate into a mere academic exercise – 'We must rethink Marxism, we must rethink man' (p. xlii). Sartre is now firmly planted in the Marxist tradition, having found a focus for his new concern for a philosophy of history. Yet, although this rethinking of Marxism naturally put him further at odds with the Communist Party, he remained convinced that it should not be completely disowned – rather, in the absence of any option, 'one can only say that a worker should enter the PC' (p. xlii). But this confusion between theory and practice was symptomatic of Sartre's post-war years, and his attempts to bring practice into line with theory were singularly unsuccessful, especially during the late 1940s.

This, I believe, was principally due to his growing *rapprochement* with the PCF during this period. In 1948 he joined the *Rassemblement Démocratique et Révolutionnaire* (RDR – Democratic and Revolutionary Movement) which was designed to provide a milieu for action as an alternative to the PCF and the SFIO (French Socialist Party). The movement was intended to be a 'concrete experience of democracy' (Sartre, 1949a, p. 28), giving everyone the opportunity to participate, in the belief that the working class needed to acquire political competence before it gained political power. Direct participation in the RDR was made possible by the closest of contacts between the central body and the base, and between different sections of the base.

Apart from this, Sartre was initially attracted by the RDR's attempt to steer a course between the USA and the USSR in the Cold War. In December 1948 he wrote, in an article in *Franc-Tireur*, that he would not fight the USSR because, 'in any case and whatever the pretext firing on the proletariat is a crime'. But on the other hand, 'We're not taking the side of the USSR against America either. We could not possibly conceive of ourselves fighting a democratic people who have often shown an admirable sense of freedom' (Contat and Rybalka, 1974, I, p. 194).

Indeed, Sartre bent over backwards to remain friendly with the Americans, against the expressed wishes of the PCF, but eventually the tensions became too great. Opinions polarised as Tito broke with the USSR, Rajk and Kostov were executed on absurd grounds, and the existence of labour camps in the USSR became common knowledge. The RDR was wound up, and Sartre moved inexorably towards the Communists. In 1951 he wrote:

To the extent that I am inspired by a rather broad Marxism, I am an enemy for Stalinist Communists...[but]...Until the new order, the party will represent the proletariat for me, and I do not see how this situation could possibly change for me for some time...It is impossible to take an anti-Communist position without being against the proletariat. (p. 254)

The point of closest contact with the PCF came in 1952 when he wrote *The Communists and Peace* in an explosion of anger at the arrest of Communist Party joint leader Jacques Duclos in unjustified circumstances. At a demonstration against the visit to Paris of NATO commander General Ridgeway, Duclos' car was found to have contained a loaded pistol, a truncheon, a wireless transmitter, and two carrier pigeons – these latter were alleged by the police to have been intended as messengers to Stalin. It transpired that the pistol and the truncheon belonged to Duclos' body-guard, the 'transmitter' was a receiver, and the pigeons were for Duclos' Sunday dinner. Nevertheless, Duclos was locked up in the Sante and charged with conspiracy.

In *The Communists and Peace* Sartre showers praise on the USSR, claiming it to be the embodiment of 'the opportunity of the proletariat, and the first state to contain the premises of socialism' (Sartre, 1969a,

p. 10), as well as arguing that 'the USSR wants peace and proves it every day' (p. 13). In providing a Leninist answer to the question of how to foster the unity of the working class (in the first of the three articles which comprise the essay, at least), Sartre was succumbing to the kind of discipline more or less guaranteed to prevent him from 'rethinking Marxism', as he had proposed in his piece on Yugoslavia in 1950.

Only 18 months later, in the third article which makes up *The Communists and the Peace*, does Sartre make some progress in this respect, and this is in his analysis of the genesis of groups. No longer is it the function of leaders to engender unity in the masses, as it was in the first two articles, rather the leaders emerge when the masses stir and 'have crystallised into some form of primary collectivity' (Sartre, 1969a, p. 194). Again, Sartre is hinting at the kind of questions to be answered in the *Critique* at the end of the decade, when this mysterious 'crystallisation' of groups – for example, during the storming of the Bastille – becomes a central part of his political anthropology, and the social and historical conditions of group-genesis are more adequately acknowledged.

Despite Sartre's proximity to the PCF during this period, his relations with the Party were always tense. Like a moth looping round a candle, Sartre would now dive in close to the light and then dart away, singed by the flame that hides itself behind the promise of illumination. The critical turning-point came on 4 November 1956 when the Soviet Union invaded Hungary (for the second time) after premier Imre Nagy announced that his country was to leave the Warsaw Pact.

Sartre analysed the Hungarian uprising in *The Spectre of Stalin*, published in *Les Temps Modernes* over three months at the end of 1956 and the beginning of 1957. Here, Sartre is concerned to demolish the notion that the Russian intervention was 'inevitable', or that it 'had to happen'; rather he writes an 'existential history' of the event, showing how the pressures of a situation, and the choices of individuals within that situation, go to make up history.

Sartre has no sympathy with PCF apologists observing dead Hungarians lying in the streets of Budapest, and then turning with a sigh, saying, 'It's got to be done, you see. We must put up with them, these dead; it is our duty' (Sartre, 1969b, p. 9). There is no question of this because 'In politics, no action is unconditionally necessary' (p. 17). On the contrary, what is 'necessary' is no more and no less than what happens as a result of the combination of situation and choices, and this is *action*. The USSR defined necessity by its actions, and it also defined socialism by these actions: 'No-one among these enthusiasts was willing to understand that the USSR *by its actions defined* its own socialism and the socialism it counts on re-establishing in Hungary' (p. 9). The notion of necessity is preserved as the ghost of Stalin, for it absolves one from responsibility, and justifies any catalogue of violent crimes. That ghost, says Sartre, is preserved in the post-Stalin Soviet leadership: 'Doubtless, the neo-Stalinists do not approve of Stalin's crimes; but they resemble him in that they do the same things "of necessity", and without noticing that they are crimes' (p. 84).

The events in Hungary heralded Sartre's break with all those in the USSR and the PCF who did not denounce what he called 'the Hungarian massacre' (Contat and Rybalka, I, p. 333–4). It is my contention that this allowed him to return to the task announced in 1946 in *Materialism and Revolution*. Released from the shackles imposed by defence of the PCF, embroiled in the Algerian question, and recognising 'in spite of the abominations, the crimes, the obvious privileges of the socialist camp, and to condemn with so much more strength the policy which puts these privileges in danger' (Sartre, 1969b, p. 91), Sartre's philosophy was approaching a new watershed.

In 1957, Sartre was asked by Jerry Lissowski, of the Polish paper *Twórczość*, to write a piece on Marxism and existentialism, which he did. De Beauvoir notes that, 'He had been pondering the subject for years, but had felt that his ideas were not yet ripe; he had needed some external stimulus before being able to take the plunge' (de Beauvoir, 1978, p. 384). Later, Sartre rewrote this piece and it became *Search for a Method*, the precursor to the *Critique of Dialectical Reason*. The latter will be looked at in detail in subsequent chapters, and it is enough to say here that Sartre had finally decided on his task: 'there is one and only one question I am asking: Do we have the means today of constituting a structural, historical anthropology?' (Contat and Rybalka, 1974, I, p. 340). For Sartre, Marxism remains the philosophy of our time, but 'lazy' Marxism is inadequate – inconsistent in itself and a failure as a revolutionary philosophy, at least in the hands of the PCF. Sartre's task is to reawaken Marxism; to found the historical dialectic, to release subjectivity, to turn passivity towards praxis, and to analyse the revolutionary moment in all its particularity. At last he felt he had the means to make an explicit attempt at answering the questions first posed by his attack on sterile materialism in *Materialism and Revolution*.

The following year, Sartre wrote a preface to André Gorz's *The Traitor*, entitled 'Of rats and men'. In his book, Gorz uses Sartre's method, developed in relation to studies of Baudelaire and Genet, in an attempt 'to understand ... on the basis of his life history, the source of his choices, his singularity and the movement of his thought' (p. 347). To this extent, Gorz has taken on the role of the observed turned observer, and as such is confronting the problems of historical materialism which Sartre had revealed. First, he attempts to make sense of the dialectic in which we act on the world as it simultaneously acts upon us; and second, Gorz gives flesh to the particularity of the life of an individual, which historical materialism traditionally ignores. Near the beginning of his superb, if enigmatic, commentary on Gorz's book, Sartre sums up the problematic at which he had arrived by 1958, and which, once developed, promised the greatest enlightenment:

I read science fiction occasionally, and always with pleasure. These stories give the exact degree to which we fear ourselves. One tale among others delighted me: men land on Venus. These future colonisers have hardly left their space ship when they joyously set off to hunt the natives of the planet, their future subjects, who, at first, do not appear. We can imagine the pride of the lords of creation, drunk with triumph and new freedom. But soon everything crumbles in the face of the intolerable evidence: the conquerors are in a cage. Their every move has been charted, the roads they discover have been marked out for them. Bent over this glass cage, invisible, the inhabitants of Venus are subjecting these superior mammals to intelligence tests. This, it seems to me, is our common condition, with this difference – we are our own Venus dwellers and our own guinea pigs. (Sartre, 1965b, 'Of rats and men', pp. 337–8).

We act as we observe, our observations become part of our actions, and our actions are swallowed up in the experiment – where, then, is the truth?

# 4     The *Critique* (1) – the dialectic

---

> I came to feel that I ought to tackle the fundamental problem – whether there is any such thing as a Truth of humanity.     (Sartre, 1978a, p. 822)[1]

In 1957, the year after his split with the French Communist Party over the invasion of Hungary Sartre, as we have noted, published a slim volume entitled *Search for a Method*. Three years later a much bulkier work, the *Critique of Dialectical Reason*, appeared. Taken together, Sartre's intention in these books was, 'to raise one question, and only one: do we now possess the materials for constituting a structural, historical anthropology?' (*CDR I*, p. 822).

The relationship between *Search for a Method* and the *Critique* is ambiguous. Most commentators follow the chronological order, using the first as an introduction to the second – an approach which Sartre commends 'from a dialectical point of view' (*CDR I*, p. 821). However, he also says in the same preface that, 'Logically, the second should have come before the first, since it is intended to provide its critical foundation' (*CDR I*, p. 821). In the collected French edition of the *Search for a Method* and the *Critique*, Sartre only observed the chronological order because he 'was afraid that this mountain of notes might seem to have brought forth a mouse' (*CDR I*, p. 821). Contrary to traditional habit, I propose to take the two works in reverse chronological order, and this for two reasons. First, as well as having links with the *Critique*, *Search for a Method* is also a guide to the method used in Sartre's historical biography of Flaubert, *The Family Idiot*. The *Flaubert*, together with the other biographical exemplars of Sartre's developing historical method, will be examined in the final chapters of this book. It seems wise, then, to hold over examination of the *Search for a Method* until it is most applicable. Second, this approach will enable us to follow Sartre's suggestion that we understand the mechanics of the methodology before seeking its implications.

---

[1] *Critique of Dialectical Reason*, I; hereafter referred to as *CDR I*. Full-length discussions in English of this volume of the *Critique* can be found in Aron, 1973; Desan, 1974; Chiodi, 1978; Poster, 1979; and Catalano, 1986.

The next three chapters, then, deal with the three topics relevant to our pursuit of Sartre's theory of history and its political significance which emerge from the *Critique*. First, we shall be concerned with Sartre's attempt to 'prove' or 'found' the materialist dialectic. Although I have argued that an understanding of Sartre's political position helps towards a fuller understanding of the *Critique*, it ought to be stressed too that the move from *Being and Nothingness* to the *Critique* has 'purely' philosophical motivations. In 'thinking against himself' Sartre realised that the radical separation of subject and object enshrined in the former (book) was inadequate for an understanding of their relationship in the temporal (or 'diachronic') plane. In other words, he had no way of treating the relationship between the individual and the world through time. The first topic to concern us here, then, in this context, is Sartre's attempt to 'prove' or 'found' the materialist dialectic.

Second, Sartre knew that the isolation of individual human beings enshrined in *Being and Nothingness* could neither account for the universally observable phenomenon of co-operation, nor provide the basis for a complete philosophical anthropology. Relationships between human beings therefore receive much more sophisticated treatment in the *Critique* than in the earlier work. From this perspective I shall study Sartre's analysis of the genesis of groups.

Finally, I shall consider his comments on a double alienation – the alienation among ourselves, and the alienation between us and our environment. This second topic arises as a consequence of the first. The dialectical relationship between the individual and the world can generate unintended consequences of actions, which Sartre defines as alienation. His discussion of this form of alienation – as well as the alienation we suffer among ourselves – bears on his view as to the effectiveness of our action in the world in relation to the plans we make. Does he believe that it is possible to change the world for the better or not?

Sartre begins the *Critique* with the affirmation that he wants to prove the dialectic: 'It must be proved that a negation of negation can be an affirmation, that conflicts ... are the motive force of history', (*CDR I*, p. 15) and hence that the 'materialist dialectic' is 'true'. The aim – which must be seen fundamentally as a political one – is to show that 'dialectical investigation (*l'expérience dialectique*) ... [is] ... *praxis* elucidating itself in order to control its own development (*CDR I*, p. 220). We shall consider the extent and status of this control in the chapter on alienation. At times, Sartre refers to this materialist dialectic as 'historical materialism', and he bemoans the fact that 'The totalising thought of historical materialism has established evrything except its own existence' (*CDR I*, p. 19). Sartre agrees unreservedly with the characterisation of historical materialism as expressed by Marx: 'Men make their own History...but under circumstances...given and transmitted by the past', and goes on,

If this statement is true, then both determinism and analytical reason must be categorically rejected as the method and law of human history. Dialectical Rationality, the whole of which is contained in this sentence, must be seen as the permanent and dialectical unity of freedom and necessity. (*CDR I*, p. 75)

Sartre's task, then, is to found the dialectical rationality of historical materialism, and it is essential to grasp his conviction that this can only be done from within history itself, and not from some spurious transcendent position outside it.

It ought to be pointed out at the outset that no conclusive proof, as such, is forthcoming in either volume of the *Critique*. Sartre's remarks on this score are almost entirely cast in the conditional 'if...then' form, and this in two senses. First, in the sense that *if* the dialectic exists, *then* certain conditions (ontological and epistemological) must obtain; and second, that *if* we are to show that the dialectic exists, *then* we need to be able to show that certain hypotheses (e.g. about the nature of history) are true. So with respect to the first, for example, Sartre writes that,

a dialectic exists if, in at least one ontological region, a totalisation is in progress which is immediately accessible to a thought which unceasingly totalises itself in its very comprehension of the totalisation from which it emanates and which makes itself its object. (*CDR I*, p. 44)

And as for the second,

If there is to be any such thing as the Truth of History (rather than *several* truths, even if they are organised into a system), our investigation must show that the kind of dialectical intelligibility which we have described above applies to the process of human history as a whole. (*CDR I*, p. 64)

Those who look for an explicit resolution of either form of these conditionals in Sartre will be disappointed. However, his widespread use of the tactical assumption that the dialectic does exist, thus opening the way to further exploration and hypothesis on that basis, strongly suggests that his inclination is to work with an *a priori* resolution of these conditionals, and to leave the heuristic value of the categories and concepts to do the job of persuasion on his readers. This is the burden of the following remark from volume two of the *Critique*:

Our aim is solely to establish if, in a practical ensemble riven by antagonisms (whether they are multiple conflicts or these are reduced to a single one), the very rifts are totalizing and entailed by the totalizing movement of the whole. But if we actually establish this abstract principle, the materialist dialectic – as movement of History and historical knowledge – needs only to be proved by the facts it illumines, or, if you prefer, to discover itself as a fact and through other facts. (Sartre, 1991, p. 15)[1]

Corroboration is thus continually deferred, both to volume two (see *CDR I*, p. 69), and even (though not explicitly) to his biography of Flaubert, *The Family Idiot*, which follows the explanatory outlines of the *Critique*, and which builds on the insights of the latter's concern with 'finding the intelligible foundations of a structural anthropology' (p. 15). As Ronald Aronson rightly observes in his commentary on volume two of the *Critique*, 'it is of the very nature of the dialectic that it can be methodologically validated only if it is substantively true, and it is substantively true only if history itself turns out to cohere as a totalization of envelopment' (1987, p. 197). The second hypothesis is never fully redeemed, although, as I shall show, there is more than enough evidence in the texts available to indicate that – given sufficient time – Sartre believed he could have redeemed it.

In the first volume, the strongest positive statement as to the dialectic's existence is to be found in Sartre's discussion of *need* (*CDR I*, pp. 79–88). There he explains that, were it not for need, our actions in the world would not exhibit dialectical characteristics – which he describes as 'the negating transcendence of contradiction, the determination of a present totalisation in the name of a future totality, and the real effective working of matter' (*CDR I*, p. 80).

Need is first experienced by the human organism as a lack in respect of the requisites to sustain life. The contradiction to be transcended is that what the organism lacks is not something like itself, but rather, 'inorganic and less organised elements or, quite simply...dead flesh' (p. 80). The contradiction is resolved by, on the one hand, the human organism making itself like inert matter so as to 'modify the material environment' (*CDR I*, p. 82), and, on the other, Nature is itself turned simultaneously into a 'false organism' by the human organism's attempt to satisfy its needs in it. 'Negativity and contradiction come to the inert through organic totalisation', writes Sartre, and so, 'As soon as need appears, surrounding materiality is endowed with passive unity' – a unity which is normally characteristic of the organism rather than inert matter (*CDR I*, p. 81). Sartre continues: 'The oscillation which opposes the human thing to the thing-man will be found at every level of dialectical investigation' (*CDR I*, p. 90).

---

[1] *Critique of Dialectical Reason*, II; hereafter referred to as *CDR II*. A full-length discussion in English of this volume of the *Critique* can be found in Aronson, 1987.

Thus we have the contradiction and its resolution, both founded on need, and the whole process has the dialectical characteristic of the negation of a negation in that the satisfaction of need is the negating of that which threatens the organism's survival – for example, the taking of food negates hunger. Moreover, this negation of negation is not circular, because the transcendence effected by the human organism is aimed at a totalising end. If it were not, then the negation of negation would merely be a return to a starting point. In the context of totalisation, though, 'the negation of negation becomes an affirmation' (*CDR I*, p. 86) – precisely what Sartre set out to show.

From another point of view, the problem he faces in the attempt to found the dialectical rationality of historical materialism will not be new to those acquainted with the intellectual foundations of Marxism. Sartre expresses it thus: 'How can a man who is lost in the world, permeated by an absolute movement coming from everything, also be this consciousness sure both of itself and the Truth?' (*CDR I*, p. 30). In other words, how can the foundations of the movement of history be identified by a historical actor who is him- or herself a part of that movement?

The *Critique* is littered with references to this problem: 'if the search for the Truth is to be dialectical in its methods, how can it be shown without idealism that it corresponds to the movement of being?' (*CDR I*, p. 25). And, 'In reality, the hypothesis which makes the critical investigation feasible is precisely the one which the investigation seeks to prove' (*CDR I*, p. 70). Sartre is confronted with the difficulty of being a situated observer. The 'n + 1 dimensional observer does not and cannot exist' (*CDR I*, p. 708), and so Sartre cannot stand outside the object with which he is concerned, any more than the scientist can. Indeed, he was particularly fond of pointing to the twentieth century discovery that, at the sub-atomic level, the scientist is as much a part of his/her experiment as, for instance, Sartre is a part of the history with which he is dealing.

Before describing the nature of the proof he is to offer, Sartre first turns to the crude-Marxist solution to the conundrum. Having recognised that it is human involvement in history-making which makes it difficult to say anything objective about history, Marxists simply ignore the human element altogether so that 'Being *no longer manifests itself* in any way whatsoever: it merely evolves according to its own laws' (*CDR I*, p. 26). On this reading, human beings play no active part in the revelation of the dialectic, and the world develops by itself, 'and to no-one'. Sartre says that he will call this interpretation '*external*, or transcendental, dialectical materialism' (*CDR I*, p. 27). It is external because it has performed the sleight-of-hand of dissolving the human in the unfolding dialectic of Nature, and then taking up an external position *vis-à-vis* that dialectic in order to pronounce upon its existence. In other words, the dialectic cannot unfold before the human being, because the human being has disappeared in the dialectic; consequently a transcendent position is required from which to posit it.

This is, of course, the materialism criticised by Sartre in *Materialism and Revolution* (see pp. 46–9) and it offends Sartre for two reasons. First, it involves a direct rebuttal of his desire to prove the existence of the dialectic 'without idealism'. From Sartre's perspective, Marxists claim to have a materialist philosophy, yet it has been established through idealism – i.e. (on his understanding of the word) by placing the observer in a transcendent position beyond history. Sartre believes that it is necessary to found the dialectic from within, not from without. Second, the crude Marxist position has the flaw of eliminating the human subject. A continuing theme of Sartre's work is the crucial nature of the activity of human beings in the world. Men and women create meaning in the world, and without them, there would be no history as we conceive it. To dissolve the human is to rob history of its makers.

The political point in Sartre's position is vital. In his desire to preserve the activity of human beings, Sartre is affirming that history is not something which just occurs, beyond us and beyond our control. Exploitation and oppression are not merely phantom circumstances, but situations which human beings influence – even if indirectly. In stressing this, Sartre is attempting to return control of history to people – to help them understand that history is to be made, not passively suffered. When he uses words like oppression and exploitation, it is essential to understand that he has in mind the human basis of these processes – the active way in which they are implemented.

He is particularly hard on Engels in this context. Referring to the correspondence between Engels and Dühring, he says, 'Engels makes fun of Dühring for speaking somewhat hastily of oppression. But, in trying to correct him, he goes to the opposite extreme: economism.' If we succumb to a crude economistic interpretation, then, 'The resulting opposition between capitalists and wage-earners does not merit the name of *struggle* any more than that between the shutter and the wall it beats against' (*CDR I*, p. 711). Sartre is stressing that the struggle between capital and labour is not inhuman, but, on the contrary, is human-implemented.

The implication that follows is that, as such struggle has a human origin, it is subject to purposive human intervention and therefore, perhaps, abolition. But of course it is entirely possible that the human agent is merely a vehicle for an uncontrolled and uncontrollable historical process. Indeed, in his criticism of Engels' crude materialism, Sartre is expressing the human inspiration of oppression, yet as we move on in the *Critique*, we discover that the control that Sartre here implies for human beings over their situation is diluted in their confrontation with worked matter (i.e. matter worked upon and transformed by human beings), or the 'practico-inert'. We shall come to discover the extent of this dilution in our investigation of alienation. For the moment, we have established that Sartre wants a proof of historical materialism that will have recourse neither to a dialectic of Nature, nor to the dissolution of men and women. In what realm of Being might this proof lie?

The clues lie in the assessment we have just made of Sartre's criticisms of crude materialism. He stressed both that the truth must come from within (i.e. not from a transcendent 'without'), and that it must take account of the activity of human beings in their social world. In looking for a place to found historical materialism, then, we might expect Sartre to establish it in the active social relations of men and women. This is his explicit claim:

In short, if there is to be any such thing as dialectical materialism, it must be a *historical* materialism, that is to say, a materialism from within; it must be one and the same thing to produce it and have it imposed on one. Consequently, this materialism, if it exists, can be true only within the limits of our social universe. (*CDR I*, p. 33)

In looking to the social world as the arena in which to found historical materialism, Sartre is placing the foundations firmly within history, rather than outside it, as well as stressing that it is the social activity of human beings which reveals those foundations.

Indeed, it is this notion of activity which provides us with the nature of one of the conditions for proof that Sartre offers. Towards the end of the *Critique*, he again refers to the problem of the situated observer which I discussed earlier: 'Now it may be suggested that the struggle in itself, that is to say, the temporalisation of reciprocity, although it creates both dialectical experience and the consciousness of it, may transcend the dialectical comprehension of the agent, observer, or historian' (*CDR I*, p. 805). In other words, a viable characterisation of the historical process might elude us because we are part of history ourselves. Sartre goes on, 'We must reply to these theoretical questions like Diogenes, by walking' (*CDR I*, p. 806).

This is essential to the emergence of the truth of historical materialism. We must not impose an interpretation on the development of history, as the transcendental materialist does, rather we must let it take its course freely: 'we must take the object as it is given and allow its free development to unfold before us' (Laing and Cooper, 1971, p. 93). But even Laing and Cooper's gloss is not quite accurate (even though Sartre says something very similar: 'We must accept the object as it is and let it develop freely before our eyes' (*CDR I*, p. 17)), for it implies a history external to its makers. Sartre is adamant about the need to avoid a pre-experiential *a priori*: 'The "*a priori*", here, has nothing to do with any sort of constitutive principles which are prior to experience. It relates to a universality and necessity which are contained in every experience but which transcend any particular experience' (*CDR I*, p. 35). So-called 'speculative' philosophers of history – those, like Sartre, who claim to have discovered the mechanisms that drive the historical process – are often criticised for deriving their positions from a series of logical abstractions rather than empirical data. In short, they are censured for the *a priori* nature of their investigations. The remark above constitutes Sartre's riposte to such criticism. It is not that he claims to provide a wealth of empirical historical data for his theory (although the *Critique* does contain detailed discussion of historical examples), but that it is experience itself that confirms the truth of the dialectic. It is wrong, then, to say with Alistair Davidson that in the *Critique* Sartre tried 'to capture [the world] through a system of contemplation: to understand the world through mental processes' (in Charlesworth, 1975, pp. 114–15). This deprives Sartre's text of the very practical sense of corroboration that he is trying to develop.

Indeed, this is the first of 'five conditions under which a dialectic can be established' that Sartre sets out (*CDR I*, p. 34). Rejecting Kantian transcendentalism and Husserlian phenomenology, he writes that, for dialecticians, 'it is necessary to find our apodictic [i.e. certain and incontrovertible] experience in the concrete world of History' (*CDR I*, p. 35; my parenthesis). In other words, human beings become aware of the 'a priori' truth of historical materialism as they move through the world. In this sense, it is not independent of human beings, but is rather 'constituted' by their practical awareness of the conditions of their actions.

So it is not simply a matter of 'letting the world unfold before us', as Laing and Cooper seem to suggest, because we shall encounter the dialectic only through our active participation in the world. 'The dialectic as the living logic of action is invisible to a contemplative reason', writes Sartre; rather, the dialectic, 'appears in the course of *praxis* as a necessary moment of it' (*CDR I*, p. 38). The person who tries to take up a position outside history will tend to perpetuate analytical, rather than dialectical, reason, because events will only appear to be related externally.

So when 'action in the course of development begins to give an explanation of itself' (*CDR I*, p. 38), the rationality governing action 'appears' to the individual as dialectical rationality. This means that individuals recognise that the past, or historical, *praxis* of others is the condition for their own present *praxis*, and that the rationality of their present *praxis* is both transparent and opaque – transparent in that it produces them, and opaque to the extent that it is produced by others. This amounts to a 'reciprocity of coercions and autonomies' whose 'law' appears as 'dialectical Reason' (*CDR I*, p. 39).

The dialectic is experienced as necessary in that, 'if the dialectic exists, it is because certain regions of materiality are *structured* in such a way that it cannot not exist' (p. 39). Moreover, the specific nature of this relation is that of 'totalisation' – denoted by relationships of 'interiority' rather than 'exteriority'. As ever, Sartre's language is neologistic, but precise. Here, relationships of interiority are those between elements which are modified by their membership of a group or ensemble, while relationships of exteriority are those between elements unmodified by such membership, or 'inert', as Sartre might say. So 'the dialectic, if it exists, can only be the totalisation of concrete totalisations effected by a multiplicity of totalising individualities' (p. 39).

But it cannot simply be *stated* that such regions of materiality exist, because this would be to lapse into some form of the hyper-empiricism earlier criticised by Sartre. In other words, such a statement could never constitute the grounds for the 'proof' of the dialectic that Sartre is seeking. Instead he makes the (possibility of the) intelligibility of dialectical reason the grounds for the proof of existence of the dialectic. So he writes, 'If...dialectical Reason has to be grasped initially through human relations, then its fundamental characteristics imply that it appears as apodictic experience in its very intelligibility' (*CDR I*, p. 44). He continues, in a crucial sentence, that, 'It is not a matter simply of asserting its existence, but rather of directly experiencing its existence through its intelligibility, independent of any *empirical discovery*' (p. 44). So if the dialectic exists, 'as the reason of being and of knowledge', it 'must include its own intelligibility within itself' (p. 44).

But this is still not quite enough, for we do not yet know in what this intelligibility would consist, or how we would recognise it. At this point Sartre asserts that, 'the basic intelligibility of dialectical Reason, if it exists, is that of a totalisation' (p. 44). This is because if totalisation were *not* the basic intelligibility of dialectical Reason, then the dialectic could not properly be said to exist because 'thought, as the *praxis* of the theoretician, would necessarily be discontinuous' (p. 44). If, then, we can identify an arena in which totalisation is the constituent fact of life, we will be in an arena in which we can 'directly experience' the existence of dialectical reason. This is why Sartre writes that, 'It is therefore necessary for the critical investigation to ask the fundamental question: is there a region of being where totalisation is the very form of existence?' (*CDR I*, p. 45).

Sartre's treatment of this problem mirrors his dealings with the dialectic. He chooses, first, to work on the assumption that there is a particular region of being where totalisation is the very form of existence; second, to map out the ontological and epistemological consequences of such a state of affairs; and, third, to prompt us towards judgements as to the explanatory superiority of this (dialectical) approach over other (analytical) ones.

So he writes, for example, that 'we assume' that 'the region of totalisation is, for us, human history' (*CDR I*, p. 50). A region of totalisation is further described as one in which the totalisation, 'while radically distinct from the sum of its parts, is present in its entirety, in one form or another, in each of these parts, and which relates to itself either through its relation to one or more of its parts or through its relation to the relations between all or some of them' (*CDR I*, p. 45), while at the same time being a '*developing* activity' (*CDR I*, p. 46). In other words, history is a region of totalisation, and the agents of totalisation are individuals. So Sartre translates his abstract remarks above into the language of history and individuals: 'if there is such a thing as the unity of History, the experimenter must see his own life as the Whole and the Part, as the bond between the Parts and the Whole, and as the relation between the Parts' (*CDR I*, p. 52).

Most importantly, the bonds between the parts (individuals) in a region of totalisation (history) are described by Sartre as bonds of interiority rather than exteriority, or, better, that bonds of exteriority are a moment of the dialectical process in which 'the *bond of exteriority* (analytical and positivist reason) is itself *interiorised* by practical multiplicities' (*CDR I*, p. 57). Analysing the bonds of interiority between parts takes account of the 'constantly shifting hidden conflict which modifies each part *from within* in response to internal changes in any of the others' (*CDR I*, p. 92) in a way which analytical reason (which deals only in 'molecular dispersion' (*CDR I*, p. 93)) can never do, and to this extent 'dialectical Reason includes and transcends analytical Reason' (*CDR I*, p. 92). I shall have more to say on the relationship between analytical and dialectical reason shortly.

So human beings find themselves, ontologically, in a region of totalisation and, epistemologically, in a situation in which 'dialectical knowledge [is] itself a moment of totalisation' (*CDR I*, p. 47). The implication of this is that knowledge-acquirement is a very democratic affair. In principle, says Sartre, 'anyone' can carry out the investigation because it 'can and must be anyone's reflexive experience', where 'reflection' is understood as '*praxis*' (*CDR I*, pp. 48–9). In other words, anyone who cares to reflect upon the nature of his/her relationship with their fellow human beings and with the world, will discover that relationship to be dialectical.

However, Sartre is careful to stress that the investigation could not have been carried out at any *time*. He writes that, 'If the totalisation produces a moment of critical consciousness as the necessary incarnation of its totalising *praxis*, then obviously this moment can only appear at particular times and places' (*CDR I*, p. 50). In particular, Sartre notes that such a moment has its principal precondition in the 'Stalinist idealism [that] had sclerosed both epistemological methods and practices' (p. 50). With this, Sartre refers to a 'new divorce between *praxis* and the knowledge which elucidates it' (p. 50) – the first divorce presumably being that effected by Descartes. So Sartre qualifies his original remark by writing that, 'Thus, when we claim that *anyone* can carry out the critical investigation, this does not mean that it could happen at any period. It means anyone *today*' (p. 50).

In respect of the question as to whether Sartre is developing a theory of histories or History here, it ought to be pointed out that the implication of what I have described so far is that the historical process is not open-ended. If it is true that, as Sartre writes, 'Each of the so-called "laws" of dialectical Reason is the *whole* of the dialectic', and so, 'the basic intelligibility of dialectical Reason, if it exists, is that of a totalisation' (*CDR I*, p. 44), then every individual act must be understood to be in both exterior *and* interior relation to all other individual acts, and those relations go to make up the ongoing totalisation. The apparent relationship of exteriority of individual acts is a myth engendered by the persistent use of analytical reason to understand them.

The idea is that history is a totalisation, and that individual *praxis* is the totaliser. History is a 'whole' which comprises a myriad of individual actions in the temporal (or 'diachronic') and spatial (or 'synchronic') planes. It is important to recognise that all this implies a very specific understanding of the unity of history for Sartre. Most people will agree that actions and the events they produce are related to each other in some way, and that therefore the historical process is a unified one. From an analytic point of view though (the one that Sartre rejects), these actions and events are related in a way analogous to the relations between discrete objects such as molecules. In terms of the historical process, actions and events on this reading follow one another as in a chain, and with similar sorts of relations between them as between links in a chain.

From a dialectical point of view, too, actions and events follow one another in a temporal sequence, but the relations between them are not like those of links in a chain. The dialectical claim is that while action A is followed by action B and then B by C, the relations between them are such that action B *contains* action A, and action C contains both B and A. In Sartre's terminology, action B *totalises* action A, and action C totalises action B. Again using Sartre's terminology, the relations between actions

A, B, and C from a dialectical point of view are relations of *interiority*, and this, according to Sartre, is the point of view required to understand the historical process.

These reflections enable Sartre to make the apparently startling claim that each individual action contains the whole of human history – that there is an *identity* between an individual and History and between History and an individual life. So he writes that, 'My life itself is centuries old', (*CDR I*, p. 54) and, more extravagantly, that each of us is 'simultaneously, individual and the whole of human history' (*CDR I*, p. 57). Such claims are less startling, though, if one accepts the basic dialectical proposition that actions and events are related by bonds of interiority, and that each and every human action is totalising in the sense outlined above. From this it is clear that dialectical unity differs from analytic unity to the degree that actions and events are bonded in a different way. For the dialectician, actions do not simply succeed each other, but rather – in the classic formulation – 'transcend and preserve' each other. The unity is one in which each historical action contains all other historical actions, rather than one in which each historical action merely follows previous ones.

In this context some have argued that Sartre is agnostic as to whether there is History or only histories. However, the dialectic itself – if it is true, and Sartre implicitly thinks that it is, even though he explicitly protests that it is yet to be proved – seems to demand the unity of History as a condition for its existence. The totalising nature of individual actions makes for dialectical intelligibility, and the bonds of interiority which make dialectical reason the right reason to 'read' history ensure that nothing is left 'outside' the 'totalisation without a totaliser' which is History.

The all-embracing nature of the totalisation is made clearer in Sartre's discussion of culture(s) in the introduction to the *Critique*. On the condition, he writes, that there *is* a 'developing totalisation' (which, once again, he indicates is yet to be proved, but whose existence he continually tacitly accepts), then '*bodies of knowledge*, however disparate their content or the dates of their appearance ... are linked by *relationships of interiority*' (*CDR I*, p. 53).

He explicitly rejects the possibility (if the hypothesis of the existence of totalisation proves to be right) of 'cultural regions' as a mere 'collection, or, at the very most, a superimposition of strata whose only bond (the superimposition itself) is external' (p. 53). If the bonds are bonds of interiority, as Sartre suspects, then, 'I find myself dialectically conditioned by the totalised and totalising past of the process of human development: as a "cultured" man ... I totalise myself on the basis of centuries of history.' And just in case we were in any doubt as to the inclusive nature of this dialectical conditioning, Sartre notes that 'cultured' man is 'an expression which applies to *every* man, whatever his culture, and even if he is an illiterate' (*CDR I*, p. 54). For those who have tried to portray Sartre as anticipating some of the themes of post-structuralism and post-modernity, this kind of sentiment must be hard to explain. Nothing could be further from this, for example, than Jean-François Lyotard's proposal concerning the incommensurability of language games.

This is an appropriate place to introduce rather more formally another issue raised by Sartre's description of the historical process – necessity. There are two principal forms of necessity in the context of the philosophy of history. The first refers to actions or conditions which are necessary in order to achieve a certain goal or bring about a given outcome. Thus Stalin, and the characteristics he embodied, could be said to have been necessary for the survival of the Russian Revolution in the face of internal and external threat.

The second meaning involves the claim that such-and-such an outcome was necessary in that the antecedent conditions were sufficient to make it necessary and unavoidable. In this sense, Stalin could be seen to have been the necessary outcome of antecedent conditions that gave rise to him. The sense of *sufficiency* is central here, for we are not saying that there was a series of conditions *necessary* to the emergence of Stalin, but that at the same time someone else could have become leader of the Soviet Union. The point is, precisely, that the conditions were such that their sufficiency led to the inevitable emergence of the particular individual called Stalin. This sense of necessity is evidently a threat to the notion of free and purposive human action, and we shall see Sartre on occasions apparently subscribing to it. If this seems to clash with his view of the individual as rational and purposive (as in his portrayals in *Being and Nothingness* and the biographies of Baudelaire and Genet based upon it), then this is symptomatic of a tension throughout his work generated by his embracing of Marxism without abandoning the tenets of existentialism. The former stresses sufficient antecedents while the latter stresses free and purposive individual actions. Sartre's intention is to combine these two approaches in a higher synthesis, and the stresses and strains produced by this project are in evidence throughout his later work.

The last question to be asked of dialectical reason, at this stage, is why Sartre spent so much time and effort founding and expounding it. By 1960, Sartre was as much a political animal as a philosopher, and it would be surprising if we did not find a profoundly political point behind the *Critique*. The political commitment in the *Critique* is to use the dialectic as a weapon to wrest from the bourgeoisie their hold on *truth*. Sartre sees analytical reason as a bourgeois weapon, used against the working class. Analytical reason is an 'oppressive praxis' (*CDR I*, p. 804) in that it relates things only in exteriority, and so sets up an atomistic (and hence divisive) world-view. On the other hand, says Sartre, the worker must 'recreate Reason, dissolve analytical rationality in a larger complex' (*CDR I*, p. 801), and this 'larger complex' is indeed dialectical reason. In this sense, class-conflict is a 'conflict of rationalities' and, 'The bourgeois class conceals the operation of the dialectic under the atomising rationality of positivism, whereas the theorist of the proletariat will demand explanations in the name of the dialectic itself' (*CDR I*, p. 802).

Workers will discover the dialectic through action and through the experience of exploitation, and will be led to a rejection of the atomism which analytical reason encourages. It is plain enough to see how Sartre arrives at this conclusion – competition comes about in a competitive society and to the extent that analytical reason splits things apart rather than recognising their interior bonds, the analytic provides a philosophy tailor-made for competing individuals rather than co-operative groups. Conversely, says Sartre, the dialectic is 'a transcendence of contemplative truth by effective practical truth, and of atomisation...towards the synthetic unity of the combat-group' (*CDR I*, p. 803). Sartre's vision is that of a co-operative society, and he sees the founding the historical dialectic as fundamentally instrumental in achieving that end.

All the while, however, we must realise that there are two views of analytical reason put forward in the *Critique*. One, as I have described, is that of a weapon of war in the bourgeois armoury; the second is that analytical reason was, and is, a necessary moment of the investigation. To this extent, it is analytical reason as deployed by the positivists with which Sartre is in disagreement, rather than analytic reason itself. Sartre says, for instance, that the dialectician 'rejects *a priori* the purely analytical reason of the seventeenth century, or rather, he treats it as the first moment of a synthetic, progressive Reason' (*CDR I*, p. 20). On the whole, however, dialectical reason is heralded as the technique by which we shall gain control over our political lives: 'At its most immediate level, dialectical investigation has emerged as *praxis* elucidating itself in order to control its own development' (*CDR I*, p. 220).

Some have pointed to the irony in Sartre's attack on analytical reason given that it employs many of the strategies of analytical reason itself. Lévi-Strauss, for example, makes much of the apparent paradox of Sartre using analytical reason to write a critique of dialectical reason: 'the work entitled *Critique of Dialectical Reason* is the result of the author's exercise of his own analytical reason: he defines, distinguishes, classifies and opposes' (Lévi-Strauss, 1972, p. 245). Anthony Manser, though, thinks that Sartre has overcome the problem of using analytical language to introduce a dialectical theory. The solution, he says, is to talk in a new language – a language which will make dialectical rationality accessible. This language will grow up out of our present language:

> there are no mentionable matters which we cannot discuss in our ordinary language. We are quite able to talk of 'wholes which are more than the sum of their parts' even if they do not seem to fit the categories of normal logic. (Manser, 1971, pp. 353–4)

In any case, as I pointed out above, Sartre's opposition to the use of analytical reason is not total – indeed, he describes it as 'indispensable' (*CDR I*, p. 93). He merely wants to domesticate it, or to 'put it in its place' – to point out both the dangers of its political implications and its poverty in respect of describing and explaining a process such as human history which is, simply, dialectical, and therefore not fully susceptible to analytic treatment.

In conclusion, then, Sartre argues that dialectical reason will provide a better explanation of the historical actions of individuals than will analytical reason, because it recognises that there is more to the relationship between human beings and the world than the merely external relations between objects. Sartre asserts this in the spirit of an attack on bourgeois 'truth', and yet the political implications of dialectical reason are ambiguous – an ambiguity born of the equivocal nature of historical materialism itself. We make history at the same time as we are made by history; we live a destiny. We control our political lives at the same time as we do not control them. It would be wrong, though, to overstress the disadvantages of this lack of control – indeed, for Sartre, the experience of it is a condition of the intelligibility of history. Yet there is clearly a danger that destiny may seem to take over – a danger to which Sartre saw modern Marxism succumbing. Occasionally he offers a similar pessimism: 'Historical experience has shown quite undeniably that the first moment in the construction of socialist society...could only be the indissoluble aggregation of bureaucracy, of Terror, and of the cult of personality' (*CDR I*, p. 662). These remarks on the Russian Revolution and its aftermath smack of the same mechanicism of which he found Communist commentators guilty after the 1956 invasion of Hungary.

With respect to the conclusions of 'totalisation' that Sartre draws from dialectical reason, he was once asked, 'How can individual acts result in ordered structures, and not a tangled labyrinth – unless you believe in a sort of pre-established harmony between them?' Sartre replied that there is a level of 'generality' which must be considered, and then put off a concrete answer until the second volume of the *Critique*: 'In the second volume, I was going to take an elementary example of a battle, which remains intelligible after the confusion of the two armies engages in combat in it' (Sartre, 1974a, pp. 55–6). In an extract from this projected second volume, published in the *New Left Review*, Sartre asks a relevant series of questions: 'Is history, at the level of large ensembles, an ambiguous interpenetration of unity and plurality, of dialectic and anti-dialectic, of sense and non-sense?' More directly, 'Are there, depending on the circumstances and on the particular ensemble in question, several totalisations related only by co-existence or some other external relations?' (Sartre, 1976b, p. 163). Sartre, at this point, has no concrete answer to give, and the introduction to the extract concludes correctly that, 'It remains to be proved that history is not composed of unconnected totalisations' (p. 139).

The question of a 'pre-established harmony' then, remains unanswered. However, we shall be in a better position to discuss this point after considering volume 2 of the *Critique of Dialectical Reason*, and the harmonious wholes that Sartre creates of the lives of Baudelaire, Genet and Flaubert.

# 5    The *Critique* (2) – groups

*It is seriality* which must be overcome in order to achieve even the smallest
common result.                                                     (*CDR I*, p. 687)

In the previous chapter I suggested that Sartre's foundation of the dialectic
constituted a political statement. His contention was that analytical reason
splits things up, while dialectical reason brings them together, by revealing
their bonds of interiority. Why is this a political statement? The image of
the political spectrum as a line stretching from right to left is a familiar one.
Typically, we would place conservatism towards the right-hand end of the
line, and socialism towards the left-hand end. Yet this simple picture soon
becomes inadequate when, for example, we want to illustrate the difference
between liberal and socialist politics. Both of these would, presumably, be
found left of centre on the horizontal spectrum (in respect, for example, of
their support for various forms of egalitarianism), but this would serve to
obscure, rather than reveal, an accurate presentation of their positions. To
the left–right line it is possible to add a vertical axis, whose parameters we
might call 'individualism' and 'holism'. By individualism we mean a
political theory which is founded on the individual; and by holism, we
mean a theory based on groups. This added dimension enables us to make
more sense of the differences between socialism and liberalism – the liberal
left is individualist, and the socialist left is holist.

The distinction between individualism and holism has had profound
effects on arguments within the left as to the tactics to be adopted for
progressive social change. Liberals believe that change must be founded on
the actions of the fundamental social unit – the individual – while socialists
seek progress through the activity of a group or groups – usually the
working class.

In his early days, inasmuch as he was concerned with politics at all,
Sartre would have to be classified as an individual leftist, and it was this
which brought him into conflict with the PCF from the early 1940s
onwards. In the context of its political programme, the PCF was a classic
representative of the holist left. It believed that mass action, particularly

working-class mass action, would be the source of radical social change. I have already argued that the combination of his experiences in the Second World War, together with his altercations with the Party, encouraged Sartre to the same opinion. As he moved towards class politics, Sartre understood that his philosophical individualism was an inadequate tool for understanding the phenomenon of solidarity. He knew of events like the storming of the Bastille. He had experienced – and marvelled at – the joyous unity displayed at the Liberation of Paris in 1944. How was he to come to terms with this phenomenon of co-operation and solidarity – 'Why is it that, as sometimes happens, individuals in a given case do not quarrel over food like dogs?' (*CDR I*, p. 350).

Sartre became aware that an adequate political theory required an understanding of the relationship between human beings, and between human beings and their environment, and he found the key to this understanding in dialectical reason. The dialectic, by stressing internal bonds rather than external relationships, is a form of reason which lays waste the myth of individualism, and provides the foundation for an understanding of group action. Analytical reason is untenable because it treats human beings as molecules. In a discussion of the mechanics of the free-market he says,

I have taken the example of the pure competitive market because it illustrates what Hegel called 'the atomised crowd': but in fact the quantitative relations between physical molecules are radically different from the relations between social atoms. The former act and react in the milieu of exteriority; the latter in that of interiority. (*CDR I*, p. 285)

These relations of interiority indicate that dialectical reason is the right tool to use to understand them. The use of analytical reason here would have the effect of both leading to misunderstanding, and to reinforcing the 'absolute separation' between people which is so crucial to the re-production of domination of the 'individualistic bourgeoisie' (*CDR I*, p. 97). The political point is clear – Sartre's socialism demands an understanding of sociality, both as political phenomenon and as political tactic.

There is also a reason internal to the economy of the *Critique* for why Sartre moves to his study of the philosophical anthropology of groups. If History is totalisation – which it must be if dialectical intelligibility is to be possible – then Sartre must show not only how individuals incarnate this totalisation, but also how those same individuals are linked by bonds of interiority in the 'various forms of human ensembles' (*CDR I*, p. 65). In these respects, Sartre's discussion of groups is a central contribution to his attempt to 'prove' the existence of the dialectic.

He begins his survey with what he calls 'collectives', which are 'the most obvious, immediate and superficial gatherings of the social field' (*CDR I*, p. 252), and which he describes as 'the basis of all individuation as well as unity' (p. 250). Already, in his discussion of scarcity and history, Sartre has shown that in a world (such as ours) characterised by scarcity, 'everyone within the particular social field still exists and acts in the presence of everyone else', and so far as each individual is concerned, 'the other members of the group...exist for him *collectively*, in that each of them is a threat to his life' (*CDR I*, p. 128).

It is important to note right at the outset that Sartre does not see one form of sociality – for example, collectives – necessarily developing into another form along a pre-ordained temporal path. He is merely concerned to reveal the different types of sociality that might emerge under certain historical conditions: 'I have claimed that the inert gathering with its structure of seriality is the basic type of sociality. But I have not meant this in a historical sense, and the term "fundamental" here does not imply temporal priority' (*CDR I*, p. 348).

Sartre's well-known example of the characteristics of a collectivity is that of a queue of people waiting for a bus in the Place Saint-Germain. Any one individual in the queue could be replaced by any other and the serial unity of the collective would not be disturbed, for no one is 'necessary' to that unity. In the context of scarcity – for example, if there are not enough seats on the bus to accommodate the numbers in the queue – this inter-changeability takes on a concrete meaning: that 'every individual' is 'dispensable' (*CDR I*, p. 260). But, at the same time, the people in the queue realise 'the impossibility of deciding which of the individuals are dispensable in terms of the intrinsic qualities of the individuals' (*CDR I*, p. 261). Nevertheless, competition is an evident possibility, and in this sense, 'The visible unity...is only an appearance' (*CDR I*, p. 264).

Typically, Sartre has begun his treatment of sociality with a picture of isolated individuals; yet in a crucial section of the *Critique*, entitled in Sheridan-Smith's translation, 'Duality and the Third Party', he seeks to show that individuals are fundamentally related even though they might appear isolated:

Since we began with the dispersal of human organisms, we shall consider individuals who are completely isolated by institutions, by their social condition, or by accidents of fortune. We shall try to reveal in this very separation, and therefore in a relation which tends towards absolute exteriority, their concrete historical bond of interiority. (*CDR I*, p. 100).

There are two ways, both correct, of viewing these remarks. First, Sartre plainly *needs* to show that this bond of interiority exists, otherwise social gatherings of this sort will not be accessible to dialectical intelligibility.

This refers us back to suggestions I made regarding the 'proof' of the dialectic in the previous chapter. Second, as Fredric Jameson observes, the existence of bonds of interiority, if shown to exist, means that all action takes place against a background of 'society', and that, 'human life is, in its very structure, collective rather than individualistic' (Jameson, 1971, p. 207). This marks a signal difference from the perspective of *Being and Nothingness*, and its implications, in terms of the political distinctions drawn at the beginning of this chapter, are clear.

Sartre develops these ideas by means of what he calls the 'trinity'. By way of example, he conceives of himself as a bourgeois intellectual at his desk observing two labourers, working in ignorance of each other, separated by a wall. To begin with, he says that, 'my initial relation to the two workers is negative: I do not belong to their class, I do not know their trades, I would not know how to do what they are doing, and I do not share their worries' (*CDR I*, p. 100). The fact of his being of a different class to the labourers precludes the intellectual from partaking of a solidarity which they share by virtue of their social situation. These apparently isolated workers have much in common compared to the bourgeois intellectual who observes them: 'they are both manual workers and they are both from the country; they differ from each other less than they differ from me and, in the last analysis, their reciprocal negation is, for me, a kind of deep complicity. A complicity against me' (*CDR I*, p. 103).

Despite this, however, a basic understanding of their situation arises in that the intellectual recognises that the labourers are pursuing ends. Without such a recognition, he would not be able to compare his ends with theirs: 'The basis of comprehension is complicity in principle with any undertaking, even if one then goes on to combat or condemn it' (*CDR I*, p. 101). The implication is that the intellectual discovers him- or herself as a member of *society* through an identification of the labourers' ends. We must note immediately, however, that this sociality is unstable. The understanding of the labourers that the intellectual gains through identification with their 'end-pursuing' may be undermined if those ends contradict his own. In this context, we remember from *Being and Nothingness* that it is precisely the other's project-forming capability which defines him or her both as human – as the *same* as me – and as a threat to my project, and so *other* than me.

As an example of the activity of what Sartre calls a 'third party', the intellectual participates in relations in two ways. First, the perception s/he has of the two labourers provides for unification of the field – but Sartre is clear that this is an 'ideal act', (*CDR I*, p. 101) and so cannot result in concrete relations. More importantly, the intellectual provides an objective existence for the labourers which they can constitute as potentially hostile, (i.e. 'not-labourer'), 'and in interiorising this designation, I become the objective milieu in which these two people realise their mutual dependence outside me' (*CDR I*, p. 103). For Sartre, the trinity is an essential feature of human existence: 'this trinity is not a designation or ideal mark of the human relation: it is inscribed in *being*, that is to say, in the materiality of individuals' (*CDR I*, p. 109). In other words, with the trinity, Sartre has established a basic form of sociality on which to build his analysis of groups and collectives. I shall say more on the substance of these foundations in the next chapter.

Seriality, however, has within it the seeds of its own dissolution. Under certain conditions of extreme need, serial multiplicity becomes simply an impossible manner of living. The presence of *need* is crucial: 'without the original tension of need as a relation of interiority with Nature, there would be no change; and, conversely, there is no common *praxis* at any level whose regressive or descending signification is not directly or indirectly in relation to this original tension' (*CDR I*, p. 349). As need grows, serial separation proves to be untenable, and the first stirrings of the 'group' are engendered as a response to this 'impossible' situation: 'in so far as the individuals within a given milieu are directly threatened ... by the impossibility of life, their radical unity ... is the inflexible negation of this impossibility ... thus the group constitutes itself as the radical impossibility of living, which threatens serial multiplicity' (*CDR I*, p. 341). In other words, the 'impossibility of life' within the given 'milieu' (i.e. the milieu of scarcity) engenders a negation of that situation, and the group, as 'radical unity', may arise.

Sartre then proceeds to a concrete example of how a group can emerge from the ashes of seriality and separation. In 1789 the people of Paris contrived a passive acceptance of the hunger that was imposed upon them. Of course, they had an assembly and, 'The electoral assembly was the active unity, as the being-outside-itself-in-freedom, of the inert gathering' (*CDR I*, p. 351), but because of its passivity, the assembly could never be satisfactory. Elections themselves ('in bourgeois democracies'), says Sartre, 'are passive, serial processes' (*CDR I*, p. 351). At this stage, the government of France represented a unifying factor as far as the Parisians were concerned, because Paris was 'constituted ... as a totality from outside' (*CDR I*, p. 352) – i.e. by the government. Now a form of 'quasi-reciprocity' (*CDR I*, p. 353) began to grow up in the city: 'the totality of encirclement can be described as being lived in seriality. It was what is known as enthusiasm: people were running in the streets, shouting, forming gatherings, and burning down the gates of the toll houses' (*CDR I*, p. 353). At this point, every individual saw every other individual as a potential victim of government troops, and so mutual identification in danger arose.

Sartre is quick to point out, though, that this identification is not the serial identification 'between *one* man and *one* multiplicity' (*CDR I*, p. 368), which an analytic investigation of the phenomenon might lead us to suggest. This 'common-sense' view has it that in the face of a common danger, previously dispersed individuals come together to confront that danger. Sartre writes that 'this kind of rationalism is not dialectical, and, though Marxists sometimes make use of it, its analytical, utilitarian origins are quite apparent' (p. 368).

Such an analysis is inadequate, argues Sartre, because it cannot explain how sociality is created from dispersal. After all, the designation of the threatened group *as* a threatened group is received by its individual members 'in seriality', and so therefore Sartre suggests that both practical unity and the dialectical intelligibility of that unity can only be possible on the basis of some structure of interiority – i.e. the third party. This is the reason for Sartre insisting, in the Parisian example, that, 'As the possibility of repression in the Quartier Saint-Antoine appeared increasingly probable, residents of this district, *seen as third parties*, were directly threatened' (*CDR I*, p. 367; my emphasis). This confirms the importance of those third-party relations which I described earlier. Here they are elevated to the status of 'the only possibilities of making intelligible the appearance of a constituted *praxis*, in and against the passive field' (*CDR I*, p. 366).

Everyone under these circumstances is therefore both a serial individual and a third party. The serial individual responds to clear and present danger by 'contagious processes' such as flight and panic (*CDR I*, pp. 369–70), while the individual as third party totalises his/her immediate circumstances and recognises that these circumstances (locality, friends, and other features of the multiplicity of which s/he is a part) constitute a 'totality in danger' (*CDR I*, p. 369). But at the same time, and crucially, 'he will find himself thereby designated by this threat as integrated into the totality which he has totalised' (p. 369). It is at this point that everyone, 'as a *third party*, [becomes] incapable of distinguishing his own safety from that of the other' (*CDR I*, p. 368).

Both volumes of the *Critique* contain examples of how a dialectical investigation implies the reassessment, and even abandonment, of standard categories and tools of understanding. Here, the 'mutual identification' of which Sartre speaks should not be conceived of in terms of 'altruism and egoism' (p. 368). The identification, rather, is 'engraved in the practico-inert field' (p. 368) and is produced by the dialectical relationship between the *praxis* of an oppressing group and the progressive integration of individuals as third parties into a totality which comes to be the oppressed (or, here, 'fused') group.

In the face of this common enemy, the crucial step which transformed this identification into group action in Sartre's Parisian example was that of the people taking up arms:

> the ... factor – which was soon to create the revolutionary *praxis* of the group – was that the individual act of arming oneself, in so far as it was in itself a complex process, whose aim, for every individual, was the defence of his own life, but whose motive force was seriality, was reflected, both of itself, and in its result, as a double signification of freedom. (*CDR I*, p. 355)

Now we are confronted with 'a united group which had performed a common action' (*CDR I*, p. 355). This is an 'apocalyptic' event – 'throughout a city, at every moment, in each partial process, the part is entirely involved and the movement of the city is fulfilled and signified in it' (*CDR I*, p. 357). Each is a third party for all the others, everyone is indispensable for the protection of the group, and the being of the group is to be found in each of its individual members. This is the climax of political solidarity, as presented in the *Critique*. To have remained in a state of separated, serial multiplicity would have been to succumb to annihilation by government forces. The 'impossibility' of living that situation is what transformed the collective into the group.

Sartre is careful, however, to warn us that this transformation was not at all a case of 'organised common action' (*CDR I*, p. 354), but of a series of self-interested actions, based on self-preservation, which only in retrospect came to be seen by its participants as common and not dispersed. The policy of the government was designed to quell resistance by force, but the effect of this, in the field of *praxis*, was that '*the people of Paris armed themselves against the King*' (*CDR I*, p. 355). Only at this point did the Parisians recognise themselves as 'a united group which had performed a concerted action' (p. 355).

As far as Sartre's general anthropology of groups is concerned, this is a specific case of his general thesis that groups are only ever constituted 'by the synthetic relations among other groups' – i.e. even if the group to be constituted is not directly affected by the actions of other groups (*CDR I*, p. 363). At the same time, any group-in-constitution is self-determined in the sense that its recognition of itself as Other (in respect of other groups) needs to be realised by itself (p. 362).

However, the heady excitement of this danger-filled atmosphere does not last for ever. Once the conditions that generated the group have died down, how is the group to be preserved? Sartre hints that under certain conditions this may not be a pleasant task: 'if the group is really to constitute itself by an effective *praxis*, it will liquidate alterities within it, and it will eliminate procrastinators and oppositionists' (*CDR I*, p. 403). And these undesirable elements will be a central feature of any apocalyptic event such as the one just described. For, as Sartre says: 'the theoretical schema which I have sketched does not apply in reality: there are procrastinators, oppositionists, orders and counter-orders, conflicts, temporary leaders who are quickly reabsorbed and replaced by other leaders' (*CDR I*, p. 403).

The problem, as the group begins to disintegrate, is how to neutralise the threat of seriality. At the moment of the apocalypse, the individual identifies wholly with the collective – its interests are his/her interests. Sartre is clear that this is an unstable situation. Imagining the position of the isolated lookout, charged with defending the group's position, he says: 'My courage and endurance, during my lonely watch, will be proportional to the permanence within me of the group as common reality' (*CDR I*, p. 418). Referring back to Sartre's distinction between totality and totalisation (*CDR I*, pp. 45–7), we can see that this amounts to a specific instance of his general notion that a totality will dissolve into its constituent parts unless it is continually totalised by the 'synthetic labour' of totalisation (*CDR I*, p. 46). The fused group clearly constitutes a totality (or, rather, 'a totality which is perpetually detotalised' (*CDR I*, p. 443)), in which the whole 'is present in its entirety...in each of [its parts]' (*CDR I*, p. 45), but is always threatened by dissolution and seriality.

At this point, Sartre introduces the idea of the 'pledge' as the means by which to tie the individual to the group. When an individual proposes the oath 'Let us swear', 'he claims an objective guarantee from the other third party that he will never become other' (*CDR I*, p. 420). The penalties for breaking the pledge are harsh: 'To swear is to say, as a common individual: you must kill me if I secede' (*CDR I*, p. 431). It is essential, says Sartre, to have these extreme sanctions because the basis of the pledge is *fear*. The fused group was originally born of fear guaranteed by the presence of an external danger. In threatening dire consequences for the 'oppositionists', each third party in this new 'statutory' group produces its own fear (grounded in the fear of dissolution) so as to preserve solidarity: 'The fundamental re-creation, within the pledge, is the project of substituting a real fear, produced by the group itself, for the retreating external fear, whose very distance is deceptive' (*CDR I*, p. 430). In this context, we might remember Trotsky's response to the 'procrastinating' sailors of Kronstadt in 1921. In attempting to return to the ideals of 1917, the sailors were deemed to be behaving in a counter-revolutionary fashion. The survival of the group (i.e. the Bolshevik regime) took precedence over the luxury of dissent, and the sailors were massacred.

But such violence can be read as confirmation of the continued existence of bonds of fraternity in the pledged group. The lynching of a traitor confirms both the bonds of 'love' between the lynchers (*CDR I*, p. 439), and the status of the traitor as a pledged member of the group – right up until the moment of his death:

He remains a member of the group in so far as the group – threatened by betrayal – reconstitutes itself by annihilating the guilty member, that is to say by discharging *all its violence* onto him. But this exterminating violence is still a link of fraternity between the lynchers and the lynched in that the liquidation of the traitor is grounded on the positive affirmation that he is *one of the group*; right up to the end, he is abused in the home of his own pledge and the right over him which he acknowledges in the Others. (p. 438)

It needs to be pointed out, though, that these remarks on fear, terror, and violence are made by Sartre in the context of a very specific case of group formation, i.e. 'groups which have defined themselves in combat and by the liquidation of the old seriality of impotence' (*CDR I*, p. 442). The fused group emerged from the direct threat, and use, of violence by another, already constituted, group. Sartre has already pointed out, though, that groups may be formed without the direct threat of violence from another or other group(s) – although threat of some sort is always present in that fear is driven by need resulting from scarcity. Given that it is clear in the context which Sartre has been describing that fear generated within the group is needed to replace the fear which was instrumental in fusing the group in the first place, but which has dissipated as the enemy withdraws, it is possible that other motivations, less inscribed in violence (but always founded on need), could lead to group formation, thus obviating the necessity for disciplinary violence to provide for cohesion.

In sum, Sartre's reflections on Paris in 1789 seem also to be reflections on post-Revolutionary Russia, and his remarks on the fused and statutory group can be read as an anatomical description of Stalinism. Stalinism, though, is evidently not the only form of society possible; indeed, it is not even the only authoritarian form of society possible, and as far as non-authoritarian societies are concerned, only in volume 2 does Sartre begin to confront the problem of the intelligibility of 'totalisation in [what he calls] non-dictatorial societies' (*CDR II*, pp. 428–41).

A major characteristic of the groups we have considered is that every individual in the group is capable of performing every necessary task. To this extent, the group is a very simple social formation in which the need for the division of labour (for instance) has not arisen. Now Sartre proceeds to consider a second classification of group in which specialisation is demanded. The first type is the 'organisation', which Sartre defines as 'a distribution of tasks' (*CDR I*, p. 446). An example of the organisation would be a football team in which, for the players, 'From the moment when the real struggle begins, his individual actions... no longer appear meaningful apart from those of the other members of his team' (*CDR I*, p.

457). The organisation is still a collective which has a readily identifiable unity, but the community now consists of a myriad of specialist 'positions' instead of a web of socially mobile individuals: 'Thus the creation of forms of differentiation treats the group as a transition from homogeneity to a calculated heterogeneity or, more commonly, from a less differentiated state to a more differentiated one' (*CDR I*, p. 493).

Sartre notes that the organisation, despite the hardening of social relations which it involves, has certain advantages over the pledged group. The differentiation which defines the organisation is a source of possibilities which are not open to members of the pledged group, in which the only possibility 'was for everyone to preserve the group from all kinds of internal and external threats' (*CDR I*, p. 467). In the organisation the individual is presented with the possibility of 'doing more than' accomplishing the mere fulfilment of his/her functional demands. In the organisation as football team, for example, '*a good goalkeeper* [Albert Camus?] is individualised as a common individual in so far as he produces himself in the future through his past actions as capable of *doing more* than is expected of everyone at the normal level of organisation' (*CDR I*, p. 462). This individualisation of free *praxis* amounts to a move 'beyond the task and the pledge' (*CDR I*, p. 463).

The organisation is also an improvement on the individual in terms of the possibilities of action. 'To resemble a guard in square formation', says Sartre, for example, 'one would have to have eyes all around one's head, and arms in one's back'. In this sense, 'an organisation does not *reproduce* an organism, but is meant to be an improvement on it by means of human invention' (*CDR I*, p. 534). Sartre's emphasis here on the capability of human beings to *create*, is characteristic. In cases like this, he is being clear that human beings are able to take the raw material which is their situation in the world, and construct something better from it. The organisation is not something provided by God or produced by History, but is rather created by human beings.

However, submerged in the apocalyptic fervour of the fused group, and held in thrall by the institutionalised terror of the pledged group, the individual – basis of all sociality – now reappears as a threat to the survival of that sociality. The differentiation allowed in the organisation can 'collapse in a moment into a statute of accidental heterogeneity (of exteriority)' (*CDR I*, p. 545). Because the individual is the 'regulatory schema and untranscendable limit of the constituted dialectic' (*CDR I*, p. 559) – in other words, of the organised group – 'there is a constant danger that the current will cease to flow' (*CDR I*, p. 545).

In a sense, the possibility of this breakdown was anticipated by the necessity for the pledge which, 'occasions a first contradiction in that it becomes the basis for the heterogeneity of functions' (*CDR I*, p. 577). Now, by living the new possibilities generated by the organisation, and in a move of dialectical irony, the individual 'can realise his fidelity in the group only through a transcendence which removes him from the common statute and projects him into the object outside' (*CDR I*, p. 585). This is experienced by the individual as fear of exile, and this, 'in reciprocity, gives rise to the fear that the group may be dissolved, as inessential, in the essentiality of individual actions' (p. 585). Further, because this new danger 'arises from ... pledged fidelity' (p. 585), the pledge itself can offer no protection against it.

In an attempt to preserve its unified character in the face of schisms appearing at the level of the organisation, a second form of group based on specialisation appears: the institution. The institution conceives 'new practices':

The group reacts to this permanent danger, appearing at the level of the organisation, with new practices: it produces itself in the form of an institution-alised group; which means that 'organs', functions and powers are transformed into institutions; that, in the framework of institutions, the community tries to acquire a new type of unity by institutionalising sovereignty, and that the common individual transforms himself into an institutionalised individual. (*CDR I*, p. 591)

It is clear that Sartre holds the institution in less high regard than any of the other types of group he has described. Although he claims that his description of institutions as 'degraded forms of community' is not intended to constitute a value-judgement, his surmise that 'the movement of the [dialectical] investigation may possibly be circular' in that the institution appears to be a return to the 'collective statute' and 'towards the practico-inert from which Freedom-Terror removed itself a little earlier' (*CDR I*, p. 591), constitutes unmistakable signs of disapproval – or, at least, dialectically founded resignation.

At this level, then, authority begins to emerge in its full development, and constitutes a form of alienation:

the sovereign reigns through and over the impotence of all; their living practical union would make his function useless, and indeed, impossible to perform. However, his proper activity is to struggle against the invasion of the group by seriality, that is to say, against the very conditions which make his office legitimate and possible. We have seen how the contradiction is resolved, in practice, by a new form of alienation: that of each and all to one person. (*CDR I*, p. 628)

Sartre concludes his 410-page discussion of groups with what reads as a rather undialectical appeal to the Soviet Union to loosen up its social and political structures. As I have suggested, his reflections on the fused group, the statutory group, the organisation, and the institution can be read as a dialectical history of the structures which emerged in the Soviet Union between 1917 and 1960. In Sartre's assessment of them, the 'move' from one structure to another is carefully explained in terms of the overcoming of contradiction, and the subsequent solution of these contradictions in a new structural form. At this last moment of the discussion, however, dialectical contradictions seem to be replaced by a relatively uncomplicated voluntarism. In fact, the conclusion suggested by Sartre's dialectical investigation is that 'institutionalisation' in the Soviet Union 'will [necessarily] lead to bureaucratisation' (*CDR I*, p. 660), and that this involves (among other things), 'mistrust and serialising (and serialised) terror at the level of the peers; and the annihilation of organisms in obedience to the superior organism' (*CDR I*, p. 658).

True, Sartre does say that any attempt by a 'sovereign institutional group' (for example, the Communist Party of the Soviet Union) to regroup serial individuals will not result in their taking on the statute of the 'being-of-the-group', but will rather constitute these individuals as a potential group either 'outside the state' or 'in opposition to the state' (*CDR I*, p. 661). However, there is no necessity for this, and in the end Sartre seems to appeal to the goodwill of the Communist Party itself to loosen the shackles: 'the sovereign must gradually abandon its *monopoly of the group*' (p. 661).

In other words, Sartre's dialectical investigation has led him to a place that he does not favour, but the dialectic itself offers no way out. Instead, he can only rather lamely conclude that the 'first stage in the construction of a socialist society', which 'could only be the indissoluble aggregation of bureaucracy, of Terror and of the cult of personality', now 'seems to be approaching its end' (*CDR I*, p. 662). Sartre gives no clear indication, here, either of why the end happens or what might come next.

Roger Garaudy's conclusions about Sartre's treatment of groups in the *Critique* are not complimentary: 'Social relations are hardly more than a multiplication of personal relationships: that, it would seem, is the fundamental postulate of the *Critique of Dialectical Reason* (Garaudy, 1970, p. 91). This rebuttal does not do justice to the complexity of Sartre's analysis. For instance, his system of 'revolving thirds' is a clear indication of an attempt to introduce the dialectic into social relationships. At the same time, it would be wrong to say (as some have) that Sartre has drawn up an abstract and analytic 'anatomy of revolutions'. He has certainly taken historical events – i.e. the French and Russian revolutions – and distilled their essence. But he is not saying that all revolutions will necessarily move from fused group to pledged group to organisation to institution. 'This', he writes, 'is of course not a historical sequence; and indeed we shall see that – on account of dialectical circularity – any form can emerge either before or after any other and that only the materiality of the historical process can determine the sequence' (*CDR I*, p. 583).

What we are left with are the foundations of the 'structural anthropology' which Sartre was seeking, but without the historical bedrock in which to place it. Sartre hoped to provide the History in the second volume of the *Critique*, but even there, as we shall see, the historical examples are limited, and Sartre never found himself able to complete the task promised by the two volumes: the attempt to 'establish that there is *one* human history, with *one* truth and *one* intelligibility ... by demonstrating that a practical multiplicity, whatever it may be, must unceasingly totalise itself through interiorising its multiplicity at all levels' (*CDR I*, p. 69). Sartre's earlier concern at the unmanageable enormity of this task seems to have been borne out: 'I am far from believing that the isolated effort of one individual can provide a satisfactory answer – even a partial one – to so vast a question, a question which engages with the totality of History' (*CDR I*, pp. 40–1). I do not believe, though, that this remark should be read in anything like a postmodern manner. Sartre is suggesting neither that the individual is *constitutively* incapable of engaging with the totality of History, nor that such a totality does not exist, but rather that the *practical* obstacles to such an intelligibility through *praxis* are so immense as to defy resolution.

Despite all this, the solid emphasis on groups is itself a significant feature of Sartre's thought at this stage of his development. The political point of this is reiterated: 'I have tried above all to indicate that the government apparatus and its sub-groups for constraint and propaganda are careful not to occasion what might be called *organised action* within inert gatherings. Every organisation disturbs them in so far as it dissolves seriality' (*CDR I*, p. 654). Seriality represents political impotence, solidarity represents political strength.

But was anyone listening to Sartre's gargantuan affirmation of socialist strategy? Certainly the *Critique* was not well received by the Communist Party, primarily because Sartre had 'unkind' things to say about the working class. He variously refers to it as an 'inert collective being', and an 'inorganic common materiality' (*CDR I*, p. 251). He writes that 'even in revolutionary periods', the 'transformation of a class into an actualised group has never actually appeared' (*CDR I*, p. 679). Furthermore, the Trade Union organisation, 'is typical of the organised group which becomes institutional and sovereign (and is in constant danger of bureaucratisation)' (*CDR I*, pp. 679–80).

Certainly, Sartre's evident admiration for the organised turmoil of the apocalypse – the taking of the Bastille, or the storming of the Winter Palace – is better suited to the 'spontaneous uprisings' favoured by anarchists, than to any disciplined approach to social change. In this context, Sartre's treatment of the apocalypse has sometimes been seen as the blueprint for the libertarian uprisings in France – particularly Paris – in 1968. Clearly many of the students had read Sartre, but both he and de Beauvoir have disclaimed any such extravagant responsibility on the part of the *Critique* for the May disturbances. Beauvoir summed up the reaction thus: 'The *Critique of Dialectical Reason* was published; attacked by the Right, by the Communists, and by the ethnographers, [but] it gained the approval of the philosophers' (de Beauvoir, 1978, p. 511). To the extent that philosophers have only interpreted the world and never changed it, the *Critique* is no guide to social revolution.

We are united by the fact that we all live in a world which is determined
by scarcity.                                              (*CDR I*, p. 136)

In the context of the *Critique* as a book aimed at revealing the roots of
political emancipation, we have seen Sartre discovering effective, if
unstable, political action in the temporary cohesion of the group. His
anthropology of the group assumes a sociality which he seeks to develop in
the reciprocal activity of third parties. I have already noted, however,
Sartre's suggestion in the *Critique* that *conflict* is as basic a feature of the
human condition as is solidarity. Of course it is precisely such conflict that
engenders the possibility of cohesion, and it is to be expected in a dialectical
investigation that conflict and alienation will have positive aspects. But the
question is whether Sartre envisages an eventual resolution of conflict and
alienated relations. In this crucial political context his view of alienation
between human beings needs to be explored thoroughly.

A similar question can be asked about the relationship between human
beings and their environment – particularly between human beings and the
surrounding materiality they have worked on and created. What happens
to the work we do in the world? Does it remain ours, or does it escape us?
Sartre suggests that the instruments we create in the world may elude us by
taking on a 'life of their own'. In this sense, the surrounding world
becomes a threat – but does it have to be so? If this perverse behaviour of
worked matter is a fundamental feature of our condition, then our control
over our lives would seem to diminish accordingly. At every stage of the
dialectic, our actions would escape us and amount to a threat to our
emancipation. How far, in other words, does Sartre think we control our
actions in the world? How far, to reiterate a point referred to earlier,
(p. 67), can *praxis*, once it has elucidated itself, actually 'control its own
development'? First we must consider the possibility of alienation between
human beings.

We have already seen that, under certain conditions, need is the motor
force for the formation of the group. Indeed, for Sartre, need is at the root

of all explanation: 'Everything is to be explained through *need*; need is the first totalising relation between the material being, man, and the material ensemble of which he is a part' (*CDR I*, p. 80). However, the conditions that allowed the group to form were very specific: the presence of an external danger made living in seriality 'impossible'. Seriality was overcome and, momentarily at least, alienation between human beings disappeared with it in the '*united group which had performed a concerted action*' (*CDR I*, p. 355).

But scarcity is a two-edged sword. It has been a constant factor in human history, says Sartre: 'the whole of human development, at least up to now, has been a bitter struggle against *scarcity*' (*CDR I*, p. 123). Inevitably, the fact of scarcity (which is ever-present) is the basis for potential conflict because, '*There is not enough for everybody*' (*CDR I*, p. 128). Under these conditions, 'Man exists for everyone as non-human man, as an alien species...the mere existence of everyone is defined by scarcity as the constant danger of non-existence both for another and for everyone' (*CDR I*, p. 130).

This is a far cry from the seductive, solid picture of the group presented elsewhere in the *Critique*. Sartre graphically portrays the uncomfortable condition of scarcity – and we must remember that this lack has characterised the whole of human history 'up to now':

Nothing – not even wild beasts or microbes – could be more terrifying for man than a species which is intelligent, carnivorous and cruel, and which can outwit and understand human intelligence, and whose aim is precisely the destruction of man. This, however, is obviously our own species as perceived in others by each of its members in the context of scarcity. (*CDR I*, p. 132)

The potentiality for conflict is made yet clearer in Sartre's discussion of positive and negative reciprocity. Reciprocity itself, he says, is in principle completely opposed to alienation, but it can take either of two forms, under different conditions. Positively, within reciprocity, 'the end may be shared (a collective undertaking or work), everyone making himself the other's means in order that their collective effort shall realise their single transcendent aim' (*CDR I*, p. 113). This sounds very much like the attitude existing in the group. However, reciprocity can also be negative so that, 'each refuses to serve the other's end, while recognising his own objective being as a means within the adversary's project, he uses his own instrumentality in others to make them an instrument of his own ends in spite of themselves. This is struggle' (p. 113).

But what decides whether struggle will ensue? What conditions are necessary for conflict? Sartre supplies the answer: 'The origin of struggle always lies, in fact, in some concrete antagonism whose material condition is scarcity' (p. 113). Bearing in mind Sartre's affirmation that scarcity has been an enduring feature of the human condition, then the short-lived apocalyptic solidarity of the French Revolution, for instance, is put into some sort of perspective. If we take at face value Sartre's references to scarcity as the foundation of conflict, then the chances of political emancipation would seem to be slim. There is the permanent possibility – even likelihood – of conflict in the field of scarcity.

But is this scarcity removable? If we can show that scarcity is, in principle, eradicable, then the possibility of reducing the incidence of conflict between human beings remains open. Without scarcity, the prime force making for conflict is removed (although so are the conditions for cohesion, given that need drives group formation). In a 1975 interview, Sartre seems relatively optimistic about the future. He says that 'true social harmony' will come, 'once there has been a change in the economic, cultural, and affective relations among men. It will begin with the eradication of material scarcity – which, as I showed in the *Critique of Dialectical Reason*, is for me the root of the antagonisms, past and present, among men' (Sartre, 1978d, p. 13).

In the same interview, however, he goes on to affirm that the future may also hold other, unforseeable, antagonisms to militate against complete harmony. In the *Critique* itself he is even more guarded. He never says that scarcity is definitely eradicable, but only that it is possible to imagine an alternative state: 'relations of immediate abundance between other practical organisms and other milieux are not inconceivable *a priori*' (*CDR I*, p. 735).

So a world without scarcity can be conceived, and in this respect scarcity is contingent. But such a world would be so radically different from the present one, writes Sartre, that 'our quality as *men*' would disappear, 'and since this quality is historical, the actual specificity of our History would disappear too' (*CDR I*, p. 124). Since Sartre continually stresses that he is investigating our specific history, and not some putative alien one, he bases all his remarks in this context on the assertion that 'in spite of its contingency, scarcity is a very basic human relation' (*CDR I*, p. 123). So it is not just a question of whether the eradication of scarcity would reduce conflict, but of how it would remove, at a stroke, the principal condition for the possibility of human history.

There is thus no unqualified assertion of the possibility of the eradication of scarcity in the *Critique*. Indeed, in a different, but relevant, context in the *Search for a Method*, Sartre suggests that the elimination of scarcity is a situation beyond our comprehension: 'As soon as there will exist for everyone a margin of real freedom beyond the production of life, Marxism will have lived out its span; a philosophy of freedom will take its place. But we have no means, no intellectual instrument, no concrete experience which allows us to conceive of this freedom or of this philosophy' (Sartre, 1968, p. 34). The fact is that, in the *Critique*, there is enough scarcity to go round.

For Sartre, the role of scarcity in exploitation is fundamental:

if workers produce a *little more* than society really needs, and if they are administered by a group which is freed from productive labour and whose members, necessarily few in number, can share out the surplus, there seems no reason at all why the situation should ever change. However, if we assume that differentiation occurs in a society whose members always produce a *little less* than everyone needs...so that the constitution of an unproductive group depends on general malnutrition, and so that one of its essential functions is the selection of the surplus population to be eliminated – if we assume all this, then, it seems to me, we will have grasped the very framework of the transformations, and their intelligibility. (*CDR I*, p. 149)

The unproductive group (capitalists) depends on the goods and services provided by the productive group (workers) for its survival. As – according to Sartre – the productive group provides a little less than everyone needs, the unproductive group siphons off what it needs to survive, leaving too little for the producers. The producers thus find themselves exploited. Furthermore, Sartre does not seem at all optimistic with regard to the eradication of this exploitation – as we saw in the quotation from the *Search for a Method* above, we cannot conceive of a situation in which we do anything else other than 'produce a little less than everyone needs'. It ought also to be noted that Sartre is using the fact of scarcity to drive what he calls 'transformations'. In a situation of surplus, 'there seems no reason at all why the situation should ever change', but relations founded on scarcity are fundamentally unstable and subject to dialectically intelligible flux. Scarcity, then, drives (our) history.

The fact remains that in Sartre's view, scarcity can, and most probably will, bring individuals into conflict with one another. This speculation receives an element of support from parts of the *Critique* where the separation between human beings appears to run deeper than that provided by the apparently contingent state of scarcity. For example, in *Being and Nothingness* Sartre gives the example of a man, sitting on a park bench, who constitutes the focus of the world around him. At a certain point, another man enters the park and the man on the bench is aware that all the objects in the park now have an alternative focus, and that, 'We are dealing with a relation which is without parts, given at one stroke, inside of which there unfolds a spatiality which is not my spatiality; for instead of a grouping toward me of the objects, there is now an orientation which flees from me' (*BN*, p. 254).

In the same way, when in the *Critique* Sartre is working through the implications of the Duality/Third-Party situation, he says of the labourers that, 'their material environment eludes me, in so far as it is made the object or the means of their activity...[it is] an *objectivity-for-the-other* which escapes me' (*CDR I*, p. 102). This '*glissement*' or 'point of haemorrhage' would seem to be irreducible. Sartre makes exactly the same point elsewhere in the *Critique* while talking about how far the unification of two totalising consciousnesses is possible. 'The limit of unification', he says, 'lies in the mutual recognition which occurs in the process of two synthetic totalisations: however far the two integrations are carried, they *respect one another, there will always be two* of them, each integrating the entire universe.' (p. 114). To this extent, the separation of individuals would seem to be fundamental to their condition, with the solidarity of the group only providing temporary relief, under very specific conditions, from alterity. Further, the ignorance represented by this 'haemorrhage' is fundamental to dialectical intelligibility – if it did not exist we could not think dialectically.

Far from being the place of sociality and reciprocity suggested in parts by the previous chapter, then, Sartre's social universe is peculiarly Janus-faced. Isolation is as much a feature of existence as sociality. Certainly the cohesion that he recognises as essential for political action is not easy to come by, and even when it happens it is in permanent danger of dissolution.

Nor does the potential alienation of human beings end with their social relations. Sartre also says that we can become dominated by the unintended consequence of our actions: 'man has to struggle...against his own action as it becomes other' (*CDR I*, p. 124). For example, we might perform a task with one end in view, only to find that the end is subverted within the new situation that our actions engender.

In his own words, Sartre would say that *praxis* acts on the world, and this gives the world the status of the 'practico-inert' or, as the *Critique*'s glossary helpfully defines it, 'matter in which past *praxis* is embodied' (*CDR I*, p. 829). The practico-inert may then turn back on *praxis*, subverting its intentions and creating an 'anti-praxis'. Sartre describes the same process by using the terms 'finality' and 'counter-finality'. In this case *praxis* conceives an aim (a finality) and acts on the world in order to bring it about. This *praxis* is embodied in the world (practico-inert) which turns back on *praxis* and produces – in place of the intended finality – a counter-finality. In other words, the activity of human beings – as well as having the potentiality for creating a better world – can also be counter-productive. The practico-inert, in its power to frustrate, is a place of 'violence, darkness and witchcraft' (*CDR I*, p. 318). As ever with Sartre, though, we need to be aware that what on the face of it is counter-productive is also often the condition for progress. This is, of course, a feature of the dialectic, and it is essential that words like 'counter-productive' are understood dialectically. Here, he will say that the very experience of frustration and the necessity it embodies is a precondition for the (dialectical) intelligibility of history.

At one point in the *Critique*, Sartre provides a very simple example of the machinations of the practico-inert. Due to pressure on arable land, he says, Chinese peasants have been in the habit of deforesting large areas to provide more clear soil for crops. The positive result of this is indeed that more ground becomes available for planting, thus providing temporary relief from shortage. However, the deforestation has a negative result too: 'since the loess of mountains and peneplains is no longer retained by trees, it congests the rivers, raising them higher than the plains and bottling them up in their lower reaches, and forcing them to overflow their banks'. Catastrophic flooding is the result. Sartre goes on: 'If some enemy of mankind had wanted to persecute the peasants of China as a whole, he would have ordered mercenary troops to deforest the mountains sys-tematically. The positive system of agriculture was transformed into an infernal machine' (*CDR I*, p. 162). This sort of event turns our actions against themselves, and the unforeseen consequences of the practico-inert may be disastrous. The Chinese peasants set out to create more farming land, and end by being flooded out of their homes.

On the face of it, what Sartre calls the hell of the practico-inert is an inevitable attendant feature of our actions in the world. To illustrate this issue further, we can turn to another example of the practico-inert to which Sartre refers. He notes that gas-lighting was made easily and cheaply available in the nineteenth century by the use of coal as a source of energy. As well as having obvious benefits – for example, use in the home, or for street-lighting – gas-lighting also meant that employers could ask their workers to be productive for up to 15 or 16 hours a day. For the work-force, this is evidently an unfortunate, unforeseen consequence of the discovery of coal in the context of the industrial revolution.

Now, says Sartre, 'we do not quite know whether it was the industrial ensemble dominated by coal which, through the medium of the men it produced, required a working day of sixteen hours, or whether it was the industrialists, in the coal-based economy, who used gas-lighting to increase production' (*CDR I*, p. 160). The importance of the answer to this question lies in the fact that if we are to blame the workers' long hours on 'industry', then their suffering appears somehow to be written into history, as a necessary aspect of the thing called 'The Industrial Revolution'. If, on the other hand, we are to hold the industrialists themselves responsible for this new practice, then the suffering appears more readily accessible to eradication. To this extent, to be at the mercy of historical forces is measurably worse than to be subject to the contingent whims of industrial capitalists, for, in the second case, emancipation is a more likely proposition. However, Sartre's options for explanation do not end there. As well as industry and the industrialists, he asks whether, 'the two formulations do not refer to the two aspects of a single dialectical circularity' (p. 160). It is clear that this is the explanation he favours, and just what it means – as well as its implications for emancipation – we can discover from a third example taken from the *Critique*.

Sartre notes that one consequence of the industrial revolution was a rapid increase in the incidence of air pollution. This pollution was bad for the work-force for three reasons. First, working people tended to live nearest to the source of the pollution (and also downwind of it – this is why, in a country like Britain where the prevailing wind is from the west, the salubrious parts of towns and cities are always to be found on their western edges); second, they were exposed to the foul air for a large proportion of the day because low wages forced them to work long hours, and finally, noxious fumes were particularly dangerous because of the workers' weakened state – brought about by the lack of an adequate diet, sanitation, and so on.

Sartre also says that the pollution had unfortunate consequences for the employers themselves. First, they too had to breathe bad air, although admittedly the employer, 'has sufficient means to spend his evenings and his Sundays out of town, in his country cottage' (*CDR I*, p. 194). Second, pollution is costly for the employers – a certain sanitary standard has to be maintained, and this diverts capital which could be used elsewhere. Pollution, then, as an unintended consequence of the advances made during the industrial revolution, is bad for both the work-force and the employers.

As before, the question is – could anything have been done about it? Or did pollution merely 'appear', in the same way that gas-lighting was suggested simply to have 'appeared'? Sartre is clear that in the same sense that the industrial revolution would not have occurred without the activity of human beings, so pollution (for instance) has a human origin. Consequently, its effects were susceptible to human intervention: 'From the outset means were in fact available of lessening the pollution if not of ending it entirely. Franklin had already suggested that coal smoke could be reused, since it was really just incompletely consumed carbon' (*CDR I*, p. 195).

Sartre's emphasis on the responsibility of human beings is a familiar refrain. It was a central theme of *Being and Nothingness*, and here we find it resurfacing 15 years later. Towards the end of the *Critique*, Sartre goes

into some detail in two historical examples to illustrate this responsibility
– first in the colonial situation of the pauperisation of Muslim com-
munities; and secondly, with reference to exploitation in Victorian England
coal-mines. Violence in a colonial situation, he claims, is not *inscribed* in
things, rather violence is *practice*. It is true that, 'The son of the colonialist
and the son of the Muslim are both children of the objective violence which
defines the system itself as a practico-inert hell' (*CDR I*, p. 717). But this
violence was only first used when the system itself was installed: 'It is man
who inscribed violence into things as the eternal unity of this passive
mediation between men' (p. 718).

Sartre makes the point even clearer in the example of the exploitation of
wage-labour. He says that the demand for coal (based on need) 'produced
the mine owners as major capitalists' (*CDR I*, p. 738). By way of
demonstrating the environmental and historical conditions that created
exploitation, Sartre points to,

Scientific discoveries, technical innovations immediately put to use, customers as
seriality; no more was necessary for the mine to emerge as a fabulous inheritance,
owned by one man; for the first machines to appear there, overthrowing techniques
and imposing a set of exigencies and constraints on both capitalists and workers.
(p. 738).

'No more was necessary', that is, except the activity of human beings:
'what concerns us is that this process established itself against a
background of scarcity...and *by men*...The transformation of the mine
owner *comes to him from outside*, but he has to interiorise it and realise it
practically' (*CDR I*, p. 739). The mine-owner's recognition of himself in
other mine owners, and through this his anticipation of competition,
imposes demands upon him 'from outside'. But the situation is also one of
'a *praxis* of systematic oppression' (*CDR I*, p. 743). The owner must
recognise the workers as free in order to practise oppression, in the same
way that the colonialist recognises the humanity of the indigenous
population before he can treat them as sub-human. The force of Sartre's
position lies in the fact that he sees oppression as *deliberate*, and not simply
an automatic reaction to exterior circumstances. It is completely wrong, he
writes, 'to interpret the cruelty of the English employers as indifference,
blindness or contempt: it was in fact quite deliberate' (p. 743).

In the discussion of the machinations of the practico-inert, however, the
centrality of the responsibility of human beings is displaced. For sure, we
are responsible for conceiving projects and working towards their
fulfilment, but we are also implicated, by proxy, in the *subversion* of our
projects because that is in the nature of the dialectical operation of the
practico-inert.

For instance, in the pollution example, Sartre notes that the unintended consequence of foul air was not eliminated, despite the fact that techniques were available to do so. The reason, says Sartre, is that on balance the employers preferred to allow the pollution to continue, as it was one way of being constituted as a distinct class. Their refusal to eliminate pollution, coupled with their position as the only people who could do it, characterised them as a 'special group' (*CDR I*, p. 195). He says quite clearly that these 'archaic' industrialists 'had the power to alter the situation' (*CDR I*, p. 196), but that, given the impossibility of 'transcendence' of the situation at this level, in the struggle between 'pros and cons' the cons won out. In this way, 'The counter-finality which *has to be removed*... becomes *a finality which had to be maintained*' (p. 196). In other words, the employers found that they could turn the counter-finality of pollution into a finality – i.e. the project of retaining their grip on the workforce.

At the end of his discussion of this example, Sartre confirms that this toing and froing between actions and unintended consequences is both a fundamental feature of the human condition, and one of the conditions of its intelligibility:

To sum up, the intelligibility of material contradictions within a developing process is due to the fact that, through negation as a material unity within the social field, every finality is a counter-finality; and to the fact that, on the other hand, to the extent that all movements of matter are sustained and directed by men, every counter-finality is objectively, at its own level, and from the point of view of particular practico-inert ensembles, a finality. (p. 196)

In other words, every action we perform will have unintended consequences. They may be dire (for example, the Chinese deforestation), or they may not. In any case, we will always act towards a certain end (finality), find that that project has been subverted (counter-finality), and then rearrange our actions in the light of the new situation. The subversion of our actions appears to be an untranscendable feature of our existence.

This is what Sartre refers to as a Hegelian form of alienation (*CDR I*, p. 227), according to which 'alienation ... [is] ... a constant characteristic of all kinds of objectification'; in this case, that 'man' '*returns to himself as Other*' (p. 227). But he says in the same passage that we must distinguish between *this* form of alienation and *Marx's* sense of it, according to which alienation 'begins with exploitation' (p. 227). Sartre says surprisingly little in the *Critique* about the causes of exploitation and the possibility of eradicating them, although as we have seen, in an attenuated sense, early industrialists could have alleviated problems associated with air pollution. We can only conclude that alienation as objectification is an untranscendable feature of the human condition, and that we are given insufficient indication as to whether alienation born of exploitation is transcendable or not.

To conclude, Sartre's position on the alienation of human beings among themselves is hardly encouraging. The group is presented as the means of escape from seriality: 'the project of removing man from the statute of alterity which makes him the product of his produce, in order to transform him hot [*à chaud*], by appropriate practices, in a *product of that group*, that is to say – as long as the group is freedom – *into his own product*' (*CDR I*, pp. 672–3). However, the group as 'freedom' is permanently threatened with instability: 'It is formed in opposition to alienation, in so far as alienation substitutes the practico-inert field for the free practical field of the individual; but it cannot escape alienation any more than the individual can, and it thereby lapses into serial passivity' (*CDR I*, p. 668).

In other words, 'the necessity of freedom implies the progressive alienation of freedom to necessity' (*CDR I*, p. 672). This dialectical see-saw is reflected, too, in the alienation between human beings and their worked environment. In necessarily engendering counter-finalities as the unintended consequences of our actions, we participate in our own alienation. We *can* act to turn a counter-finality into a finality, but that project, too, will be subverted. This is not to say that Sartre thinks the human condition to be utterly hopeless. In his stress on our responsibility and our ability to create new situations, he affirms his belief that a measure of improvement is possible. If I set out to build a house, then competition from other people or the demands of the environment might force me to alter the design or make the house expensive to build. However, the chances are that I will end up with a roof over my head where there was none before, and to this extent my situation is improved. Similarly, as I pointed out earlier in the chapter, the very experience of the unintended consequences of our actions is a condition for understanding the historical process. At the same time as I am cast down by my failure I am lifted up to a higher level of understanding. In this sense, failure is a condition of success.

These reflections have merely enabled us to see historical materialism at work – we make history at the same time as it makes us: 'In so far as … we understand that we have actually done something else and why our action has been altered outside us, we get our first dialectical experience of necessity' (*CDR I*, p. 222) – and this, of course, is a practical instance of Sartre's conviction that the critical investigation required to establish the dialectic 'can and must be anyone's reflexive experience' (*CDR I*, p. 48). Nothing is necessary except the necessity of the dialectic. To the extent that the operation of the dialectic locks us into the counter-finalities of the practico-inert, and turns our actions into satanic representations of intention, then alienation would seem to be both a permanent danger within the human condition, and (in a dialectical twist), the source of the possibility of understanding it. Is this, then, as Wilfrid Desan would have us believe, 'an eloquent plea for the cause of freedom' (1974, pp. vii–viii)? Elsewhere, as I have pointed out, Sartre affirms that, 'dialectical investigation has emerged as a *praxis* elucidating itself in order to control its own development' (*CDR I*, p. 220). If human freedom consists in establishing the intelligibility of history, then alienation can be read as a condition of emancipation. If, however, freedom involves the rational control of human development, then alienation – on Sartre's account – would seem to comprise a permanent threat to it.

# 7 The second *Critique*

> If the plurality of epicentres is a real condition of *two* opposed
> intelligibilities...how could there be *one* dialectical intelligibility of the
> ongoing process?                                                    (*CDR II*, p. 5)

For a long time it looked as though the promised second volume of the
*Critique of Dialectical Reason* would never appear. Scattered remarks
about it in the first volume (see for example *CDR I*, pp. 39, 69, 824) came
to be read as a typically Sartrean promissory note – one that would not be
redeemed. Thus volume two seemed likely at the time to constitute the
latest and most important of a long list of Sartre's unfinished projects, to
be followed notoriously by the missing fourth volume (on *Madame
Bovary*) of his Flaubert biography.

It was clear, though, that Sartre had begun work on the projected second
volume towards the end of the 1950s, and a tantalising glimpse of its
content was given when he sanctioned the publication of 25 translated
pages of it in the *New Left Review*'s centenary edition (Sartre, 1976b). This
glimpse, it turns out, was representative of the whole, for it is entitled
'Socialism in one country' and deals with Stalin and Stalinism – as do
nearly half of the pages of volume two itself. Finally, in 1985, Gallimard
published the second volume in its entirety (Sartre, 1985a) and this was
followed in 1991 by Verso's publication of Quintin Hoare's translation
(Sartre, 1991). Mention ought also to be made of Ronald Aronson's
illuminating English-language commentary (1987), published after a
lengthy study of Sartre's original manuscript.

There is, of course, a question as to how much one can legitimately make
of a posthumously published piece of work which Sartre himself evidently
never wanted to appear. Is it fair to draw conclusions as to the nature and
direction of his thought from a text which he presumably considered short
of the requirements for public consumption? In my view the question turns
on what these requirements might be, and how short Sartre had fallen of
them. He might, for example, have been concerned at either a lack of
quality or a lack of completeness. As far as quality is concerned the second

volume is at least as impressive as the first, particularly in its introduction of new and instructive technical terms, and there is the additional bonus of a dazzling, if idiosyncratic, interpretation of Stalinism.

Clearly, however, the second volume is incomplete in that it fails to fulfil the first volume's promise to 'establish that there is *one* human history, with *one* truth and *one* intelligibility' (*CDR I*, p. 69). Interestingly, though, this failure is not rooted in any error (as such) on Sartre's part, but is born of his own thoroughness. He knew that the demonstration of unique intelligibility meant 'demonstrating that a practical multiplicity, *whatever it may be*, must unceasingly totalise itself through interiorising its multiplicity at all levels' (p. 69; my emphasis). When he finally got down to trying to do so, it became plain that he was involved in a task of monumental proportions because 'practical multiplicities', in the guise of societies and their sub-groups, take on many forms, and the demonstration of unceasing totalisation would demand different techniques and approaches in each case.

Put crudely, Sartre decided to split these multiplicities up into two groups, which he called 'directorial' and 'non-directorial' societies. His analysis of Stalinism amounts to an attempt to show how a directorial society unceasingly totalises itself, and he is clear that it is easier to do so for these societies, with their 'obviously less complex structures' than in non-directorial bourgeois democracies (*CDR II*, p. 187). In this second volume he simply does not get around to dealing with non-directorial societies, except in note form in the Appendix, let alone with the problem of international interaction and the interaction of groups and organisations not bounded by national boundaries. In short, it must have become clear to Sartre that his project would remain incomplete, and perhaps he thought that the second volume made such a small impression on the overall task that it was not worth having it subjected to public scrutiny. At the very least, this vertiginous sense of incompletion was probably at the root of his decision to abandon the line of dialectical enquiry in this particular form.

All this is by way of establishing that if, as I suspect, it was not lack of quality, but lack of completeness, that caused Sartre to hide away his manuscript, then we are surely entitled to take it as seriously as any other piece of his published work. There is certainly much to admire here: a deepening of the understandings reached in volume one, organised around the introduction, explanation, and deployment of new technical terms; fruitful analyses of boxing and Stalinism; and further reflections on the issue of dialectical necessity and the associated theme of the extent of human control over the historical process. All of these considerations take

Sartre constructively beyond the limits of volume one and demand close inspection.

This position on the legitimacy of such inspection is reinforced by Arlette Elkaïm-Sartre's editorial remark that the text 'takes the form of a final draft – one last reading might have removed a few stylistic flaws' (*CDR II*, p. ix), although she also writes that the 'status' of the notes included in the 57-page Appendix (made around 1961–2) 'remains in doubt' because they clearly represent Sartre thinking on his feet, and that she 'hesitated before publishing them' (*CDR II*, p. 395). As I pointed out above, these notes contain reflections on important issues such as that of totalisation in non-directorial societies, and it is as well to be aware that these remarks need to be approached with caution. The Appendix aside, though, I propose to discuss volume two as I would any of the texts published during his lifetime – free of concerns as to its status within his *œuvre*.

Sartre closes volume one with the belief that, 'the regressive moment of the critical investigation has demonstrated the [dialectical] intelligibility of practical structures' (such as groups, organisations, and institutions), and the observation that these are only 'elementary formal structures'. This constitutes what he calls the regressive arm of the investigation. Now, 'These structures must ... be left to live freely, to oppose and to co-operate with one another.' This is the progressive investigation, through which he hopes to show 'the double synchronic and diachronic moment by which History constantly totalises itself' (*CDR I*, pp. 817–18). If he can show this, then he will have reached the twin goals of revealing History as a 'totalisation without a totaliser' (*CDR I*, p. 817), and demonstrating its dialectical intelligibility. As Aronson remarks, 'In volume one we have repeatedly seen individual or group praxis totalise, but volume two returns to the real historical world of fragmented, contending, and conflicting praxes. Can there be a totalization without a totalizer ... ?' (1987, p. 3). Again volume two, 'bears the urgent substantive burden of establishing that the scattered and separate multiplicities do indeed produce a single history' (p. 37). In fact, the real historical world receives less attention than Aronson signals, but this should not surprise us as Sartre has warned that volume two will still comprise a 'formal project' (*CDR I*, p. 818).

Nevertheless, the proof of singularity is essential to Sartre's project because it bears firmly on his desire to demonstrate dialectical intelligibility. History's 'oneness' is a condition of its intelligibility in that history-making is totalising, and totalisation is a movement of synthesis and integration. Put differently, dialectical intelligibility would not be available if history did not constitute a totalising movement of synthesis and integration. This is a perspective that Sartre is clearly not prepared to countenance. He asks whether,

History [is] not perhaps, at the level of large ensembles, an ambiguous interpenetration of unity and plurality, dialectic and anti-dialectic, meaning and meaninglessness? Are there not, according to the circumstances and ensemble in question, *several* totalizations – with no relation between them other than coexistence or some other relation of exteriority? (*CDR II*, p. 120)

But, 'If we were to accept this thesis, we should be returning by a detour to historical neo-positivism' (p. 120). As we know, relationships of exteriority are not dialectical relationships and so, unless embedded in relationships that are bound by bonds of interiority (which of course Sartre believes they are), they will not be open to dialectical intelligibility.

Volume two can therefore profitably be read as an attempt to substitute unity for plurality at the level of history, not – as in volume one – through the formal demonstration of the dialectical intelligibility of 'practical structures' (groups, organisations and institutions), but by revealing the dialectical intelligibility of *struggles*. His successive analyses of boxing, of competing sub-groups within a group, of the battle between Stalin and Trotsky, and of Stalinism itself, are all intended to show how what Sartre calls 'rifts' do not amount to irreducibly separate totalisations, but can be shown to be moments of a wider totalising movement.

In its most general form, Sartre's project is to show the totalising movement at the heart of even the most apparently disunited society – one riven by class struggle for example: 'if the class struggle is to be intelligible to the historian's dialectical reason, one must be able to totalize classes in struggle – and this comes down to discovering the synthetic unity of a society riven through and through' (*CDR II*, pp. 15–16). In every single case of apparently (dialectically) meaningless disunity that Sartre encounters he wants to be able to arrive at the same conclusion as that reached after his discussion of struggle between sub-groups:

We have shown that the struggle is intelligible. Basically, the fact is that unity is dissociated within a vaster unity, i.e. that of the totalization-of-envelopment. The intelligibility of the struggle appears as soon as it is deciphered on the basis of this totalization, and in the perspective of the common praxis. (*CDR II*, p. 85)

Once again it is important to stress the political project that informs such an apparently abstruse debate on the dialectic. In chapter 3 I pointed out how Sartre believed that Marxism had 'sclerosed' by failing to recognise the need to establish its own truth. As he puts it here, 'it is precisely when the machine seems jammed that it is appropriate to unravel the formal difficulties hitherto neglected' (*CDR II*, p. 16). The formal difficulty is that of demonstrating dialectical intelligibility, which itself turns on revealing the totalising movement that gathers up apparently irreconcilable 'practical multiplicities' in wider syntheses. So it is a question of establishing the truth of Marxism and, 'Marxism is strictly true if History is totalization. It is no longer true if human history is decomposed into a plurality of individual histories; or if, at any rate, within the relation of immanence which characterizes the fight [here, a boxing match] the negation of each opponent by the other is on principle detotalizing' (p. 16).

Having outlined Sartre's aims in volume two of the *Critique* I propose to divide what follows into roughly three parts. First, I shall look at Sartre's analysis of boxing as an example of his demonstration of the dialectical intelligibility of struggles. Second, I shall reflect on the issue of dialectical necessity through his discussion of Stalinism, and third, we need to know where all this leaves us as far as the question of 'one History' is concerned.

The general problem, of which boxing is a particular example, is expressed as follows. Sartre claims to have already demonstrated (in *CDR I*, pp. 735ff.), 'that antagonistic reciprocity is a bond of immanence between epicentres, since each adversary totalizes and transcends the totalizing action of the other' (*CDR II*, p. 5). But what happens in the case of '*two* conflicting enterprises'? Each enterprise appears to have an intelligibility all its own, so can there be an overarching intelligibility? Thus: 'If the plurality of epicentres is a real condition of *two* opposed intelligibilities (inasmuch as there is a comprehensive intelligibility in each system and based on each praxis), how could there be *one* dialectical intelligibility of the ongoing process?' (p. 5). Or, to bring us into the presence of Sartre's example, is a boxing match a 'real unity or an irreducible duality'? (*CDR II*, p. 6).

I pointed out in chapter 4 that Sartre's 'proof' of the dialectic was based on the redeeming of hypotheses, couched in the form that 'if X then Y must be the case' (see pp. 56–7). He employs a similar strategy here:

If it is established that the fight, whatever it may be, is the present retotalization of all fights; if it is clear that it can be decoded only *by them*; if it has meaning only in so far as it is put back in the *real* perspectives of contemporary boxing … then it will easily be understood that *boxing in its entirety* is present at every instant of the fight as sport and as technique. (*CDR II*, p. 20)

Sartre's first and largely unspectacular point is that the 'rift' represented by the two totalising and seemingly independent praxes is only apparent. The rift is only possible because of boxing itself. Boxing, with its rules, acquired techniques, and organising bodies, is presupposed by the struggle. Without the history of boxing, the particular fight would not make any sense. But it would be wrong, claims Sartre, to see this particular fight as a mere example or representation of the general art called boxing.

The relationship between the general and particular is tight and dialectical. Indeed, to use terms such as general and particular is already to distort Sartre's position, because there can be no unchanging 'general' of which the particular might be an example. Rather, the general (for example, boxing) is totalised by every particular fight and becomes something different to what it was before. Each fight is the transcendence of boxing in that if boxing was not transcended by each bout then it would have only an 'abstract being... an ensemble of possible meanings and practices' – so each fight concretises the possibility. But at the same time boxing transcends each fight 'since each punch is understood and foreseen on the basis of that ensemble [i.e. boxing]' (*CDR II*, pp. 20–1). Thus 'the boxer transcends boxing, and boxing envelops the boxer since it itself requires that transcendence' (p. 21).

We can express this process differently by introducing a technical term of which Sartre makes persistent use in volume two of the *Critique* – 'incarnation'. Incarnation is usefully defined in the glossary as the 'process whereby a practical reality envelops in its own singularity the ensemble of totalizations in progress' (*CDR II*, p. 457). Translated into the field of boxing, this means that each particular bout incarnates, in the sense of individuates (*CDR II*, p. 28) or singularises, boxing as a whole. Thus, 'in every fight, boxing is *incarnated*, realized, and elapses as it is realized' (*CDR II*, p. 22). It is essential to grasp that the bout does not merely *represent* boxing, but actually *is* boxing in that it gathers all of boxing up and retotalises it through the contending praxes of the boxers. As Sartre puts it, 'It follows from this that the relationship between the singular features [the bout] and the incarnated total [boxing] can no longer be defined as that between contingencies and the concept or essence' (*CDR II*, p. 34). Most emphatically, 'each fight is all of boxing' (*CDR II*, p. 21).

With reference to Sartre's original question, then, as to whether a bout comprises a 'real unity or an irreducible duality', his conclusion is that it is a unity in the important dialectical sense that the contending praxes totalise (or rather retotalise) the ensemble of techniques and organisations called boxing. Further, given that 'dialectical intelligibility... is defined through totalisation' (*CDR II*, p. 3), then this particular form of struggle (if not yet *all* forms, for example, class struggle) is shown to be intelligible.

Given that our brief was simply to indicate how Sartre demonstrates the intelligibility of struggle in the case of a boxing match, I could now pass on to the second theme of this chapter – the question of dialectical necessity. But, in simply demonstrating its intelligibility, Sartre has not exhausted the dialectical implications of boxing, and it is worth gesturing at the direction he goes on to take. For the violence of an individual bout, he writes, points beyond the hall in which it takes place, and even beyond the ensemble of boxing itself, to society at large. 'It is worth noting', he says, 'that the violence of boxers is linked to ongoing conflicts in two different ways: that is, directly and via a series of mediations' (*CDR II*, p. 22).

The direct linkage is the less interesting, and is simply a case of the fight relating, 'without any intermediary, to the interhuman tension produced by the interiorization of scarcity' (p. 22). In the case of mediations, however, boxing refers us rigorously to the ensemble of social relations which reciprocally produce and are produced by it. Boxing, writes Sartre,

was born in our bourgeois societies and must first be studied in this guise. If it is true, moreover, that such societies are divided into classes [Sartre's tentativeness is disingenuous – he clearly thinks they are], some exploiting and oppressing the others, bourgeois boxing must be studied on the basis of the real structures of the exploitative system. (*CDR II*, p. 35)

The critical moment, for Sartre, is the 'contractual moment' when the boxer (most probably from the working class) sells his violence to the promoter. At that point, his violence, the original location of 'his value and his freedom', the 'rage which makes him so combative' (*CDR II*, p. 43) is transformed. Rather than 'the easy demonstration of a brutal superiority', the boxer's violence turns into a 'painful and dangerous labour', and loses its character as 'a wild and liberating passion' (p. 43). The promoter, on behalf of the bourgeoisie, converts proletarian violence into discipline and reproduces the commodification, competition, and alienation of capitalism. By this process, moreover, proletarian violence is individualised, and the resistance it represents is prevented from being expressed in social form – for example, trade union organisation (*CDR II*, p. 36). Clearly, too, the bourgeoisie will derive pleasure from 'providing the rules' according to which its opponents beat each other up, rather than combine to resist bourgeois domination (*CDR II*, p. 47).

Each boxing match, then, is not simply the incarnation of all boxing, but the incarnation of all violence, whether directly incarnated as the immediate expression of the interiorisation of scarcity, or mediated by the structures of bourgeois society. Sartre does not shrink from the startling conclusion implied by this theory of incarnation:

Everything is given in the least punch: from the history of the one who delivers it to the material and collective circumstances of that history; from the general indictment of capitalist society to the singular determinations of that indictment by the boxing promoters; from the fundamental violence of the oppressed to the singular and alienating objectification of that violence in and through each of the participants. (*CDR II*, p. 48)

The entire thrust of this argument has been to stress the singularity and specificity of the bout as at the same time replicating and transcending its concrete universal (boxing). There is a political point here. Sartre bemoans the typically one-sided Marxist analysis that involves 'a procedure of decompressive expansion which starts off from the object to arrive at *everything*' (*CDR II*, p. 49). In other words, an event is seen (correctly but unduly partially) as referring centrifugally to the events around it which give it significance. This is a perfectly respectable dialectical procedure, but Marxists 'unfortunately... too often limit themselves' to it (p. 49). The second procedure is what Sartre calls a 'procedure of totalizing compression' which, 'by contrast, grasps the centripetal movement of all the significations attracted and condensed in the event or in the object' (p. 49). In the first case, the event is dissolved in its mediations and is therefore unintelligible, while the second, 'which alone is capable of grasping the dialectical intelligibility of an event', both preserves it and demonstrates its necessity as incarnation (p. 49).

So Sartre's discussion of boxing has allowed him, to his own satisfaction at least, to demonstrate the dialectical unity that lies at the heart of apparent plurality, and thus to show how struggle (at this simple level) is dialectically intelligible, as well as to indicate how the singular event is determined by the bonds of interiority linking it to its general determinations. Without these determinations the singular event would not be possible, but the event itself is also a (re)totalisation of those determinations. Behind all this lies the fundamentally political motivation of 'unjamming' Marxism by addressing the problem ('otiose, or at any rate premature' for most Marxists [*CDR II*, p. 16]) of the 'formal intelligibility' of both struggle and the individual event.

How successful has Sartre been? Even on his own terms he has at this point fallen some way short of resolving the question outlined at the beginning. His original aim was to show how 'History constantly totalises itself' (*CDR I*, pp. 817–18). So far, at the very most, he has shown how boxing totalises itself through the totalising actions of boxers in individual bouts. Crucially, and worryingly for Sartre, this has involved demonstrating totalisation taking place within an ensemble that is already a totalised unity – boxing. Although his examples of struggle become more complex as volume two progresses (sub-groups within a group, workers vs. managers during rapid industrialisation in the Soviet Union, Stalin vs. Trotsky) they, too, are characterised by taking place within an already-existing unity. He never reaches the position of being able to deal with the intelligibility of rifts which appear truly to constitute the limits of intelligibility rather than totalising features of a pre-existing unity.

To press the point, after his discussion of the struggle between Stalin and Trotsky, organised around the slogan 'Socialism in one country', Sartre comments that:

The foregoing example has only a limited scope, since struggle appears in it only as the avatar of an already integrated group. What we have basically shown is that if synthetic unity already exists...[then]...internal conflict...is only an incarnation and historialisation of the global totalisation. (*CDR II*, p. 118)

And he makes similar remarks in the case of disputes between workers and managers in Soviet society (*CDR II*, p. 148) and Soviet society itself under Stalin (*CDR II*, p. 183). In all these examples, struggle is intelligible to dialectical reason because of the pre-existence of an identifiable unity, be it boxing, the unity of a group within which struggle takes place, or the sovereign-as-dictator imposing unity.

The big challenge is to show History totalising itself where no such unity is to be found – for instance in what he calls 'non-directorial societies' – but he never gets round to doing more than gesture at how such an investigation would proceed. In the Appendix he hints that he would have focused on 'worked matter' as the mediator: 'elements interior to the [practical] field are – as worked matter – elements of unity...At this level, everyone is already an *incarnation*' (*CDR II*, p. 433). Effectively though, his search for History as a totalisation without a totaliser ends less than half-way through volume two with the following remark: 'Before going on to the examination of a non-dictatorial society, however, a number of points ought to be clarified' (*CDR II*, p. 183). There follow further reflections on the Soviet Union and on various ontological questions, but the promised examination of non-dictatorial societies never takes place.

So the question posed earlier – 'what could be the historical unity of a society chopped up by class struggles?' (*CDR II*, p. 50) – remains unanswered, but there is more than enough in what we do have to suggest strongly that Sartre would have found a way to demonstrate such unity. His impulse is totalising – even totalitarian – and his avowed intention to allow structures to 'live freely' (*CDR I*, p. 818), and his apparent willingness to keep an open mind as to the unity or plurality of totalisation(s), is compromised by his desire to demonstrate the truth of Marxism. And Marxism is not true, we remember, if 'human history is decomposed into a plurality of individual histories' (*CDR II*, p. 16). Hence the overriding need to demonstrate dialectical unity at every turn.

As I pointed out earlier, almost half of volume two is taken up with a discussion of Stalinism. This illuminating analysis could be approached in a number of ways, but in keeping with one of the themes of this book I propose to look at it for what it can tell us about the nature of necessity in a dialectical context. I outlined two senses of historical necessity in chapter 4 and they can both be found here.

It was a political worry in volume one that the various forms of alienation discussed by Sartre seemed unsurmountable in any concretely possible human history (see chapter 6 above). More particularly, it was a political worry for Sartre himself that some Marxists in the 1950s chose to absolve themselves of responsibility for their actions by referring to 'necessity'.

He takes precisely this line in *The Spectre of Stalin* where he analyses the Soviet 'pacification' of Hungary in 1956: 'Doubtless, the neo-Stalinists do not approve of Stalin's crimes: but they resemble him in that they do the same things "of necessity", and without noticing that they are crimes' (Sartre, 1969b, p. 84). This ringing rejection of such evasion of responsibility seems categorical, so how is it that Ronald Aronson, in his commentary on Sartre's second *Critique*, is able to write of his treatment of Stalinism that, 'He...takes refuge in a combination of moral neutrality and necessitarianism. His emphasis on the ways in which the evolution of Bolshevik praxis seemed necessary to its agents and is dialectically intelligible echoes too many sophisticated justifications of Party and Stalin' (Aronson, 1987, p. 179)?

I agree with Aronson's assessment, but two remarks need to be made about it. First, it has become clear that dialectical intelligibility is irremediably a function of dialectical necessity. The totalisation that is History is only intelligible because the events that make it up are linked by bonds of interiority – and these bonds are tight and not subject to appeal. Second, Sartre's position on Stalinism cannot be called a 'justification' (and Sartre repeatedly says himself that it is neither a justification nor a condemnation) because justifications have no place and no meaning in the context of necessity.

But is Aronson's characterisation a fair one? Sartre writes that, 'our intention here is not to defend them [the Soviet leadership]. That they sinned all the time and everywhere is obvious' (*CDR II*, p. 150). But then, echoing my remark about justification above, he goes on: 'It will be necessary to ascertain later on what a sin is, and our historical investigation will doubtless lead us to pose this question from a formal point of view' (p. 150). Arlette Elkaïm-Sartre, in an editorial footnote, comments that 'this gives a hint that the whole investigation of the *Critique* is a long detour in order to tackle once more the problems of ethics in history, raised in 1947 in *Cahiers pour une morale*' (p. 150, fn., and see also Verstraeten, 1990). The implication is that ethics has no secure place in the *Critique* – an unsettling thought given that half of this volume is concerned with events that demand an ethical judgement. In the meantime, though, and in the absence of a clear position on sin, the investigation apparently neutrally explores the meaning of the oppression of the Soviet worker:

In the historical circumstances of Russian industrialization, the *meaning* of their praxis [i.e. the leaders' praxis] (which does not mean its truth or its justification) was to destroy those workers as free practical organisms and as common individuals, in order to be able to create man out of their destruction. (*CDR II*, p. 150)

Terror, collectivisation, and forced industrialisation are all portrayed as performed by concrete individuals, but made necessary by circumstances:

So the leaders' praxis was *qualified* as oppressive, by virtue of the necessities it engendered within it in the internal milieu of its totalization…For…it was genuinely necessary to obtain 'at all costs' (Stalin's watchword in 1928) an almost unendurable tension of the working-class forces. (*CDR II*, p. 151)

The question remains, was any other course of action possible?

On the face of it, Sartre says that we do not know: 'At the level of dialectical investigation we have reached, we do not…have the right to say that it was impossible to proceed otherwise (nor, moreover, the opposite right: we simply do not yet know anything about the possibles)' (*CDR II*, p. 183). Once again, the issue of 'the possibles' is one to which Sartre never formally returns, but certain remarks can be made on the basis of what he does say about Stalin.

He temporarily entertains the possibility that things could have been different – that, while authoritarian procedures might have been required by the situation, the bloody repressions that went with it were not. In Sartre's own words: 'Let us concede – which seems most likely by far – that the exigencies of the process did not entirely justify Stalin's procedures' (*CDR II*, p. 206). Again, the rapid industrialisation demanded by the need to compete with hostile and encircling capitalist nations meant enormous quantitative increases in production, but 'ten million tons of pig-iron obtained by threats and bloody measures of coercion (executions, concentration camps etc.) were *on no account* comparable to ten million tons of pig-iron obtained in the same perspective and by an authoritarian government, but without coercive measures' (*CDR II*, p. 207). In other words, there is a difference between authoritarianism and bloodily enforced authoritarianism. But was the latter necessary in the context of the Russian Revolution? Again, Sartre provisionally says perhaps not. On this reading, Stalinist excesses are rooted in Stalin himself and lie outside totalising necessity: 'In so far as the purges and trials have to be blamed on Stalin…the deviation resulting from them must be attributed to factors that were personal, and for that very reason *extraneous* to the revolutionary totalization' (p. 207).

This all seems clear: there is room to applaud the survival of the Revolution through (for example) rapid industrialisation, while condemning the purges, repression, and propaganda that accompanied it. 'However', writes Sartre presagingly, 'let us have a closer look' (p. 207). In the first place, he is adamant that the survival of the Revolution demanded the exercise of sovereignty by one individual:

*What came* from praxis itself was the fact that, through its temporalization, it had engendered circumstances such that the organs of sovereignty had no other means of subsisting and acting than to resign their powers into the hands of *one* individual. (p. 207)

Then, crucially, 'But *from the moment* when praxis demanded the facticity of the individual sovereign, it contained within it – as an immediate counter-finality – the need to bear the mark of an individuality' (p. 207). What this means is that, once the survival of the Revolution involved its future being directed by one individual, it was inevitable that the stamp or mark of that individual would be imposed upon the Revolution. This is an example of what Sartre is fond of calling the 'necessity of contingency'.

Of course, none of this would matter if it could be shown that another individual other than Stalin could have driven the Revolution through. In other words, while we accept that the sovereign individual was a necessity, we do not accept that Stalin was a necessity. This would, once again, leave room for recognising the necessity of contingency – that the Revolution would bear the mark of the sovereign – without accepting the contingencies embodied in Stalinist repression. 'But', writes Sartre, 'if it is true that by being incarnated in this way praxis gave itself a deep structure of *contingency*, it is not true that any old individual – as contingent – was fit to become its sovereign' (*CDR II*, p. 214).

The Revolution thus demanded a quite specific contingency (i.e. individual), argues Sartre. Trotsky was rejected because he incarnated internationalism (p. 214) and this was no good because, precisely, 'Socialism in one country' had become the slogan through which the Revolution was to be carried forward. So those who say that 'Trotsky was more intelligent, more cultured and, moreover, an excellent organizer' (*CDR II*, p. 209), and would therefore have carried out a gentler defence of the Revolution, miss the dialectical point. 'Contingency – i.e. the individual qualities of the sovereign praxis – was circumscribed and determined', writes Sartre (p. 214). The Revolution 'demanded' a 'dogmatic opportunist', a 'militant known by the militants', a leader who was 'inflexible, coolheaded and unimaginative' (*CDR II*, p. 215). Sartre's conclusion, which I shall quote at length, runs as follows:

So we should be wrong to claim that the system required *a man*, as an indeterminate bearer of *praxis*, rather than Stalin. In fact (and even in this form we shall see that it is only half true), if the system requires a man, the latter will in any case be a strict synthesis of specific determinations (transcended in his idiosyncratic temporalization). The individual required by the system will be determined, and will determine praxis by his very determination. All that can be said, in such a case, is that his determination is certain, but – in relation to the exigency of praxis – indeterminate. As a consequence, the idiosyncratic determination of the totalizing praxis – and of the system through it – is *inevitable*, although at the outset it remains indeterminate … Those jolts, those accelerations, those brakings, those hairpin bends, those acts of violence which characterized Stalinism – they were not all required by the objectives and exigencies of socialization. Yet they were inevitable, inasmuch as that socialization demanded, in its first phase, to be directed by an individual. (*CDR II*, p. 209)

This can be read as powerful evidence of the 'necessitarianism' behind which Aronson feels Sartre takes refuge, and which makes the 'problem of ethics in history' (*CDR II*, p. 150 fn.) so intractable. While at first sight Stalin's individual idiosyncracies might seem to have been extraneous to the revolutionary totalisation, as Sartre suggested above, on closer inspection the Revolution demanded a sovereign individual and Stalin was drawn ineluctably into the role. 'Can we say, then', asks Sartre, 'that Stalin was required, even in what was most singular about him, even in the determinations that came to him from his milieu, from his childhood, from the *private* features of his adventure … Was *that Georgian former seminarist* really necessary? There will be a temptation to answer yes …' (*CDR II*, pp. 215–16), and Sartre gives us little cause to think otherwise.

But he does not quite leave it at that, and the twist he gives to the story emerges from the deployment of a favourite Sartrean category – scarcity. Sartre wants to preserve a sense of the *difficulty* of defending and pursuing the Russian Revolution. Surrounded by hostile forces, faced with internal strife, burdened by antiquated production techniques, isolated from help, the survival of the Revolution demanded great abilities from the sovereign individual. We have already seen that Stalin ensured the continuation of the Revolution, but at the cost of severe repression and extreme sacrifice. Sartre needs a way of condemning – or at least bemoaning – Stalinist excesses while recognising their necessity, and he finds it by constructing an – ultimately unsatisfactory – distinction between two types of need: need in the sense of what was minimally demanded by the survival of the Revolution and need in the sense of dialectical necessity. The gap between the two is explained by the scarcity of men 'able' to carry out the tasks demanded of the sovereign individual.

He opens his account by remarking that, 'we must recognize … that … when the ensemble requires of the sovereign-individual a genuine *ability* – human history is no longer defined merely by the scarcity of products, tools, etc., but *also*, suddenly, *by the scarcity of men*' (*CDR II*, pp. 219–20). This introduces the first sense of need, referred to above: 'The men History makes are never entirely those needed to make History, be they even as unrivalled as Stalin or Napoleon' (*CDR II*, p. 221). The implication of this is that there are some objectively discoverable criteria for action which Stalin and Napoleon failed to identify and act upon. For example, although 'peace was *required*' in post-Revolutionary France, Napoleon was constitutively unable to deliver it, and Stalin the isolationist deepened his country's isolation at the moment when it was no longer necessary (*CDR II*, pp. 221–2).

However, this sense of necessary (which it is surprising to find in Sartre given his opposition to the positivistic and analytical calculations involved in it), is different from the second sense: 'It is a strict necessity that History, when it is determined by scarcity of men, should be totalized by a sovereign whose relative unfitness for his functions incarnates and singularizes that iron law of scarcity' (*CDR II*, p. 220). In other words given the scarcity of men, the sovereign individual will always be necessarily (dialectic) unfit to carry out the necessary (analytic) tasks.

The whole notion of 'unfitness', though, is curious in a dialectic context. How is unfitness to be judged? How are we to know what the prosecution of the Revolution objectively demanded? We can accept that the historical process is not defined by a 'transcendental dialectic' (*CDR II*, p. 226), but it is defined by an immanent one with human praxis as its vehicle, so in what sense can any praxis be deemed 'unfit'? Sartre writes that, 'there are not enough men to make a rigorous history on a daily basis' (*CDR II*, p. 227), but what could be more rigorous than the necessity of contingency and, in this case, the incarnation of the Russian Revolution in Stalin?

Any inadequacy of Stalin would have to be judged against a putatively undeviated historical process, but Sartre himself writes that we have no way of knowing what this would be like:

It remains to be signalled, of course, that the existence of a diachronic meaning of History is not even implied by the foregoing arguments, at this stage of our investigation. And by diachronic meaning we merely mean the axial direction in relation to which one might define (and correct) any possible drift, today and in the infinite future of interiority. We shall return to this problem, which requires intellectual tools that we have not forged for ourselves. (*CDR II*, p. 335)

The problem is indeed returned to, but only in some illuminating yet inconclusive notes in the Appendix (*CDR II*, pp. 402–24). Sartre has devoted all his intellectual energy in the *Critique* to solving the problem of intelligibility, and he is well aware that demonstrating the intelligibility of the historical process (and we should remember that he falls someway short of doing even that) allows us to say nothing about its direction or how to judge progress. If Ronald Aronson is right to suggest that deviation is the key analytical theme and political question (Aronson, 1990, p. 97), then Sartre has left us pretty much bereft of ways of dealing with it. His remarks on factional sub-groups are equally applicable to the ascendancy of Stalin over Trotsky:

But this investigation of intelligibility should not make us, therefore, fall prey to optimism. It is true that victory comes to the victor via the mediation of the whole group, and that it incarnates a moment of the totalizing activity as praxis-process. But this does not mean that it realises the progress of the group towards its own objectives: a priori we can decide nothing. (*CDR II*, p. 86)

In other words we cannot judge – at this stage of the investigation – either the progress towards an aim nor the desirability of that aim. With Stalinism, Sartre is faced with a phenomenon some aspects of which he clearly abhors (and which he roundly criticised elsewhere) and yet on which he is incapable of passing judgement in the *Critique*. Aronson, for one, looks for 'human standards' (Aronson, 1987, p. 179) in volume two. But he looks in vain, for having focused on intelligibility, and having discovered it in dialectical necessity – even to the challenging point of the necessity of contingency – Sartre allows himself neither space for, nor the intellectual possibility of, developing the 'problem of ethics in history' (*CDR II*, p. 150 fn.).

Finally, in this chapter, I propose briefly to discuss where all this leaves us in respect of Sartre's views concerning the nature of History as such. This refers us back to his desire, announced in volume one, 'to establish that there is *one* human history, with *one* truth and *one* intelligibility' (*CDR I*, p. 69). As this remark suggests, the establishing of dialectical intelligibility is bound up with establishing the 'oneness' of history – if intelligibility is established, then the unity of history is too. Put more precisely, for dialectical intelligibility to be possible, the bonds between actions and events must be bonds of interiority (as explained in chapter 4). And if the bonds between actions and events *are* bonds of interiority, then history is unified in the special dialectical sense outlined, again, in chapter 4. Therefore, if dialectical intelligibility is shown to be possible, history must be unified in this special sense. I have already pointed out how productive it is to read volume two as an investigation into the intelligibility of struggles at increasing levels of complexity. The successful resolution of this investigation inevitably lends weight to the suggestion that History is indeed a seamless web, constituting, as Sartre points out, 'an intelligible totalisation from which there is no appeal' (*CDR I*, p. 817). In this respect no more needs to be said about intelligibility except to underscore the fact that its availability means that human history is not 'decomposed into a plurality of individual histories' (*CDR II*, p. 16), and that therefore the oneness of History is implied, if not proved, by everything that is said in volume two of the *Critique*.

A further gloss can be put on this question by referring to a guiding thread in this volume, the technical term 'totalisation-of-envelopment'. The importance of this notion is not in doubt, for as Sartre remarks in a footnote: 'We do not even know yet if the totalisation-of-envelopment can exist. We shall see further on that it is the foundation of any intelligibility of History...' (*CDR II*, p. 33 fn.). This is because the totalisation-of-envelopment comprises the 'integration of all concrete individuals by praxis' (*CDR II*, p. 86), and such integration is a condition of dialectical intelligibility. Once again, it would be wrong to look for – or at least expect to find – a comprehensive statement confirming the existence of the totalisation-of-envelopment, for such a statement would presuppose having demonstrated the dialectical intelligibility of *all* rifts, and not just the limited cases treated here.

Nevertheless, just as we might surmise that Sartre *would* have demonstrated such intelligibility, given time, so we can securely assume the reality of the totalisation-of-envelopment. Clues as to how he might have shown it are to be found throughout this volume. In discussing the rift between factional sub-groups, for example, he writes that, 'the practical existence of that other [sub-group] is a danger *not just for the identical and opposed sub-group...but also for the totalization-of-envelopment*' (*CDR II*, p. 64). However, the rift is closed by showing how struggle is intelligible in that 'unity is dissociated within a vaster unity, i.e. that of the totalization-of-envelopment' (*CDR II*, p. 85). In other words, unity is preserved, and the totalisation-of-envelopment as the integration of concrete individuals remains a secure possibility.

Elsewhere Sartre makes a stronger claim for its existence: 'the practical reality of the totalisation-of-envelopment is proved by the dialectical investigation itself' (*CDR II*, p. 188). I have already described how, in his analysis of boxing, Sartre stresses the way in which each bout is the compressive incarnation of the whole of boxing – indeed, of all violence. For it to be so, the bout must also be determined by the general social and historical ensemble: 'it refers back in a decompressive blossoming to the ensemble of practical significations which determine it in its belonging to the social and historical field' (p. 188). It is this ensemble that comprises the totalisation-of-envelopment, and which makes possible the individual bout as an event with a particular meaning. 'What counts', writes Sartre, 'is the simultaneous twofold reference to the interiority of the singularization and to the totality that envelops it' (p. 189). The dialectical investigation has revealed this twofold reference, and thus implicitly reveals, too, the existence of the totalisation-of-envelopment. Everything points to dialectical unity; and everything therefore points to *one* history, *one* truth, and *one* intelligibility.

If this gloss on volume two is correct, then Sartre may not have redeemed the extravagant promises made in volume one concerning unique intelligibility and the totalisation-without-a-totaliser, but he has made progress towards doing so, and left us with a clear idea of the path he would have followed. The stumbling-block, he believed, lay in demonstrating the dialectical intelligibility of struggle, and in the cases he has confronted here the arguments are clear and the conclusion unambiguous: History should not be regarded as a plurality of individual histories, but as a developing and unitary synthesis.

Second, it would be good to think, with Aronson, that, 'Praxis...is autonomous, original, and determinative, and not simply the carrying out of a preexisting hyperorganic reality' (1987, p. 79). While it is clear from my reading of Sartre's analysis of Stalin in this volume that there is indeed no pre-existing hyperorganic reality, the extent of the autonomy of praxis must be in question. The situation is precisely that of the woman in the Dop shampoo factory encountered in volume one: 'when the woman in the Dop shampoo factory has an abortion in order to avoid having a child she would be unable to feed, she makes a free decision in order to escape the destiny that is made for her'. But, Sartre goes on, 'this decision is in itself completely manipulated by the objective situation: she *realises* through herself what she *is already*; she carries out the sentence, which has already been passed on her, which deprives her of free motherhood' (*CDR I*, p. 235). In the same way, Stalin can be conceived of as carrying out the sentence passed on the Russian Revolution – an ugly deviation, but one called for by dialectical necessity and the 'scarcity of men'.

*Part Two*

# 8    Biographies and histories

'Aren't the people you fully respect the ones who have a "thirst for the absolute", as they used to say in the nineteenth century?'
'Yes, certainly: the ones who want everything. That's what I wanted myself.'                                                                   (Sartre, 1978d, p. 61)

By the time the *Critique* was published in 1960, Sartre had written two completed studies of literary figures – Baudelaire and Jean Genet – as well as reflections on Mallarmé, Tintoretto, Giacometti, and Kierkegaard, and a film script for John Huston's film on Freud. The Baudelaire, shorter than the Genet, appeared in the bookshops in 1947 – 3 years after the liberation of France and at the height of the popularity of existentialism. It will be remembered that this was the year in which Sartre delivered his famous lecture 'Existentialism is a Humanism' at the Club Maintenant, and which was to help make him a cult figure in the turbulence of post-war France. Compared to this lecture's intentionally 'popular' stance, the Baudelaire seemed to have little to do with Sartre's existentialism, and nor did it appear to have any relevance to his growing political awareness, which took root in the founding of the *Rassemblement Démocratique et Révolutionnaire* in 1948.

The Genet was published 5 years after the Baudelaire, in 1952, and coincided with the beginning of Sartre's temporary *rapprochement* with the French Communist Party. This was the year of General Ridgeway's visit to Paris, the subsequent arrest of Communist Party leader Duclos, and the relative failure of the PCF demonstrations in May and June. Sartre announced his (conditional) support for the PCF in his articles collectively entitled *Communists and Peace* – an angry denunciation of those on the Left who chose to ignore the political claims of the Communist Party (see pp. 50–1). This amounted to a clear indication that politics now constituted an important focus for Sartre. What, then, was he hoping to achieve by publishing the biography of the unfinished life of a French poet and novelist?

Again, by 1957, the same year in which *Search for a Method* was published and which was to lead to detailed explanation in the *Critique*, Sartre had already been at work for some years on a study of Gustave Flaubert: 'At the present moment, the book on Flaubert is long and still not finished' ('The Purposes of Writing' in Sartre, 1974a, p. 11). Indeed, the third and (as it happened) final volume of the Flaubert study was not published until 15 years later, in 1972. What relevance did these thousands of pages have to Sartre's professed political struggle? Sartre was often led to admit that the Flaubert seemed to stand outside his political concerns:

Even though I have always protested against the bourgeoisie, my works are addressed to it, are written in its language, and contain elitist elements – or at least the earliest ones did. For the last 17 years I have been engaged in a work on Flaubert which can be of no interest to the workers, since it is written in a complicated and definitely bourgeois style. Furthermore, the first two volumes of this work were read by bourgeois reformists, professors, students and the like. It was not written by or for the people; it was the product of a bourgeois philosopher's reflections over the course of most of his life. (Sartre, 1978f, p. 185)

Taking into account his political concerns around the time of the writing and publication of the Flaubert, it is even harder to see why he should have devoted so much time to such a work. In 1965 he cancelled a lecture tour in the United States in protest against American involvement in Vietnam, and 2 years later he joined Bertrand Russell in heading the International War Crimes tribunal investigating alleged American crimes in South East Asia. After the 'events' in France in 1968 he decided to throw in his lot with the radical students and workers, and became ever more closely associated with Maoist groups advocating violence as the only route to socialist emancipation. He made a much-publicised visit to Stuttgart to visit members of the Baader-Meinhof 'gang', and some of the most famous photographs of Sartre were taken while selling the Maoist journal *La Cause du Peuple* on the streets of Paris (and being bundled into a police van shortly afterwards).

In an interview with John Gerassi in 1971 he created the distinction between the 'left-wing, or classical, intellectual' and the 'leftist intellectual', and argued that 'the difference is one of action. A leftist intellectual is one who realises that being an intellectual exempts him from nothing. He forsakes his privileges, or tries to, in action' (in Barnes, 1974, p. 139). How is this to be squared with thousands of pages on a dead bourgeois poet?

From this perspective, a number of critics have come to see Sartre's biographies as peripheral to the main body of his life's work. For instance, Mark Poster says that, these studies present themselves as personal investigations, remote from social concerns. Perhaps at bottom, Sartre always reserved part of himself for art and culture, safe from the noise of politics. One might surmise that only with this anchor in cultural life could he preserve his equilibrium in the intense world of Leftist politics. (Poster, 1975, p. 195)

On the contrary. Sartre himself gave various reasons for writing his biographical studies, but never once gave the impression that he was creating a haven for himself, safe from the traumas of 'leftist politics'. On the one hand, of course, by the time of the student revolt of 1968 he had already spent some 15 years working on the Flaubert and was by then 65-years old. To have abandoned such a long-standing project at such an advanced age was unthinkable and unrealistic. Among the more positive reasons he gave for his biographies was that he wanted to understand how a person came to write: 'The reason why I produced *Les Mots* is the reason why I have studied Genet or Flaubert: how does a man become someone who writes, who wants to speak of the imaginary?' (Sartre, 1974b, p. 63). In this context, it is no coincidence that the three subjects he chose for major study are all literary figures.

Given this, Michael Scriven has argued persuasively that Sartre's biographies amount to his attempt to come to terms with what Scriven terms a 'post-literary' situation in France – i.e. one in which 'the sacrosanct nature of bourgeois literary and cultural achievements' (Scriven, 1984, pp. 27–8) had come into question. Sartre, of course, by training, early inclination, and literary production, was bound up with these achievements, and Scriven reads the biographies as Sartre's effort to 'free himself from [their] alienating grip' (p. 28). On Scriven's interpretation they provide a 'critical alternative to the traditional bourgeois novel', which Sartre rejected for its methodological naivetée and the bourgeois nature of its form and content (p. 43).

Similarly, Scriven produces a useful account of the general political conditions under which the Flaubert, if not the other biographies, was produced. Given that Sartre was calling himself a Marxist by the time he began working seriously on the Flaubert, Scriven points out the differences in orientation between the generation of Marxists such as Lenin and Kautsky, and that of Adorno and Benjamin. The former were mostly preoccupied 'with the political structure of the capitalist state', while the latter concentrated on 'problems of literature and art, aspects of the social superstructure that are furthest removed from the economic mode of production' (p. 34).

According to Scriven, Sartre followed the example of the second generation – and for similar reasons: 'a flight from ... unpalatable political reality' (p. 35). He suggests that:

It is highly unlikely that a book of this sort [the Flaubert] could have been written outside a globally pessimistic historical conjuncture when self-proclaimed Marxists of bourgeois class origins, sensing consciously or unconsciously that practical political activity would serve little purpose, turn inward on themselves and attempt to assess the significance of the cultural products of past and present epochs. (p. 34)

This is a fruitful line of thought, but it can be taken too far, and I think Scriven does so. To call the Flaubert a flight from unpalatable political reality is to underestimate its political content – particularly the political implications of the method that informs and sustains it. In other words, I think that Scriven is right to resist any desire to link Sartre's biographies too closely to his novels, and to urge us in his own specific (and largely convincing) way 'to take account of the function of these books in Sartre's literary project' (p. 44), but we shouldn't allow this to blind us to the function they have in his *political* project. In remaining firmly lodged in the territory of the literary, Scriven moves usefully beyond Mark Poster and Susan Sontag (below) by showing how Sartre's biographies are central rather than peripheral to his development, yet refuses himself the possibility of interpreting this development in the widest possible way – not only literary, but political too. Christina Howells similarly refers to Sartre's biographies as 'part of his continuous tussle with literature' (1988, p. 179) and, while this at least does them the credit of locating them correctly at the centre of his concerns, it is too one-sided a view as long as it does not take sufficient account of his political tussles as well.

It is significant that neither Scriven (1984, p. 29) nor Howells (1988, pp. 169–79) nor Poster (1979, pp. 118–19) feel a need to distinguish more than in passing between the method employed by Sartre in the Baudelaire and the Genet, and that used in the Flaubert. They feel that both methods can be subsumed under the title 'existential biography' (or, in the case of Poster, 'existential psychoanalysis'), and, while there are undoubtedly similarities between the two, I believe (as does, for example, Joseph Halpern: 1976, p. 116) that the progressive–regressive method outlined in *Search for a Method* is a move beyond that described as existential psychoanalysis in *Being and Nothingness*. This development is symptomatic of the shift in orientation experienced and practised by Sartre as a result of his coming to terms with the political challenge represented by Marxism.

In this way, Sartre's evident concern for the development of the writer conceals a deeper motivation – that of understanding the human condition as a whole: a task which has profound political implications. From this perspective, Sartre's biographies constitute a crucial aspect of his theory of history, and must be studied if that theory is to be understood. The notion of history as biography is not a new one, but the way in which Sartre attempts to relate an individual's life-story to the history and circumstances of his/her time is quite novel. For it is not simply a question of giving a serial account of someone's life, but of showing how that life continually conditions, and is conditioned by, contemporary circumstance.

In this sense Sartre attempts to reveal an identity between an individual life and its circumstances in his biographies – particularly in the Flaubert. To this extent, Susan Sontag is wrong to say that, for instance, *Saint Genet* constitutes a dead-end for Sartre. She notes that,

> After *Being and Nothingness*, Sartre stood at the crossroads. He could move from philosophy and psychology to an ethics. Or he could move from philosophy to a politics, a theory of group action and history. As everyone knows, and many deplore, Sartre chose the second path; and the result is the *Critique of Dialectical Reason*, published in 1960. *Saint Genet* is his complex gesture in the direction he did not go. (Sontag, 1967, p. 97)

Quite the opposite. *Saint Genet, Baudelaire*, and *The Family Idiot* are all very much a part of Sartre's attempt to clarify the human situation, and the conditions under which we act. As he sees it, the course of an individual's life will not only tell us about the specific conditions under which that individual lived, it may also help us to understand the limits and potentialities of the human condition in general. In this sense, the search for a historical method is clearly a political project, and it is equally plain that the biographies are a constitutive part of that search. Even when writing his autobiography, Sartre made it clear that prior to arriving at a better understanding of himself, *The Words* was, first, 'an attempt at evolving a method' (Sartre, 1957, p. 915).

From this point of view, Mark Poster misses the point when he says of the Genet, in apparent frustration, that he has 'probed the book for elements of a social theory' (1975, p. 201). It seems to me that the emergence of a historical method – and *Saint Genet* merely demonstrates Sartre's method as it had developed by 1952 – is social theory enough, particularly when we consider Sartre's burgeoning interest in Marxism, in which historical conditions are essential data by which to judge the suitability of political action. Certainly Sartre himself saw the development of a historical method as an act of political commitment. With reference to the Flaubert, de Beauvoir notes that, 'His Maoist friends condemned this enterprise to a greater or lesser degree: they would have preferred Sartre to have written some militant treatise or a great popular novel' (de Beauvoir, 1981, p. 19). Sartre's reply? 'If I look at the content...I have the impression of a flight, but if on the other hand I look at the method, I am aware of it being more rooted in the real world' (p. 19). I suggest that Sartre's biographical enterprise does not have an 'almost bizarre quality' (Scriven, 1984, p. 4) but an emphatically political one.

Why was biography so important to Sartre's historical method? Beauvoir has said of Sartre that, 'His profound idea was that at every stage in history, whatever the social and political context, it remained essential to understand men' (de Beauvoir, 1981, p. 19). In Sartre's case, it is clear that he was seeking an understanding of *individual* men, thereby hoping to throw some light on the entire human condition. In the very first sentence of *The Family Idiot* Sartre, asks, 'What can we know of a man today?' (Sartre, 1971, I, p. 7).[1] Although Sartre moved on from the ontologically isolated human beings of *Being and Nothingness* towards a theory of groups and history in the *Critique*, the individual remained a prime focus for him. In searching for the roots of Sartre's biographical method, Douglas Collins says that, 'The influence of Dilthey's romantic herme-neutics … is perhaps even more substantial than the influence of Marx', because, 'He believed that the basic unit of historical reality is not the collective mind or will, but rather the individual human being' (Collins, 1980, p. 23).

It may be true that Dilthey had an effect on Sartre's method, yet it is equally true that the momentum of Sartre's own philosophical indi-vidualism (derived from a variety of sources) was always going to lead him towards a biographical form of history-writing. In a 1960 interview concerning philosophy and the theatre, Sartre made the point in forthright fashion: 'In my opinion, what philosophy always misses is the singular as such, that is what happens to an individual' (Contat and Rybalka, 1974, I, p. 363).

More important still, from the point of view of the later dialectical method deployed in the Flaubert, Sartre will be pushed towards biography by his desire to show how individuals are 'the whole of human history': demonstrating this successfully will amount to demonstrating the success of his method. In this sense Mark Poster rather misses the point when he writes that 'the radical social theory of the *Critique* would have been served better had Sartre completed his analysis of the Soviet Union and its history in volume two than by concentrating on Flaubert' (1979, p. 119). In my view, as a demonstration of the way in which an individual totalises his history and circumstance, the Flaubert is as full a demonstration of the processes described in the *Critique* as could be hoped for.

David Cooper, heavily influenced by Sartre, even goes so far as to say that all philosophy should be biography, rejecting the idea that, 'a biographical study and a philosophical treatise are mutually exclusive types of work'. Rather, 'It might perhaps be argued with more force that all biographies must, today, be philosophical treatises (if the writer aims at

---

[1] *The Family Idiot*, I; hereafter referred to as *IF I*.

anything more than a chronological collection of facts) and that philosophy on the other hand must often assume the form of biography, as well as that of novel and theatre'. Indeed, 'Biography is the critical experiment of philosophical hypothesising...The truth of one man's life may call the bluff of countless philosophical mystifications' (Cooper, 1964, pp. 71–2).

Of course, Cooper is unjustifiably begging the question of 'the truth of one man's life' – a question which will recur throughout this examination of Sartre's biographical method. Nevertheless the point is made that biography and philosophy, or philosophy and the individual life, are intimately connected in Sartre. So the internal dynamic of philosophical individualism leads Sartre to combine philosophy and biography – this, together with a second motivation which has to do with his self-confessed 'thirst for the absolute', noted at the beginning of this chapter.

Sartre's biographies aim at far more than a 'chronological collection of facts'. He seeks (by no means always successfully) to relate the subject to a history and a society, as well as relating that history and society to the subject. He wants to show how each level of determination results in reciprocal interaction, and he wants to include each and every level of determination in his assessment. To study only individuals is not enough, for that would involve ignoring their milieu. To study the milieu is not enough, for that would involve ignoring the individuals who make the milieu. Sartre wants a method which will explain individuals and their activity; their history and their passivity. In this way, biography becomes philosophy, and philosophy becomes biography.

The method, then, is critical in Sartre. In the following chapters, I shall chart the development of his historical method as he applied it in his biographical studies. For instance, it will be apparent that the notions of activity and passivity, developed in *Being and Nothingness*, remain important but increase in complexity: passivity, for example, comes to involve conditioning by material and historical circumstances, as well as by the 'look' of the other. Childhood comes to have an increasing importance in Sartre's understanding of the evolution of the individual, and the unconscious is replaced by the notion of 'lived experience' (*le vécu*).

Although the method evolved over time, and probably not in a self-conscious, reflective fashion, two relatively distinct periods emerge (as I suggested earlier), and I intend to treat them in chronological order. First, there is the method based on the chapter in *Being and Nothingness* entitled 'Existential Psychoanalysis', which leads to the studies of Baudelaire and Genet; and then I shall look at the recommendations in *Search for a Method*, whose biographical exemplar is the three-volume work, *The Family Idiot*, before going on to assess the aims and achievements of Sartre's historical method *in toto*.

# 9    Existential psychoanalysis

Sartre had yet to demonstrate a thorough understanding of dialectical thought and Marxist materialism.    (de Beauvoir, in Collins, 1980, p. 75)

Sartre begins his account of existential psychoanalysis by making two criticisms of what he calls 'empirical' psychology – first, that it speaks in terms that are too general; and second, that it rests on facts which are held to be irreducible. As for the former, Sartre says that,

For example, we will realise the link between chastity and mysticism, between fainting and hypocrisy. But we are ignorant always of the concrete relation between *this* chastity (this abstinence in relation to a particular woman, *this* struggle against a definite temptation) and the individual content of the mysticism. (*BN*, p. 599)

I have already described Sartre's belief that philosophy ignores the individual life, and he sees 'empirical' psychology as similarly guilty. Sartre is intent on preserving particularity, and it is an issue he stresses throughout his biographies as an explanatory factor in his subjects' behaviour. An example of Sartre's use of particularity outside the biographies is to be found in a 1969 interview when discussing why his friend Paul Nizan left the Ecole Normale before he had finished his course. Sartre finds two reasons for his friend's 'escape' to Aden. At the level of generality it was because, 'he could not breathe within these institutions designed to perpetuate a monopoly of knowledge'; but more particularly because of 'neurotic problems in his personal history' (Sartre, 1974b, p. 62). Thus Sartre makes the point that although there may have been more than one person at the Ecole Normale who was ill at ease with the institution, Nizan was the only one who went to Aden, and it is this particularity that he wants to preserve and explain. Given this stress on particularity and the way in which Sartre believes his method able to deliver it in ways which other interpretative schemes cannot, the success of his existential psychoanalysis in the context of his biographies will inevitably rest on the extent to which they portray their subjects as convincing *individuals*, rather than exemplars of a method. It is essential to bear this point in mind over the next few chapters.

His second criticism of empirical psychology is that facts are presented as irreducible, without further explanation. Prefiguring his interest in Flaubert, Sartre parodies the psychologist's explanation of this novelist's reasons for writing: 'Gustave Flaubert had literary ambition, and his brother Achille lacked it. That's the way it is' (*BN*, p. 560). Sartre, on the other hand, wants to explain the why of Flaubert's literary ambition, and he points out the direction he intends to take by saying of Flaubert's action that, 'It is meaningful, therefore it is free' (p. 560). Sartre wants to reveal this meaning; he seeks a '*veritable* reducible', rather than the postulate of the psychologist, which is 'the result of his refusal or his inability to go further' (p. 560). Sartre's aim is the 'irreducible unification' which is his subject (p. 561).

What is the basis for this 'unification'? For sure, says Sartre, it is something more than an assemblage of partial drives – such seriality can never explain an action. For instance, a 'desire to row is not *only* a desire to row' (*BN*, p. 562). On the contrary,

it is a matter of discovering under the partial and incomplete aspects of the subject the veritable concreteness which can only be the totality of his impulse towards being, his original relation to himself, to the world, and to the Other, in the unity of internal relations and of a fundamental project. This impulse can only be purely individual and unique. (p. 563)

It is this 'fundamental project' which unites the actions of the subject, and is thus the 'veritable irreducible' which Sartre is seeking. Further, because every life is made 'meaningful' in accordance with its project, it follows that every action has a meaning which points beyond itself: 'in each inclination, in each tendency the person expresses himself completely... if this is so, we should discover in each tendency, in each attitude of the subject, a meaning which transcends it' (p. 563).

To this extent we cannot possibly arrive at the meaning of people's lives by a mere mechanical summing-up of their drives and tendencies: 'If we admit that a person is a totality, we cannot hope to reconstruct him by an addition or by an organisation of the diverse tendencies which we have empirically discovered in him' (p. 563). Rather, we need a 'special method' which, 'must aim at detaching the fundamental meaning which the project admits and which can only be the individual secret of the subject's being-in-the-world' (p. 564).

The project is crucial to Sartre's understanding of the individual life – it provides the unification which resides in the 'totality' of the person, and is the transcendence towards which all 'partial drives' point. The notion of the 'project' is characteristic in Sartre, who believes that we are defined as much by the future as by the past, and that meaning can only come to the world through us. We encountered Sartre developing a similar idea in his discussion of history-writing in the *War Diaries* (see p. 41). The implications of the 'project' for a biographical method are also interesting. Clearly it is intended that existential psychoanalysts should make a survey of the actions and intentions of their subjects' lives, and then allow the project of the subject to 'emerge' from the investigation. However, it is always possible that the psychoanalyst will *infer* (actively) the project, rather than let it emerge freely, with all the attendant temptation of making the facts 'fit' the method. George Schrader has said that existential psychoanalysis, 'employs a phenomenological method of letting things "speak for themselves" and of expressing things as they are' (Schrader, 1959, p. 143). This is evidently Sartre's ambition – we are already familiar with the notion of the truth 'emerging' in the context of the *Critique*. But, where there is a method, the libertarianism of emergence may be replaced by the arrogance of imposition. There is a danger that the individual subject will, in the eyes of the existential analyst, become the *existential* subject in order for the existential *method* to bear fruit.

We must now establish how we can know that everyone is susceptible to the existential method – why should it be that we are all expressive of a fundamental project? The answer lies in Sartre's ontology. He defines the for-itself as 'the being which is to itself its own lack of being', and the being which it lacks 'is the in-itself' (*BN*, p. 566). However, this in-itself 'cannot be pure contingent, absurd in-itself, comparable at every point to that which it encounters and which it nihilates', for, 'as with Hegel, the negation of the negation cannot bring us back to our point of departure. Quite the contrary, what the for-itself demands of the in-itself is precisely the totality detotalised – "In-itself nihilated in for-itself".' So, 'The fundamental value which presides over this project is exactly the in-itself-for-itself; that is, the ideal of a consciousness which would be the foundation of its own being-in-itself by the pure consciousness which it would have of itself. It is this idea which can be called God' (p. 566).

Thus the notion of the project is arrived at via an ontology which defines human-reality as a lack – as an entity which has a future to be filled. However, the *individual* characteristics (as applied to each human being) of this project cannot be arrived at ontologically, precisely because of the 'unpredictability of a free act'. The ontology is only useful because it shows that, 'we can subject any man whatsoever to such an investigation... But the inquiry itself and its results are on principle wholly outside the possibilities of an ontology.' On the contrary, 'This research can be conducted only according to the rules of a specific method. It is this method which we call existential psychoanalysis' (*BN*, p. 568).

Sartre then goes on to outline what this method entails. The principle, he says, is that, 'man is a totality and not a collection. Consequently, he expresses himself as a whole even in his most insignificant and his most superficial behaviour. In other words there is not a taste, a mannerism, or a human act which is not revealing' (p. 568). This is, of course, the strategy employed by Sartre in his discussion of the anti-Semite (see pp. 42–3), and the aim of the method is to expose the meaning of each element of behaviour by comparing them, in order to 'effect the emergence of the unique revelation which they all express in a different way' (p. 560). Sartre believes that, 'The first outline of this method has been furnished for us by the psychoanalysis of Freud and his disciples' (p. 569), and goes on to explain the similarities and differences between this 'psychoanalysis proper' and his own existential psychoanalysis. The comparison is instructive as it emphasises Sartre's disdain for any form of crudely mechanistic thought, as well as his belief that human beings must be explained as much by the future as by the past.

The basic similarity is that both forms of psychoanalysis aim at the reconstitution of a life, and that this project will necessarily recognise the situatedness and dynamism of that life in which each act symbolises the global structure which constitutes the person. Further, both methods make extensive use of documentation relating to the subject (*BN*, pp. 569–70). Sartre is most clear about his reservations concerning Freud in an interview published 26 years after *Being and Nothingness*. As well as being initially shocked by the 'biological and physical language', Sartre notes that Freud's psychoanalysis exhibits a 'mechanistic cramp'. By this he means that it is a theory of *exteriority*, or a theory which sees its subject-matter as composed of discrete and separate elements, and so treats them *analytically* rather than *dialectically*: 'Thus I would reproach psychoanalytic theory with being a syncretic and not a dialectical thought. The word "complex", indeed, indicates this very evidently: interpenetration without contradiction' (Sartre, 1974b, p. 38).

In Sartre's view, Freudian theory refuses to see that the elements under interpretation have a special form of autonomy – not an autonomy that resides in complete separateness, but one in which no element is entirely reducible to its predecessor, and which stands beyond it while simultaneously preserving it. Thus Sartre: 'While one configuration may preserve another, it can never simply be reduced to its predecessor. It is this idea of *autonomy* that is lacking in psychoanalytic theory' (p. 39).

The point of all this is that Sartre wants to give each element of his interpretation a special and *particular* status, rather than reduce them to banal levels of generality. In this way, he hopes to keep in sight the *individual* life he is trying to explain. Sartre's insistence on individual specificity – and the alleged superiority of his method in providing it –

gives us a standard against which to judge the success of his biographies he writes while deploying that method. If the method is successful, then the lives of Baudelaire and Genet (for example) should really be Baudelaire's and Genet's lives, rather than some generalised account of the human condition written in biographical form. Over against this approach, says David Cooper, stands Freudian theory which, 'remains more or less crudely reductive, dissolving the person away into an abstract bundle of unintelligible innate drives' (Cooper, 1964, p. 70). The facts that the existential psychoanalyst observes are not reducible to a set of general laws, but rather to a unique, individualised 'original choice' which informs the action of the agent and which is preserved in each element of behaviour:

> The fact that the ultimate term of this existential enquiry must be a *choice*, distinguishes even better the psychoanalysis for which we have outlined the method and the principal features. It thereby abandons the supposition that the environment acts mechanically on the subject under consideration. (*BN*, p. 572)

Sartre's second stand against Freud is taken with reference to the *unconscious*, and he is quite explicit in his condemnation: 'Existential psychoanalysis rejects the hypothesis of the unconscious: it makes the psychic act coextensive with consciousness' (*BN*, p. 570). Now we might suspect that if the psychic act is always conscious, then the project of any given subject is always immediately accessible to that subject, and the existential psychoanalyst is redundant. Not so. Sartre explains: 'if the fundamental project is fully experienced by the subject and hence wholly conscious, that certainly does not mean that it must by the same token be *known* to him; quite the contrary' (p. 570).

This reflection only constitutes 'quasi-knowledge' – it lacks the 'instruments and techniques necessary to isolate the choice symbolised' (p. 570). The reflective consciousness grasps everything all at once, and is incapable of providing the shading which will reveal the relief of this 'mystery in broad daylight'. Only 'another human attitude' [i.e. that of the existential psychoanalyst] can pencil in the shading and enable the subject 'to *know* what he already *understands*' (p. 571).

Throughout this explanation, Sartre has been referring to the inability of subjects to know their own fundamental project – otherwise there is no explicit indication that anyone should remain necessarily opaque to anyone else. However, the implication is that the existential psychoanalyst (having possession of the correct 'instruments and techniques') is in a privileged position to 'know' other people, and this is a similarity with Freud which is rarely mentioned. Both forms of psychoanalysis subscribe to the 'cult of the expert', with the existential expert comparing behavioural elements in order to discover the subject's 'fundamental choice'; while the Freudian analyst plumbs the depths of the unconscious to reveal a bundle of sexual drives, previously unknown to the subject. In both cases, the manifestations are only decipherable if the subject is 'aided and guided by a helping hand' (*BN*, p. 569).

Sartre was, in principle, intent upon preserving the freedom of the individual against the thraldom of person or psychoanalytic system. But he did not think that his method had reached any stage of perfection: 'This psychoanalysis has not yet found its Freud. At most we can find the foreshadowing of it in certain particularly successful biographies' (*BN*, p. 575). In 1944, the same year in which these words were first being read in France, Sartre wrote his study of Baudelaire. In the following chapter I believe that we shall see both that the method was indeed inadequate, *and* that the method itself menaced the person Baudelaire by demanding that he conform to its dictates. Moreover, this menace becomes so thoroughgoing that Baudelaire is threatened with disappearance, thus undercutting any hopes Sartre might have had of mobilising a critique of Baudelaire as a critique of the French literary establishment, both of the nineteenth century and of his own time. To this extent, Sartre's biographies are a graphic illustration of the tension produced by, on the one hand, the desire to let facts 'speak for themselves' and, on the other, the need to marshal them into some kind of coherent order.

# 10    The case of Baudelaire

1969. Sartre's opinion of the Baudelaire: 'very inadequate' and 'extremely bad'.
(Sartre, 1974, p. 42)

Although written in 1944, the Baudelaire did not appear until 1946 when it was published as an introduction to the poet's *Intimate Writings*. First reactions to Sartre's study were not encouraging, and he was criticised for dealing with the man at the expense of the poet – an unacceptable approach for a public brought up on Baudelaire as a national institution. This criticism, right or wrong, is an indication that the study is an exemplar of a method rather than anything else. Sartre was not writing literary criticism; he was trying to explain how a particular man came to write, and his intention was to explain it by his method of existential psychoanalysis.

Douglas Collins is of the opinion that other influences were at work in the study of Baudelaire. He refers to Angelo Hesnard's *L'individue et le sexe: Psychologie du narcissisme*, in which Hesnard provides an explanation for the phenomenon of narcissism. It is held that, from the moment of birth, mother and child form a unified whole in which the child sees the mother as an extension of itself. At some stage, the father intrudes in this relationship, the child sees its mother slipping away towards another focus, and so withdraws in order to seek compensation for itself in this loss. Collins infers that Sartre agreed with this analysis because, 'All the traits mentioned by Hesnard are found by Sartre in the life of Baudelaire. The correspondence between the two books is closer than that between *Baudelaire* and *Being and Nothingness*, which is more commonly noted' (Collins, 1980, p. 65). It may be true that Sartre read Hesnard and decided to incorporate some of his insights in the *Baudelaire*, but to say that *L'individue et le sexe* is a greater influence than *Being and Nothingness* is going too far.

Sartre's biography abounds with the language and symbolism of *Being and Nothingness* – indeed, it sometimes appears that Baudelaire existed merely to provide the perfect example of existentialist man. To this extent it is clear that the *Baudelaire* is intended as an application of existential psychoanalysis. Alfred Stern recalls that he once asked Sartre if existential psychoanalysis had any practical application, and, in a letter to Stern dated October 1948, Sartre wrote, 'I tried to apply it twice, once to the study of an individual (*Baudelaire*), the other time to the study of a collective problem (*Réflexions sur la Question juive*)' (Alfred Stern, 1968, p. 205). It seems clear, then, that *Being and Nothingness* provides the major impetus for the *Baudelaire*, and that this is the most fruitful way in which to read it. Now what does Sartre say of Baudelaire?

Sartre identifies November 1828 as the most crucial date in the poet's life, for this was when his mother remarried and he lost her undivided attention. At this time, 'Baudelaire was sent to boarding school and it was from this period that his famous "flaw" dated', because, 'He made the mortifying discovery that he was a single person' (Sartre, 1964a, p. 17).

By encountering solitude, Baudelaire discovered his freedom – a freedom which turns out to be a two-edged sword. On the one hand, Baudelaire uses this freedom to live his solitude as a *destiny*. Paradoxically, destiny does not involve passivity, but rather the exact opposite: 'He already thought of his isolation as a destiny. That meant that he did not accept it passively. On the contrary, he embraced it with fury' (p. 18). This notion of activity is crucial for Sartre because, as we saw, each element of behaviour is related to the fundamental project of the subject under consideration, and the subject actually *lives* this project which is his/her destiny. For instance, Sartre claims that Baudelaire brought his syphilis upon himself intentionally by going with 'the most squalid prostitutes', (p. 85) in order to satisfy his demand for self-punishment. The same applies to the homosexual reputation he engendered.

On the other hand, Baudelaire's freedom had rather less positive implications – because he was frightened by it, as indeed an existential man would be. He was frightened because he felt abandoned, and his freedom 'meant that he could look for no help either inside or outside himself against his own freedom' (p. 39). So the sense of freedom that he had acquired entailed 'absolute solitude' and 'total responsibility', (p. 66) and Sartre claims that Baudelaire wanted to escape from the anguish that this produced. But, at the same time, Baudelaire's 'pride could never be satisfied by a form of originality which had been passively accepted and of which he himself was not the author' (p. 65). In other words, Baudelaire could not allow himself to reject his freedom altogether, for this would involve making him the 'pure object' of the gaze of others. (p. 66) The obvious solution was for the poet to combine his freedom with the permanence that comes with objectification, so that he could, 'be free, but within the framework of a ready-made universe' (p. 67). In other words,

'He wanted to be a something whose very nature was a contradiction – he wanted to be a *freedom-thing*.' (p. 67).

How was Baudelaire to achieve this perfection in contradiction? To begin with, he chose as his guardian someone who was the 'strictest' of all the 'numerous "fathers" whom the law had given him' – Joseph de Maistre (p. 65). This was clearly an attempt by Baudelaire, says Sartre, to provide for the 'thinginess' he required if he was to be a 'freedom-thing', for, 'It is not open to anyone to choose to assert his freedom in the world of Joseph de Maistre. The paths are marked out, the aims fixed, the orders given. There is only one way for the upright man – conformity. Now that is just what Baudelaire wanted' (p. 67).

On the other hand, Baudelaire wanted to preserve his freedom at the same time as submitting to the strictures of de Maistre. In Sartre's opinion, Baudelaire's *poetry* provided the required 'supernaturalism' and resulted in the 'symbolical satisfaction of a desire for complete autonomy, of a demiurgic thirst for creation' (p. 68). Sartre goes on: 'At this point, we can begin to understand the significance of his vocation as a poet' (p. 68).

Thus, at this pivotal section of the study, Sartre has discovered why Baudelaire came to write. His poetry was a means of ensuring his free ascendency over a world fixed and given by others – a world represented by Joseph de Maistre. Baudelaire, in his particularity, has been found to conform to the ontology of *Being and Nothingness* in which it is the fundamental project of human reality to seek to embody the contradiction of the 'for-itself-in-itself', or God. There is the uncomfortable feeling that whoever Sartre had chosen to study would have been found to conform to these dictates. Is the truth emerging? Or is it being imposed? Now we know from *Being and Nothingness* that the 'freedom–thing' contradiction is impossible to sustain, and we might expect Baudelaire, in his precarious position, to plunge towards one or the other pole. But, before seeing how Sartre plays out the poet's dilemma, we must note one further concern – that of Baudelaire's *particularity* in the general ontology of freedom and brute existence, activity and passivity.

To begin with, Sartre makes a positive note of Baudelaire's dandyism and his 'cult of artificiality and frigidity' (p. 127). But this is not portrayed as something innate to Baudelaire, or even a knee-jerk response to his conditioning. Rather, his dandyism is actively assumed – a 'moral code based on effort' (p. 128). Nor is it simply our role as world-creators that Sartre is stressing here, but also the point that dandyism is Baudelaire's particular, individual response to his situation as a writer: 'In reality, Baudelaire's dandyism was a personal reaction to the problem of the social position of the writer' (p. 131). Sartre then devotes some time to explaining what this 'social position' entailed.

Before the Revolution, he says, the writer had been assimilated by the aristocracy, dependent on it 'for his income as well as his social standing'. To this degree, the writer was a *déclassé*, torn from his bourgeois, middle-class background and granted 'direct access to the aristocracy over the heads of the bourgeoisie'. However, with the coming of the Revolution, the aristocracy was swept away, leaving the writer 'completely bewildered by the fall of his protectors' and looking 'for some fresh form of justification'. Following the demise of the aristocracy, says Sartre, the bourgeoisie should have accepted the writer as their own, but the writer himself would have none of it, for two reasons. First, the writer had become accustomed to favours granted by the aristocracy which had taught him to *despise* the bourgeoisie; second (and more crucially), the writer would have become a *servant* of the bourgeoisie, intolerable for one for whom 'art for art's sake' had been the daily watchword. Baudelaire was not prepared, 'to place his talent at the disposal of his class in the same way as a barrister or an engineer' (pp. 131–3).

Sartre infers Baudelaire's dandyism is a response to this situation. Because the poet did not want to be reduced to a utilitarian artisan, Baudelaire, like many others who had refused to contract in with the bourgeoisie, resorted instead to a 'symbolical *déclassement*'. In an effort to reproduce the 'non-productive activity' which characterised the rule of the aristocracy, Baudelaire resorted to the gratuitousness of dandyism, even to the extent of 'clothes, food, manners, conversation and taste' (pp. 133–5) becoming more important than the process of writing itself: 'The exercise of the artist's profession, which still seems too utilitarian, becomes the pure ceremonial of dress' (p. 139).

This analysis is entirely characteristic of Sartre's concerns at this stage of his development. He has stressed the *active* nature of Baudelaire's being-in-the-world, as well as the *particular* characteristics of this activity. With his historical reference to the French Revolution, he also emphasises the phenomenological maxim that human beings are 'in situation', without ever getting firmly to grips with the dialectical and diachronic relationship between individuals and their situation: a weakness (in his own view) which he was to come to realise.

In observing Baudelaire living his dandyism, we see him at one of the two poles of the 'freedom–thing' contradiction that was mentioned earlier. According to Sartre, his response to this activity was traumatic: 'The aim of dandyism, the cult of artificiality and his act was to put him in possession of himself. Suddenly, he was seized with a feeling of anguish; and he abdicated. He no longer wanted anything except to be an inanimate object whose works are external.' In short, Baudelaire became 'afraid of his own autonomy' (p. 153). His reaction was to fling himself to the other extreme, to reject all responsibility for his being by succumbing to the perceived influence of forces beyond his control. On the one hand, he blamed his illness on hereditary factors – the fact that his mother and father had a 45-year age difference, making for, in Baudelaire's words, 'a disproportionate, pathological, senile union'. The poet says to his correspondent: 'You tell me that you're doing physiology under Claude Bernard. Well ask your master what he thinks of the chancy fruit of such a coupling.' (p. 153). If not his parents, then, 'On other occasions he resorted to the Devil' in order to find forces responsible for his situation and so becomes 'no more than a marionette whose strings are being manipulated'. This, then, is Baudelaire's response to his frightening situation, and from now on 'he spared no pains to transform his life into a destiny' (p. 154).

Sartre believes that as a result of this 'radical conversion', Baudelaire had decided upon his entire future by the age of 21. He had chosen a life of stagnation: 'Everything had stopped' (p. 157). Baudelaire had decided to throw away his chances:

By 1846 he had spent half his capital, written most of his poems, given his relations with his parents their definitive form, contracted the venereal disease which slowly rotted him, met the women who would lie like a piece of lead on every hour of his life and made the voyage which provided the whole of his work with exotic images. (p. 157)

Sartre's crucial observation of this wrecked life is that Baudelaire's was a consciously organised degeneration. His mistake was to try to combine the freedom of the for-itself with the brute existence of the in-itself: 'He chose to exist for himself as he was for others. He wanted his freedom to appear to himself like a "nature"; he wanted this "nature" which others discovered in him to appear to them like the very emanation of his freedom' (p. 184). This desire both to do and to be caused him to oscillate between both poles, before he finally decided to 'give his life a faded appearance' (p. 157). In conclusion, says Sartre, 'We understand now that this wretched life, which seemed to be going to rack and ruin, was carefully planned by him', and that, 'the free choice which a man makes of himself is completely identified with that which is called his destiny' (p. 184).

We are now in a position to discuss the aims, the success, and the excess of the *Baudelaire*. What was Sartre trying to do? In Christina Howells' opinion, 'Sartre's intention in his preface to the *Ecrits Intimes* was to give a picture of Baudelaire as a totality, a unique and unified whole, consistent even within apparent inconsistency, because motivated by an original choice rather than determined by chance events over which he had no control' (Howells, 1979, p. 48).

This is absolutely right, but it is unclear whether Howells thinks that

Sartre has *succeeded* in representing Baudelaire's life as a totality. We remember from the previous chapter on existential psychoanalysis that the human being is a totality, and that this is one of the principles on which the analyst depends. However, Sartre himself indicates that the task may be beyond him – at this stage at least. He claims that his description is 'inferior' to an artist's portrait of Baudelaire in that it is 'successive instead of being simultaneous' (Sartre, 1964a, p. 178). Consequently, his study does not provide a total picture of the poet. However, he says, 'It would be sufficient for us to see the living Baudelaire, if only for a moment, for our scattered remarks to be transformed into a total knowledge' (p. 178).

The implication seems to be that if biographers are dealing with a live subject rather than a dead one, then they will see a simultaneous exhibition of fundamental choice and behaviourial manifestation, rather than have to rely on the seriality provided by the study of historical documents. Certainly the existence of the totality is implied, even if it lies beyond the ken of the biographer: 'In the absence of this immediate comprehension, we can at any rate by way of conclusion underline the close interdependence of all Baudelaire's lines of conduct and all his affections, insist on the way in which by a peculiar dialectic each trait "passes" into the others or lets them be seen or appeals to them to complete themselves' (p. 178).

Sartre does not claim to have given us this totality, but he does claim to have a method which *a priori* shows us that the totality exists. As we progress, we shall see that Sartre's operational humility becomes less marked, and, by the time the *Flaubert* arrives, he is apparently making rather more extravagant claims about the possibility of communicating the totality.

The second point to which I shall be referring is that of the notion of the 'true' biography. Clearly Sartre makes much use of imagination and inference in order to reconstruct Baudelaire's life – indeed, these are the biographer's perfectly legitimate tools. For instance, Sartre remarks upon Baudelaire's disdain for the natural world, preferring the organisation of the inorganic world to that of the unworked promiscuity of the organic. This, says Sartre, was because Baudelaire was not of the country – 'As a townsman, he loved the geometrical object which was subjected to human rationalisation' (p. 101). Consequently, 'for him *real* water, *real* light and *real* heat meant those which are found in towns and which were already works of art unified by a governing idea' (p. 102). From here, Sartre develops the idea that Baudelaire's contempt for the natural world represented his fear of the gratuitousness of that world – apparently existing without rhyme or reason. Against this, Baudelaire wants to be 'a *justified* reality', and so desires to be 'a thing in the world of Joseph de Maistre', to provide him with an existence, 'in a moral hierarchy where he would have had a function and a value in exactly the same way that a de luxe suitcase or the water in jugs exists in the hierarchy of utensils' (p. 103).

At the time he wrote the *Baudelaire* Sartre was still writing novels, and this study, too, has many of the characteristics of the novel as the inferences teeter gently between fact and fiction. However, Sartre is never explicit about the fictional character of the *Baudelaire*, and it is hard to see how he could be, given that he is working to an apparently foolproof method which is intended to give us the truth of the subject. What would the status of his existential psychoanalysis be if he admitted that its use could legitimately provide that analyst with several different interpretations of the subject, with apparently no way of deciding which of them was the most 'truthful', in the sense of making Baudelaire, the individual, most wholly present to the reader? I shall return to this theme in greater detail at a later date, but my third point in this conclusion to the *Baudelaire* also bears on the status of the method.

When a history is written according to a method, as the *Baudelaire* undoubtedly is, then there is a possibility that the inferences will be made with reference to the method rather than on the basis of the material presented. The method becomes the touchstone, and the material is organised to 'fit' the method, thus preserving its integrity. We know that, for Sartre, the subject's 'fundamental choice' is supposed to emerge at the *end* of the investigation. But because this 'choice' is a crucial part of Sartre's ontology, and because we know that it will involve the subject attempting to embody the contradictory 'freedom–thing', there is the temptation to posit the 'original choice' first and then force the life to embody it. In this sense, inferences made about a life are not necessarily intended to tell us anything interesting about that life, but only to sustain the method itself.

For instance, Sartre makes much in the early pages of Baudelaire's recognition of his freedom in solitude, but nowhere does Baudelaire actually use the word 'freedom'. Instead, Sartre picks out quotations from the poems which refer to 'gulfs', or contain phrases like 'I felt giddy', and infers that Baudelaire must have been talking about his nausea in the face of his freedom. (p. 40). Is it too uncharitable to say that only existentialist man refers to freedom in these terms, and that unless Baudelaire was a self-conscious existentialist, then Sartre is merely appropriating him as one for his own ends?

Michael Scriven would agree with the gist of this interpretation, but assess it differently, as he sees Sartre's appropriation of Baudelaire's language in terms of a 'skilful merging' (1984, p. 60) which ends up constituting 'signposts beckoning him [*sic.*, the reader] towards the ultimate truth of Sartre's ideological viewpoint' (p. 61). I shall have something to say on this shortly.

Again, the Baudelaire is liberally equipped with the terminology of *Being and Nothingness*: Sartre says that Baudelaire was, 'uncreated, absurd, useless, abandoned in the most complete isolation, bearing his burden alone, condemned to justify his existence all alone' (Sartre, 1964a, p. 40). And that, 'His freedom, his gratuitousness and his abandonment which frightened him were the lot of humanity, they did not belong particularly to him' (p. 40). It seems that this is an explicit recognition that Baudelaire is the representative of humanity as described in *Being and Nothingness*. This is not so much Baudelaire the man, but 'a' Baudelaire manipulated to fit the contours of Sartre's particular ontological map. Always remembering, of course, that my quotations and inferences are as selective as Sartre's, and that this is a story of Sartre, as much as Sartre's is a story of Baudelaire.

Of course any biographer or historian is confronted with this dilemma – and it is a dilemma which cannot be resolved, but whose resolution must be attempted. Sartre, though, is forcing the method in a way that threatens both the subject and – more dear to his heart perhaps – the reader. In the same year that Gallimard released the *Baudelaire*, Sartre had also published his *What is Literature?*, in which the freedom of the reader is held to be a crucial factor in the creation of a work:

If I appeal to my readers so that we may carry the enterprise which I have begun to a successful conclusion, it is self-evident that I consider him to be a pure freedom, as an unconditioned activity; thus, in no case can I address myself to his passiveness, that is, try to *affect* him, to communicate to him from the very first, emotions of fear, desire, or anger. (Sartre, 1978e, p. 34)

It is true that in this context Sartre is referring specifically to literary works of art. However, even if we assume that the *Baudelaire* is not a 'work of art', it is hard to see how Sartre could renounce his maxim regarding the reader's freedom simply because he is writing in a different genre. What price this maxim in the *Baudelaire*?

One response to the position I have outlined here needs to be considered in some detail. Michael Scriven, in *Sartre's Existential Biographies*, writes that, 'Baudelaire and the reader are left with the unpleasant feeling that they have both been victims of existential assault' (Scriven, 1984, p. 62), and thus appears to agree with the general thrust of this chapter. He recognises that 'the language of existentialism is...overwhelmingly dominant' (p. 58), and that the biography constitutes 'a totalitarian approach to both reader and Baudelaire' (p. 57). Challengingly and ingeniously, though, he goes on to suggest that this is a strategic ploy on Sartre's part

– used to hunt down various of his *bêtes noires*, such as Baudelaire himself, the bourgeois class, Literature (with a capital 'L', i.e. the literature of the French literary establishment), and bad faith in the reader.

In other words, the abandonment of the ground rules laid out in *What is Literature?* represent Sartre's reaction to 'an impossible historical situation', in which, 'the relationship between writer and reader had reached a point of extreme antagonism' (p. 52). Seduced by an alienating ideology, Sartre's post-war French readership (and, by extension, others as well) needed to be shaken out of its torpor by a confrontational text designed to shake its cosy assumptions to the very core. Sartre does this in three ways. He takes Baudelaire, the darling of the literary establishment, and systematically degrades both him and therefore – by implication – the establishment itself. He writes a biography that is not a biography in that it 'does much more and much less than the reader of biography normally expects' (p. 52), and he exposes fatalistic thinking in both Baudelaire and the reader by insisting that, 'Men always have the life that they deserve' (p. 55), rather than allowing them to hide behind the excuse that it just happens to them.

This certainly is a productive analysis of the 'biographical illusion' (p. 58) at work in the *Baudelaire*, and its great merit is that it takes Sartre's text at face value. But the problem is that, if Scriven is right, then both Sartre's strategy and Scriven's ingenuity end up undermined by the conflicting demands of their critiques. Scriven's suggestion is that three targets are under assault: Baudelaire, bad faith, and Literature. For my purposes, these can be reduced to two because Scriven sees Baudelaire as a vehicle for attacking Literature and the class interest that sustains it. So we are left with an attack on Literature and bad faith. The problem is that the critique of the first, which involves a class analysis, conflicts with the second, which involves an existential analysis. A class analysis will only work as long as Baudelaire is continually present as a worked-up representative of his class, while the existential analysis will only work as long as Baudelaire is progressively made absent – or 'evacuated' (p. 61) – *qua* Baudelaire, and replaced by a general subject for existential psychoanalysis.

Either way, Scriven cannot afford to be quite so cavalier in implying that Baudelaire's annihilation (as a real, existing subject) does not matter, and that those of us who think that it does have simply been seduced by the liberal demands of 'traditional biographical discourse' (p. 49). For the class analysis will not work without him, and if it's only the existential analysis that is at stake, why bother with Baudelaire at all if, in principle, anyone could have been forced into the existential mould?

Further, Scriven's strategic reading of Sartre's disappearing of the 'real' Baudelaire will need to work for much more than this one text if it is to work at all. For as we have seen, and as we shall in subsequent chapters, Sartre's erasure of events and their substitution by theoretical schema are something of a working habit. As, for example, Ronald Aronson points out in respect of Sartre's discussion of Stalinism in volume two of the *Critique*, 'sometimes – notably in the discussion of Stalin singularizing the Revolution – the discussion sounds more like a deductive demonstration of an abstract theme than a specific historical study' (1987, p. 178). Are we to explain this, too, as a form of strategic totalitarianism? I think not. The fact is that Sartre needs Baudelaire, just as he needs Stalin, and the 'shock tactics' (Scriven, 1984, p. 62) of annihilation he employs backfire to the extent of endangering the very projects of historical explanation and political prescription he had set out to accomplish.

# 11    The case of Genet

Some people have objected to the length of the present study: 'When one writes so much about a living person, it is because one wants to bury him.'
(Sartre, 1963, p. 574)

Sartre and Simone de Beauvoir first met Jean Genet at the Floré in May 1944, just before France's liberation from the German occupation, and they quickly became friends. Beauvoir says of Genet that he was,

a completely free spirit. His understanding with Sartre was based on their common feeling for a freedom that nothing could intimidate, and their common abhorrence of whatever hobbled it: nobility of soul, timeless moral laws, universal justice, big words and lofty principles, and idealistic systems. (Contat and Rybalka, 1974, I p. 231)

Their friendship burgeoned, and in 1947 Sartre dedicated the Gallimard edition of the *Baudelaire* to Genet, before being instrumental in July of the same year in Genet's capture of the *Pleiade* prize for *Les Bonnes*. A year later, Sartre signed a letter with Cocteau and Picasso (among others) asking (successfully) for clemency from the President of France in relation to Genet's life sentence on the strength of ten convictions for theft. (p. 203.)

Sartre's admiration for Genet, and his willingness to be implicated in his life, was born not only of his respect for Genet's questioning of bourgeois values through his burglary and homosexuality, but because he was a thoroughly committed human being, in the Sartrean sense of *engagé*. Sartre refers to Genet and Mallarmé with equal enthusiasm, and says that he regarded them, 'with complete sympathy: both of them consciously committed themselves' (p. 281). This makes Genet 'one of the heroes of our time' (p. 262) and it is precisely this commitment that Sartre seeks to portray in his biography – not simply to record it, but to emphasise its value. By July 1949, Sartre was working on a preface to Genet (p. 16) which was eventually published by Gallimard in 1952 as volume one of the *Complete Works of Jean Genet*.

As with the *Baudelaire*, Sartre's *Genet* was hardly showered with undiluted praise – in the first instance at least. Beauvoir recalls that,

Sartre had printed several long extracts of his work on Genet in *Les Temps Modernes*; they had aroused interest. But what a fuss at the same time! Although a year earlier, *à propos* of *Deathwatch*, Mauriac had recognised Genet's talent, he now wrote an article in *Figaro* frothing with indignation at what he called 'Excrementalism'. (de Beauvoir, 1978, p. 242)

Genet's reaction to the book was not entirely laudatory either. In fact, Sartre remembers that, 'When Genet held the manuscript of my book about him in his hands, his first impulse was to throw it in the fire' (Sartre, 1978c, p. 122). Beauvoir recalls the same incident, and also notes that relations between the two men cooled off after the book's publication (de Beauvoir, 1981, p. 350), although Sartre, in conversation with de Beauvoir in 1974, claimed that Genet 'did not argue about the ideas. He thought that on the whole the things I said about him were true, and indeed sometimes their truth surprised him' (de Beauvoir, 1985, p. 273).

As with the *Baudelaire*, I am primarily concerned with the methodological issues raised by this biography. There is no doubt that it is a longer and richer analysis than that of Baudelaire, running to nearly 600 pages in the Gallimard edition. Contat and Rybalka rightly stress the book's range of intent, describing it variously as, 'a work of philosophy, a critical literary study, a treatise on ethics, a psychoanalytic biography etc.' (Contat and Rybalka, 1974, I, p. 262). No doubt this variety is due in no small measure to the fact that the Genet was published at the end of a four- or five-year period of voracious reading and critical self-examination on Sartre's part. Yet, despite claims to the contrary, Sartre's study still leans heavily on the insights and categories developed in *Being and Nothingness*, as I hope to show.

As in the *Baudelaire*, Sartre maps out the conflict between being and doing, as represented in and by the life of an individual human being. He illustrates the characteristic behaviour exhibited at each pole, and shows how the state of the subject oscillates between them. The difference between Baudelaire and Genet, however, is that the latter comes to understand this polarity and the singular loneliness it involves, and commits himself to living it to the full, thus achieving a partial emancipation in terms of Sartre's general ontology.

The bare facts of Genet's early life are that he was born in Paris in 1910, and abandoned by his mother almost immediately to the *Assistance Publique*. He was adopted by a peasant family in Morvan until, at the age of fifteen, having been caught stealing several times, he was sent to a reformatory at Mettray. The fact of Genet's being brought up in the country and the fact of his stealing are both crucial to Sartre's investigation. At the same time, Sartre sees Genet as 'contrary to nature' because he had no mother – or at least no mother that he knew – and this particular aspect of Genet's life is seen as constitutive of his homosexuality (Sartre, 1963, p. 7). Genet steals, says Sartre, because he wants to experience possession without indebtedness. Before his crisis, Genet lived in the countryside in a state of innocence, with everything he wanted being given to him. However, Genet knew that his foster-parents were not obliged to give him anything, because that responsibility lay with the mother he never knew, and this experience turns into a 'hatred of all generosity towards inferiors' (p. 9). This hatred is born of Genet's awareness that he owes a debt of subservient gratitude toward his benefactors (because of their status as foster-parents); a debt which he would not owe if the gifts came from his immediate family. Stealing is thus represented as Genet's method of fulfilling a particular desire born of a particular situation. Indeed, according to Sartre, it is an act of theft that constitutes Genet's moment of crisis.

The incident that Sartre relates is imaginary in that it never actually happened as a solitary event. Rather, Sartre telescopes all the occasions on which Genet was caught stealing into one crucial moment and somewhat arbitrarily makes it happen to Genet at the age of ten. In his mind's eye, Sartre sees Genet reaching up into the kitchen drawer. The drawer, 'is opening; a little hand moves forward'. And then: '*Caught in the act.* Someone has entered and is watching him. Beneath this gaze the child comes to himself. He who was not yet anyone suddenly becomes Jean Genet. He feels that he is blinding, deafening; he is a beacon, an alarm that keeps ringing' (p. 17).

The reason that the child who was no one is now Jean Genet is because he has become the object of Sartre's 'look' – he is the child-thief, Jean Genet. Now, 'A voice declares publicly: 'You're a thief' (p. 17), and, 'Genet, thunderstruck, considers his act, looks at it from every angle. No doubt about it, it is a theft' (p. 18).

Before this moment, Genet never realised his actions for what they were. For instance, says Sartre, masturbation as well as stealing only exist for the small child if seen by adults, for, 'to exist *is to be seen by adults*' (p. 15). Thus, 'Genet learns what he is *objectively*. It is this *transition* that is going to determine his entire life' (p. 18). However, this general ontological fact is not enough to explain Genet's reaction to the withering gaze of the adult. For, as we have noted, these adults are his *foster*-parents. Sartre conjectures that if it had been his parents who had made the accusation, then they would have reabsorbed him into the family, for, 'one doesn't rob one's family' (p. 19).

In this example, Sartre yet again emphasises that general observations about the human condition can never be enough to explain the complexity of the individual life, where particularity and generality enmesh. Similarly, Genet's age at the time he was caught stealing is crucial to an understanding of how he coped with this objectification. If he had been, say, seventeen, he could have laughed at the accusation, because, 'That is the age at which one liquidates paternal values'. He could even 'have denied the existence of values and deigned only to recognise the law of force'. But not as a child, brought up according to a religiously moral code, and for whom 'adults are gods' (p. 21).

It is clear that Sartre has no time for this particular child/adult relationship. In interiorising the adult view of him, Genet becomes lonely – a loneliness which is something more than that individuality which we recognise around the age of ten. This otherness, 'excludes any reciprocity. It is not a case of an empty and universal form but of an individual difference that has to do with both form and content. There is Genet and there are all the others' (p. 22).

Genet feels himself fully under the influence of other people and his subjectivity appears compromised beyond recovery. Indeed, it seems at this moment that Genet is merely following his ordained path to a pre-determined destiny:

Even before he emerged from his mother's womb, they had already reserved beds for him in all the prisons of Europe and places for him in all the shipments of criminals. He had only to go to the trouble of being born; the gentle, inexorable hands of the Law will conduct him from the National Foundling Society to the penal colony. (p. 31)

The objective definition of his being a criminal has corroded his subjective being to nothingness.

At this point, Sartre's perspective changes. At the very moment when he has Genet 'pinned by a look, a butterfly fixed to a cork', Sartre says that, 'He now has to live', because, 'We are not lumps of clay, and what is important is not what people make of us but what we ourselves make of what they have made us' (p. 49). In this sense, Genet is involved in a search for his Being (p. 73), and the search has led him to take on the definition that others have made of him: he has decided to live – even love – his destiny. Yet this project is doomed to incompletion, for its aims and terms of reference are in contradiction. Sartre explains. Genet once said, 'I decided to be what crime made of me', (p. 49) and Sartre points out that, 'In this seemingly very simple statement there is "to decide". But there is also "to be"' (p. 59). Decision-making, says Sartre, is intended to change the world in some way, but if you are already what you intend to be, then what can you decide?

In this context, the phrase 'to be' is ambiguous in that it 'suggests a compromise between the calm coinciding of an object with its essence and the storm-tossed development whereby a man fulfils himself' (p. 59). The reason this ambiguity arises is because, 'we are beings whose being is perpetually in question' (p. 60). This sentiment is, of course, drawn directly from *Being and Nothingness*. Because his being is in question, Genet is involved in making himself, but he has chosen to make himself what he already is for others, and thus shuttles back and forth from being to doing. Every attempt 'to be' (statically) is foiled because it can never involve inactivity: 'quietism is not so much total inaction as it is inactivity aimed at making us passive... Thus this too-deliberate passivity changes into wilfulness' (pp. 64–5).

Similarly, every decision that Genet takes in order 'to do' is bankrupted in order to fulfil the 'nature' bestowed upon him by others because, 'this signifies that he agrees to give others a hold upon him, that he voluntarily exposes himself to their gaze, in short that he utilises his freedom as a pure universal subject to lower his status to that of an object' (p. 70). Both of these categories of doing and being, in their dialectical development over the decade after his conversions, contribute 'to make the history of Genet' (p. 63). This, then, is Sartre's picture of Genet at the age of eighteen.

At about this time, Genet discovers poetry and realises the possibility of creating an illusory world. He has already found that he cannot create himself in the world, so instead he creates an illusory picture of himself in order to fulfil the fantasy that he is self-created. However, in destroying the world in this way, he has also destroyed himself by being sucked into the vortex of the imaginary world that he has made. Yet at this point in his life there is nothing else for him to do, because 'There are times... when the situation is unacceptable and we are unable to change it' (p. 344).

Then at the age of twenty-six he meets a burglar who teaches him his profession, and a whole new world of activity opens up for Genet, 'freed from his fate' (p. 402). Released from the narcissistic imaginings of his early poetry, Genet bursts into the world and finds the strength to challenge it directly, rather than derealising it in the imaginary world of poetry. He is moving from aesthete to artist: 'As an aesthete, he was a prey to derealising gestures; as an artist he invents acts which realise gestures' (p. 422). Genet has gained a crucial foothold in choosing to take those who made him an object and turn them upon themselves – he will be a subject after all.

Sartre relates that, while in prison, Genet reads a poem to his cell-mates – a beautiful poem which elicits contempt from his audience. Genet realises that he can now *live* his contradiction: he can be scorned by others, and yet be the foundation of that scorn. He is a hateful object in his writings, yet he is the subject who presents himself as such. He uses beauty to seduce his readers – the Just ones who were the source of his original condemnation – and then, through his subject-matter of crime and homosexuality, he forces the Just to look in the mirror and see that these 'crimes' are as much a part of their world as they are of his. Of course Genet is still involved in using the retreat of imagination to achieve emancipation – hardly the attitude Sartre would have condoned in his advocacy of 'committed literature'. But he is excused because he, 'is performing the exemplary act of expropriating the expropriator. The world of the Just has done him violence and he is now simply responding in kind' (Collins, 1980, p. 103).

Genet stands at a distance from his accusers and encourages them to acquiesce in their own destruction. In so doing, he achieves an emancipation –

Each of his books is a cathartic attack of possession, a psychodrama; in appearance, each of them merely repeats the preceding one, as his new love-affairs repeat the old: but with each new work he masters increasingly that demon that possesses him. His ten years of literature are equivalent to a psychoanalytic cure. (Sartre, 1963, p. 533)

In short, through his writing, Genet has realised, 'the pure freedom of the artist [who] no longer knows either Good or Evil ... Genet has liberated himself' (p. 422) – 'Genet is free, Baudelaire is not' (Scriven, 1984, p. 66). It remains to be said, however, that the liberation is partial at best, in that, although Genet has found a means of expressing his subjectivity, the subject–object dichotomy remains.

Now I turn to the methodological issues raised by Sartre's treatment of Genet. I have already suggested that the book is heavily influenced by the categories of *Being and Nothingness*. Beyond the subject–object polarity, there is also a striking similarity between Sartre's affirmation of freedom in 1944 and the way in which he shows how Genet wills his liberation through confronting a situation. Sartre himself has said that the *Genet* constitutes his most developed study of freedom: 'Perhaps the book where I best explained what I meant by freedom is, in fact, *Saint Genet*. For Genet was made a thief, he said, "I am a thief", and this tiny change was the start of a process whereby he became a poet' (Sartre, 1974b, p. 35).

We remember that freedom in *Being and Nothingness* did not necessarily involve freedom to change the world, but merely freedom to re-interpret it, and, in an interview with Simone de Beauvoir, Sartre accurately captures this form of 'diluted' freedom with respect to the *Genet*: 'Freedom is the transformation of Jean Genet, homosexual and sad infant, into Jean Genet, great writer, pederast by choice, and, if not happy, then sure of himself...[Freedom] transformed the meaning of the world in giving it another value' (de Beauvoir, 1981, p. 449).

However, while recognising these similarities with his earlier philosophical work, Laing and Cooper, among others, think that he has gone beyond it in an important way. Together with the analytic categories of *Being and Nothingness*, they find, 'an increasingly explicit and systematic concern with the relation between the individual person and the groups, institutions and class to which he belongs' (Laing and Cooper, 1971, pp. 16–17). It seems to me, though, that Genet's social and historical situation is not treated as fundamental to his development. Rather, Sartre asserts its importance – in contrast to Genet who 'cares not a rap about history' (Sartre, 1963, p. 51) – and then goes on to spend very little time demonstrating it. In fact what we discover is that he is not really talking about *history*, but about *situation*.

In chapter 2 I described how phenomenology had given Sartre a philosophy of situation, if not yet a philosophy of history. By this I meant that so long as the abstracted and ahistorical subject–object relationship prevails in Sartre's thought, then situations and the subject's response to them will always be of greater significance than the diachronic weight of history. This is so much less sophisticated and less dialectically persuasive than the account given in volume two of the *Critique* of how boxers (and each particular bout) incarnate the whole history of boxing (see pp. 99–102). An example from the *Genet* will serve to illustrate the point. At the stage where Sartre asserts the importance of history, he is concerned with explaining how Genet came to be so reviled by the villagers upon the discovery of his theft. He says: 'let us recognise that the pitiless and absurd sentence which is imposed upon the child can only come from a strongly-knit group with a system of strict and simple prohibitions. Only such a community can react with such righteous indignation... to the petty pilferings of a ten-year old thief' (Sartre, 1963, p. 52).

It is true that this explanation makes sense in itself, but it can hardly be called *historical* explanation. Rather, Sartre has taken a general observation about the 'tension between incompatible groups and ethical systems' and the individuals who live in them and applied it to the particular situation of Jean Genet. This seems to me to be better characterised by inference from situation than explanation by history. We might apply the same interpretation to Sartre's belief that Genet did not know that to be 'is also what one *makes* or does', because he had been brought up in the country – only the town (a centre of active *production*) would have taught him that. Of course Sartre has placed Genet in a situation, but he has not explained either the historical basis of that situation or Genet's relationship to that history. Indeed, Sartre himself is clear that he is trying, 'to indicate the limits of psychoanalytical interpretation and Marxist explanation and to show that freedom alone can account for a person in his totality', and goes on to invite us to judge him: 'It is for the reader to say whether I have succeeded' (p. 584).

He can hardly be said to have succeeded in demonstrating the limits of Marxism since he has devoted so little space to discussion of it. I cannot agree with Peter Caws that 'By the time of the Saint Genet a Marxist component has been added to the method' (1979, p. 190). Rather Sartre's book on Genet is best read as a more fully developed version of the essay on Baudelaire, resting on many of the same assumptions and theories. In a 1969 interview, he said that he was now critical of that approach:

It is obvious that the study of the conditioning of Genet at the level of institutions and of history is inadequate – very, very inadequate. The main lines of the interpretation, that Genet was an orphan of Public Assistance, who was sent to a peasant home and who owned nothing, remain true, doubtless. But all the same, this happened in 1925 or so and there was a whole context to this life which is quite absent. The Public Assistance, a foundling, represent specific social phenomena, and anyway, Genet is a product of the twentieth century; yet none of this is registered in the book. (Sartre, 1974b, p. 43.)

Why is there so little history in the Genet? Christina Howells gives Sartre the benefit of the doubt by saying that its absence is an intentional ploy: 'Sartre is anxious to show the limitations of a rigid Marxism which imagines it has explained a man once it has situated him in a broad historical framework... For this reason, Sartre will not stress the "Marxist" elements of his analysis until his work on Flaubert' (Howells, 1979, pp. 58–9). This may be too charitable to the state of Sartre's Marx studies in 1952. True, he had spent several years after the Second World War getting to grips with Marx, but he was also spending a vast amount of time trying to devise his own system of ethics. Similarly, it is evident from other work that he did around this time (for example, the *Communists and the Peace*) that his application of Marx's historical insights were rather naive, as I suggested in chapter 3.

I believe that the *Genet* lacked a historical dimension because Sartre had not yet acquired the means to work it out, and not because he was trying to show the limits of historical explanation. To this extent, the *Genet* is much closer to *Being and Nothingness* than it is to the *Critique*, although it stands (chronologically) exactly in the middle. The 4 years of Sartre's rapprochement with the PCF between 1952 and 1956, and his consequent contact with Communist theoreticians, were to provide a catalyst for Sartre's historical method – the fruits of which appear in his *Search for a Method*. In the context of Sartre's life it is unfair to expect the *Genet* to be much more than an extension of the *Baudelaire*, although it merits separate study because of what Genet's stubborn commitment to living his destiny can tell us of the emancipatory possibilities inherent to Sartre's early ontology.

Even the political situation and Sartre's recommendations for its improvement are couched in the language of *Being and Nothingness*, albeit overlaid with social observation. Sartre bemoans the lack of reciprocity in human life, saying that, 'it is concealed by the historical conditions of class and race, by nationalities, by the social hierarchy' (Sartre, 1963, p. 590). The perfect situation would be one in which, 'we could all be, simultaneously and reciprocally, both object and subject for each other and by each other' (p. 590). But we know that this is impossible because, 'I am a subject to myself exactly in so far as my fellow man is an object to me' (p. 590). Sartre's ontology returns to splinter our hopes on the rocks of the subject–object dichotomy.

Is there any cause for optimism? We have seen how he admires Genet's determination to live the ontological contradiction to the full, and it appears that he would want us to do the same. Certainly he warns us against taking the attitude of Bukharin (for example) who confessed 'with humility' (1963, p. 595) to the crimes others had accused him of, thus fleeing to the pole of objectivity, 'a stone amongst stones' (p. 594). Genet, on the other hand, confesses with pride, and 'proclaims in defiance of all that he is right to be wrong' (p. 595). This is how we should be. This subjectivity, for now, should be pushed to its limits. Genet provides the antidote to Baudelaire: 'The hostility that Sartre displays towards the acquiescing inauthenticity of Baudelaire has as its logical counterpart an unequivocal admiration for the self-willed authenticity of Jean Genet' (Scriven, 1984, p. 65).

Sartre writes that, 'We spend our time fleeing from the objective into the subjective, and from the subjective into objectivity. This game of hide-and-seek will end only when we have the courage to go to the limits of ourselves in both directions at once' (Sartre, 1963, p. 599). Eventually, we must seek subjectivity – involving recognition of the individual – and objectivity – stressing involvement in society. But, 'At the present time, we must bring to light the subject, the guilty one, that monstrous and wretched bug which we are likely to become at any moment.' Genet gives us the lead, he 'holds the mirror up to us: we must look at it and see ourselves' (p. 599).

To the extent that the recognition of subjectivity is an essential component of the rebellious spirit, then Sartre's message is loud, clear, political and valuable. Nevertheless, David Cooper's observation remains open to question. He says that Sartre has revealed 'the mass social process of scape-goating', whereby, 'Good folk invent ethical values and then confirm themselves as possessors of these values by electing other members of the community as scapegoats embodying the anti-value' (Cooper, 1964, pp. 71–2).

Perhaps. But does Sartre's revelation of this phenomenon also mean that, 'We must make no mistake about it: this book is a threat, a factory in which lethal weapons will be produced'? (pp. 71–2). This is a grand claim, for it implies that the *Genet* acts as a source of political emancipation in its description of the mechanics of marginalisation. But this needs to work at two levels. First, Sartre's description must convince us at a general level, such that we recognise Genet's experience as potentially or actually a common one. Second, the process of scapegoating that Cooper describes must be persuasive in the context of Genet's life itself, so that we agree it can happen to real people in particular circumstances. This, after all, is the point of Sartre's developing a biographical method that is intended to illuminate both the human condition and the particular life. The success of the method and, by implication, any political statement it is meant to contain, will be judged by how far it enables Sartre to keep both the general *and* the particular in view. If Genet 'disappears' only the human condition will remain. This may be illuminating, but it will only constitute a partial success for both the method and the politics it involves. I explained in the previous chapter how we have to believe in Baudelaire (rather than just any existential representative of Sartre's ontology) for Sartre's political points to be persuasive, and now it becomes even clearer that accepting the 'disappearance' of the biographical subject amounts to acknowledging the failure of Sartre's method and the insecurity of (in this case) his statements regarding social marginalisation.

So again we need to ask how far Sartre has succeeded in portraying and explaining Genet the man. On one level, the project is hampered by the fact that the subject is still alive at the time of writing. Contrasting Genet with Flaubert, whose life 'is a completed totality', Sartre says that, 'it is impossible to totalise a living man'. This disadvantage would seem to carry greater weight than the putative advantage that knowing Genet amounts to 'an extremely useful checking device for Sartre's own biographical hypotheses' (Scriven, 1984, p. 66).

Sartre obviously feels that his Flaubert study is fuller by virtue of Flaubert's being dead. In contrast, 'What I did in *Saint Genet*, for example, was much less complete. Living writers hide themselves: when one writes, one disguises oneself' (Sartre, 1978c, p. 122). Despite this drawback, Laing and Cooper are impressed by Sartre's achievement: 'we believe that Sartre does succeed in conveying a radical understanding of Genet as a living whole, while also evoking for the reader Genet as a real presence' (Laing and Cooper, 1971, p. 67).

However, as with the *Baudelaire*, this is probably too sanguine in the context of Sartre's habit of invention, especially in the context of a method. Laing and Cooper are not at all concerned with those parts of Sartre's exposé which rely on imaginative reconstruction. This is fair enough – imagination is one of the biographer's legitimate tools. But when reconstructions are dictated by a method rather than by the 'events themselves', there is a danger that the method will take over and the biographical subject will disappear – with all the attendant dangers described above.

Sometimes, Sartre's constructions are dubious. For instance, he claims that it is crucial for Genet's homosexuality that he was caught stealing *from behind*, in the sense that this event is mirrored in the homosexual act: 'Let there be no misunderstanding: I am not saying that his original crisis *resembles* a rape, I say that it *is* one' (Sartre, 1963, p. 79). Genet himself has said that his homosexuality predated his being a thief (Collins, 1980, p. 65) but Sartre cannot agree because of his belief that sexuality is never primary. It is essential that Sartre uses his imagination to reconstruct Genet's life, because there are gaps to be filled. But if the gaps are filled in order to preserve a biographical technique, then Genet (whose specificity Sartre explicitly set out to capture) disappears from view.

It may be, of course, that the issue can never be decided: 'We know too little about the intimate evolution of Genet the man to be able to decide whether his resolve 'to be what he was – i.e. a thief – did in fact determine the whole of his early life' (Coe, 1968, p. 14). Once again, we find ourselves in the position of criticising Sartre for using Genet as a vehicle for his ideas: 'it early becomes evident that this stupendous study is not about Jean Genet, but rather an elaborate philosophical construct of Sartre's who passes by his name, borrows his words, and shares the events of his life' (Littlejohn, 1970, p. 123).

From this perspective, Sartre's Genet is a fictional character, constructed to conform to the dictates of the existential psychoanalytic method: 'If, as they say, there were not a Genet, Sartre would have had to invent him anyway. As indeed he has' (p. 125). It seems that, as with the Baudelaire, Sartre has taken Genet as his representative of humanity. To this extent, Sartre has failed in his attempt to preserve particularity: 'What Sartre has done has been to take the historic Genet as a frame of focus for all that he himself thought about the human condition' (p. 124). Coherence has taken over from correspondence and the method tyrannises Genet's life rather than serves as a vehicle for its explanation. Susan Sontag, for one, thinks that we never really get to know who Genet is: 'He cannot catch the real Genet; he is always slipping back to the categories of Foundling, Thief, Homosexual, Free Lucid Individual, Writer.' Thus, 'The name "Genet" repeated thousands of times throughout the book never seems to be the name of a real person. It is the name given to an infinitely complex process of philosophical transfiguration' (Sontag, 1967, pp. 94–5).

This tyranny of method is particularly disturbing in the context of Sartre's intuitive libertarianism. Sartre appears to have an *inclination* to let the subject speak for him/herself, and a *method* that disallows it. The contradiction is made explicit with a concluding chapter entitled 'Please Use Genet Properly'. Dominic LaCapra points out that the message of this chapter is in conflict with the rest of the book:

Along comes an existential analyst and presents a totalising interpretation that paradoxically concludes with a plea to the reader to allow Genet to have his own 'voice' and to allow himself to be affected by the challenge of that voice. (LaCapra, 1978, p. 181)

To this extent, Sartre's oppressive use of method compromises both the subject and the reader. The subject is hidden within an intricate web of methodological entanglement, and the reader succumbs under an incessant rain of words – incapable, in the end, of making the judgement that Sartre requires of us. This book was written at the beginning of Sartre's attempt to steer the PCF away from dogmatism, but here the project is undermined by his own determination to impose.

# 12    Search for a method

The progressive–regressive method, the coming and going between conditions and project, presents no radical originality concerning the method of understanding, which has been used spontaneously by historians and ethnographers when either were forced to deal directly with lived experiences or to reconstruct them.          (Aron, 1973, p. 7)

I have argued that, despite the 5-year gap between their respective publication, Sartre's historical/biographical method exhibits no signal change between the *Baudelaire* and *Saint Genet*. I have also suggested that 1952 was an important year for Sartre – the year in which his political trajectory took him closer to the PCF than ever before, with the publication of the first two parts of the *Communists and Peace*. This proximity was to last for 4 years, until the Soviet invasion of Hungary, and it led him towards a profound reappraisal of the relationship between existentialism and Marxism. In 1957 Sartre was given the opportunity to develop this relationship. In that year, he made a trip to Poland, and one of the organisers of the journal *Twórozość* asked him to write an essay on the subject of 'Where existentialism stands in 1957' for an issue on French culture. Sartre wrote the required essay, and then rewrote it a little later, 'to suit French readers', (*CRD I*, p. 822) before having it published in *Les Temps Modernes* in September and October 1957.

The expressed aim of the book is to revive Marxism from what Sartre perceives as a stagnation brought about by its gratuitous and opportunist use in the political context. Sartre makes a radical distinction between 'original' Marxism (i.e. that of Marx himself) and the Marx of Marxists – particularly Sartre's contemporaries. Apart from one slight reservation, to which I shall refer, Sartre believed that Marx had provided the best historical framework within which to work, but that this grid had been twisted and distorted beyond recognition by his followers: 'we must be careful: the original thought of Marx, as we find it in *The Eighteenth Brumaire of Louis Napoleon Bonaparte* attempts a difficult synthesis of intention and result; the contemporary use of that thought is superficial and dishonest' (Sartre, 1968, p. 45). The aim, then, is to point out the

150

'existing contradictions' (p. xxxiii) in Marxist philosophy as it had developed in France by 1957.

The *Search* is divided into three sections. In the first, Sartre explores the relationship between existentialism and Marxism; in the second, he introduces the notion of the project and of mediations, together with a discussion of the contribution of 'auxiliary disciplines' such as psychology and sociology; and third, he explains the foundations of the progressive–regressive method. This last constitutes a move beyond the existential psychoanalysis which was the foundation of the *Baudelaire* and the *Genet*, and is crucial in this context as it represents the battle-plan for the *Flaubert*, on which he was already working.

In introducing the relationship between existentialism and Marxism, Sartre notes that cataclysmic periods of real philosophical creation are rare. He claims three such periods to be those of Descartes and Locke, Kant and Hegel, and that of Marx. Once established, they cannot easily be transcended. They have arrived for very good historical reasons, and they will only be transcended for very good historical reasons – 'there is no going beyond them so long as man has not gone beyond the historical moment which they express' (p. 7).

We should note at the outset the Hegelian tenor of these remarks. Being and knowledge are inextricably linked, and so knowledge is dependent upon the historical movement for its development: 'It is the very movement of History, the struggle of all men on all planes and on all levels of human activity, which will set free captive thought and permit it to attain its full development (p. 8). Indeed, in the preface, Sartre makes clear his indebtedness to Hegel. He says that his own philosophy of existence has inherited two requirements from Marx 'which Marxism itself derives from Hegelianism'. First, 'if such a thing as Truth can exist in anthropology it must be a truth that has *become*, and it must make itself a totalisation'. Second, 'in *Search for a Method* I have taken it for granted that such a totalisation is perpetually in process as History and historical Truth' (p. xxxiv). Sartre is working with the Hegelian dialectic of being and knowing, and this will become an important factor later when I discuss the truth-status of Sartre's biographies.

After the flowering of each of the momentous philosophies to which Sartre has referred come the 'ideologists', 'relative men' who 'get their nourishment from the living thought of the great dead'. Sartre makes it clear that in this context he considers existentialism to be an ideology – 'a parasitical system living on the margin of knowledge' (p. 8). Despite, or perhaps because of, its role as an ideology, existentialism has a part to play in the revival of Marxism, but this can only be understood by referring to the past. Sartre singles out Hegel as having presented us with the 'most ample philosophical totalisation' (p. 8), such that we are 'integrated alive in the supreme totalisation' (p. 9). He suggests that Kierkegaard fears for the individual in the face of this gigantic system and, 'is led to champion the cause of pure, unique, subjectivity against the object universality of essence, the narrow, passionate intransigence of the immediate life against the tranquil mediation of all reality' (p. 11).

For Sartre, both men are 'right', (p. 12) but they each tell only a half-truth. It is left to Marx, says Sartre, to effect a synthesis of the two, and to affirm 'with Kierkegaard the specificity of human *existence* and, along with Hegel, take the concrete man in his objective reality' (p. 14). Once Marx had died, he could do nothing about the Marxists who pillaged his work for opportunist political reasons; and Jaspers, for one, found himself confronting a Marxism between the two world wars which, in its scientific and objective pretensions, had forgotten that just as history makes people so people make history. Jaspers refuses 'to co-operate *as an individual* with the history which Marxists are making' (p. 16). However, Sartre sees Jaspers as reverting to a form of the transcendent subjectivity found in Kierkegaard – a philosophy which pays no heed to the lessons of the historical dialectic taught by Marx. The scene is almost set for Sartre himself to attempt to unite Marxist and existentialist objectives.

But first he must explain why this is necessary in the context of contemporary Marxism. We might wonder, for instance, why existentialism has not been dissolved in the great flowering of Marxism. How has it managed to preserve its autonomy? The answer, says Sartre, is that 'Marxism stopped' (p. 21). And the blame for this sclerosis lies with those who used Marxism to build the Soviet state. Threatened from all sides after the Revolution and intent on preserving the gains they had made, the leaders of the Revolution forced a wedge between theory and practice, 'transforming the latter into an empiricism without principles; the former into a pure, fixed knowledge'. Obeying the dictates of survival, 'Party leaders...feared that the free process of truth, with all the discussions and all the conflicts it involves, would break the unity of combat.' And so they 'put the doctrine out of reach' (p. 22). Practice becomes a knee-jerk response to objective conditions, and the theory becomes an idealism, fixed and transcendent. These remarks revive much of what Sartre had to say of contemporary Marxism in *Materialism and Revolution* as far back as 1946.

It is plain that Sartre finds Marx himself standing in sharp contrast to French Marxists. For instance, he notes approvingly that, 'Marx was convinced that facts are never isolated appearances, that if they come into being together, it is always within the higher unity of a whole, that they are bound to each other by internal relations, and that the presence of one profoundly modifies the nature of the other' (p. 25). This is a very neat and succinct expression of the dialectical nature of the historical process, and it implies the need for dialectical reason to understand it. In studying a historical event (Sartre cites the revolution of 1858), Marx provides the blueprint for Sartre's method in stressing the particular detail of the event while attempting to incorporate these anecdotal facts into the totality. In contrast to this patient analysis, Sartre sees Marxists turning to 'voluntarism' in an attempt to force Marxism to fit their sclerosed theory. For them, 'Analysis consists solely in getting rid of detail, in forcing the signification of certain events, in denaturing facts or even in inventing a nature for them in order to discover it later underneath them, as their substance, as unchangeable, fetishised "synthetic notions"' (p. 27).

It is into this wasteland of Marxist idealism that Sartre injects existentialism. In the context of a Marxism which seeks to 'liquidate particularities', existentialism 'has been able to return and maintain itself because it reaffirmed the reality of men as Kierkegaard asserted his own reality against Hegel' (1968, p. 28). This, then, is existentialism's contribution. It aims to preserve the uniqueness and particularity of individual people and events against the sterile universals of Marxists. This recognition is crucial to an understanding of Sartre's historical/biographical method as expressed in the *Flaubert*. There, he is at pains to show how an individual life generates, and is generated, within a general historical context. This task, he claims, would be utterly beyond contemporary Marxists because, for them, the individual life is of no account. However, Sartre stresses that existentialism must take its correct place within the corpus of Marxism proper, for Marxism, 'remains...the philosophy of our time. We cannot go beyond it because we have not gone beyond the circumstances which engendered it' (p. 30). Indeed, Marxism will only be transcended once the reign of scarcity is at an end. Thus, 'as soon as there will exist *for everyone* a margin of *real* freedom beyond the production of life, Marxism will have lived out its span; a philosophy of freedom will take its place'. But at present, 'we have no means, no intellectual instrument, no concrete experience which allows us to conceive of this freedom or of this philosophy' (p. 34). With this affirmation of Marx's pre-eminence, as well as the condition for its being superseded and existentialism's possible contribution to its demise, Part One ends.

In Part Two, Sartre shows in detail how he intends to reintroduce the individual to history, but first he introduces a discussion of the historical method of contemporary Marxists. He says that, to their credit, they attempt to *situate* the object that they are studying: 'they mean to determine for the object considered its real place in the total process; they will establish the material conditions of its existence, the class which has produced it, the interests of that class (or of a segment of that class)' and so on. For example, 'they will interpret the acts and discourses of Robespierre in terms of a fundamental economic contradiction' (p. 36). But in the end this is unacceptable, says Sartre, because 'It is *a priori*. It does not derive its concepts from experience' (p. 37).

In contrast to this economism, which Marx himself denounced (p. 43), Sartre asserts that politics is irreducible, and that we need the notion of mediations to bring this to light. He says that mediations, 'will bring into play the concrete men who were involved in it [i.e. the French Revolution], the specific character it took on from its basic conditioning, the ideological instruments it employed, the real environment of the Revolution' (p. 42). In this way, the method will preserve the real – the action of human beings – in contrast to Marxists who 'dissolve men in a bath of sulphuric acid' (pp. 43–4).

This discussion of historical method is of great political importance to Sartre for two reasons. In placing such stress on subjectivity and activity he is intent on making room for responsibility in Marxism, and the explicit political connection is made later in the book when Sartre is discussing how a French Communist described the 1956 Soviet intervention in Hungary. The writer is reprimanded for using such phrases as 'could not help' and 'could not do otherwise' because of the simplistic substitution of compulsion for the complicated dialectical relationship between freedom and necessity. As I suggested in the context of the second volume of the *Critique* in chapter 7, however, these laudable 1957 intentions to reintroduce responsibility to Marxism are by no means borne out in Sartre's own discussion of Stalinism.

Second, though, the voluntarism that lurks here behind these remarks is bound up with Sartre's enduring political utopianism. He wants to stress the active element in the human condition because the belief that we make history (even if coterminously with it making us) is an essential requirement for political action. For if we are indeed tossed hither and thither by forces beyond our control (either transcendent or 'natural'), then how can we ever hope to take rational control of our circumstances? Political action, properly speaking, would be meaningless; hence the political importance of Sartre's statement that 'It is men who *do*, not avalanches' (p. 48).

As well as failing to cater for intention in history, contemporary Marxists are also castigated for refusing to accommodate the individual in historical explanation. For instance it is not enough to explain Valéry by his generalised background, for in referring to him as a petit bourgeois, the man Valéry disappears: 'Valéry is a petit bourgeois intellectual, no doubt about it. But not every petit bourgeois intellectual is Valéry. The heuristic inadequacy of contemporary Marxism is contained in these two sentences' (p. 56).

Sartre wants to move beyond abstract determinations and false universality. He quotes Engels on the subject of the individual in history: 'That such a man, and precisely this man, arises at a determined period and in a given country is naturally pure chance. But, in the absence of Napoleon, another man would have filled his place... The same is true of all chance events and of all that appears to be chance in history' (p. 56). Sartre's opinion? 'Existentialism considers Engels' statement an arbitrary limitation of the dialectical movement, an arresting of thought, a refusal to understand' (p. 57). Sartre's plan is to overcome this limitation by developing a method in which individuals will be explained in context, but will simultaneously have their individuality preserved. It is worth taking a closer look at Sartre's intentions here, for the task he sets himself is vast and its ramifications are legion.

Essentially, he is proposing a scheme which lay beyond even Hegel's wildest intentions. Hegel, while allowing 'the particular to continue as a surpassed particularity' (pp. 48–9), never professed a method which would arrive at an understanding of individuals as existing in their own right, yet simultaneously shot through by the mediations of personal history and personal environment; social history and social environment. Sartre intends to hang the individual in an intricate web of actions and determinations. He says that, 'we assert that the part of chance can and must be reduced to a minimum', (p. 83) and makes much of various Marxist writers who, like Engels above, claim Napoleon himself to have been an accident. Sartre's aim is:

to show that *this* Napoleon was necessary... In short, we are not dealing with an abstract universal, with a situation so poorly defined that several Bonapartes were *possible*, but with a concrete totalisation in which *this* real bourgeoisie, made up of real, living men, was to liquidate *this* revolution and in which *this* Revolution created its own liquidator in the person of Bonaparte, in himself and for himself. (p. 83)

That is, of course, precisely what Sartre tries to do for Stalin in volume two of the *Critique* (see pp. 105–7), and behind this desire to preserve the particularity of every historical individual lies his profound humanism: 'Our intention is not, as is too often claimed, to "give the irrational its due", but on the contrary, to reduce the part of indetermination and non-knowledge, not to reject Marxism in the name of a third path, or of an idealist humanism, but to reconquer man within Marxism' (p. 83). Sartre is proposing the preservation of particularity in the name of humanism, and a method which will contribute to that preservation. My suggestion is that these aims harbour contradictory impulses. The *inclination* is to reclaim individuals from a Marxism which has submerged them in universality. But the *method* may still leave the individual struggling in the Sartrean spotlight which defines their place. They exchange the anonymity of Marxist generality for the definitive rigours of Sartre's method. We shall be better able to pursue this criticism after having studied *The Family Idiot*, because there Sartre makes his most systematic attempt to apply his method to an individual.

For now, we must turn to the problem of mediations, which Sartre says are essential to an understanding of the individual in the social nexus. One mediation he mentions is that of the family: 'Existentialism ... believes that it can integrate the psychoanalytic method which discovers the point of insertion for man and his class – that is, the particular family – as a mediation between the universal class and the individual' (p. 62). However, not every individual sees the family in the same way. Particularly, the child has a very specific view of it: 'The family ... is experienced, on the other hand, as an absolute in the depth of opaqueness of childhood' (p. 62). Childhood provides for Sartre's second mediation: 'It is childhood which sets up unsurpassable prejudices ... [and] ... makes us experience the fact of our belonging to a specific environment as a unique event' (p. 60). It is this very uniqueness that Marxists persist in ignoring, says Sartre, thus contributing to a dramatic loss of explanatory power: 'Today's Marxists are concerned only with adults; reading them, one would believe that we are born at the age when we earn our first wages. They have forgotten their own childhoods' (p. 62).

It is important to note, however, that Sartre is never really clear about just how important childhood is as an explanatory factor. In *Words*, for instance, it seems to override all else: 'Every man has his natural place; it is not pride or worth that settles its height: childhood decides everything' (Sartre, 1964b, p. 43). However, in an interview in 1975, he places it in a wider perspective: 'I don't believe that a man's history is written in his infancy. I think that there are other very important periods when things are added: adolescence, youth, and even maturity' (Sartre, 1978d, p. 44). Despite these changes of emphasis, the point remains that the diachronic spectrum of a life is vital to its explanation – a fact that develops through the Baudelaire and Genet to the Flaubert, as Sartre's treatment of childhood becomes more and more intense. Sociologists are criticised for concentrating on the synchronic, or 'horizontal', complex for explanation. Marxists are criticised for pursuing the *social* diachronic at the expense of the *individual* diachronic. Sartre wants to combine all of these approaches in an explanatory method that will reduce the effect of chance to a minimum.

He begins Part Three, entitled 'The Progressive–Regressive Method', with the affirmation that, 'we accept without reservation the thesis set forth by Engels in his letter to Marx' – a thesis that Ronald Hayman rightly says Sartre 'loved to quote' (Hayman, 1986, p. 325): '"Men themselves make their history but in a given environment which conditions them"' (Sartre, 1968, p. 85). In 1959, Sartre was asked to consider why he had found the precepts of phenomenology so attractive. He replied that he had wanted 'to give man both his autonomy and his reality among real objects, avoiding idealism without lapsing into a mechanistic materialism', and that he had taken to phenomenology because he was 'ignorant of dialectical materialism' (Sartre, 1974b, p. 37).

By 1957, however, he had become acquainted with historical materialism and had decided upon an unequivocal agreement with it. Yet its implications are complex. He says of Engels' text that it, 'is not one of the clearest, and it remains open to numerous interpretations. How are we to understand that man makes History if at the same time, it is History which makes him?' (Sartre, 1968, p. 85). Sartre takes two quotations from Marx himself to demonstrate that opposite interpretations are possible (pp. 85–6). The one that Sartre wants to avoid is that which lapses into an 'idealist Marxism', asserting that we are entirely determined by circumstances. Clearly this would be at odds with Sartre's notion of us as active, project-forming, intentional beings. His understanding of Engels' statement is, simply, that we are both product and producer *simultaneously*: 'If one wants to grant to Marxist thought its full complexity, one would have to say that man in a period of exploitation is *at once both* the produce of his own product and a historical agent who can under no circumstances be taken as a product' (p. 87). For Sartre, this interpretation preserves the role of human *praxis* in history-making. To be sure, we make history on the basis of prior condition, but, 'it is *men* who make it, not the prior conditions' (p. 87).

At the present time we do not fully understand this, and nor shall we, 'so long as the Proletariat, the subject of History, will not in a single movement realise its unity and become conscious of its historical role' (p. 88). For consistency's sake we might expect that Sartre does not fully understand what he is doing either, for he is as much a victim of the disunity of the proletariat as we are. No doubt he would admit to this, at least to the extent that the full complexity of History is beyond his understanding at present. However, in asserting that there will, eventually, *be* a unity, he would appear to be placing himself beyond the historical circumstances in which he is confined. In exactly the same way as Hegel and Marx did, Sartre stands beyond the dialectic of Being and Knowing in order to describe its implications. Marx has already warned us against this, and Sartre himself quotes the relevant third thesis on Feuerbach: 'The materialist doctrine according to which men are the product of circumstances and of education...does not take into account the fact that circumstances are modified precisely by men and that the educator himself must be educated' (p. 86) – and then ignores its lesson of humility. To explain.

History is 'less opaque than it was' writes Sartre, because, 'The Proletariat has discovered and released "its secret"; [and] the capitalist movement is conscious of itself' (1968, p. 90). Rehearsing themes that are to be dealt with in great detail in the *Critique* (and discussed in chapter 4), Sartre writes that History has a plurality of meanings and it is our task to reduce this plurality – a task which he is confident we shall accomplish: 'Our historical task, at the heart of this polyvalent world, is to bring closer the moment when History will have only one meaning, when it will tend to be dissolved in the concrete men who will make it in common' (p. 90). Sartre is certain that the dialectic of Being and Knowing will result in a single History. He derives this certainty in the midst of a world which is at odds with itself, and which he – on his own admission – cannot stand beyond. And yet it seems that he has, thus falling prey to the idealism which he condemns in crude Marxists. The educator of the third thesis does not need to be educated, for he has become the Educator.

If we are not merely the products of material circumstances, then how are we to understand the means by which we go beyond them in order to make history? At this point, Sartre introduces a familiar notion – that of the project: 'Only the project, as a mediation between two moments of objectivity, can account for history; that is, for human *creativity*' (p. 99). The project affirms that we are not mere things, pitched and tossed between sets of material circumstances, but rather creative beings whose character is one of 'going beyond'.

The notion of the project, and the lack which engenders it, has a long history in Sartre's thought – we remember from *Being and Nothingness* that the human being is a being whose being is in question. But now it has become rather more complex. The projects formed by individuals on the basis of what they lack are not now plucked from thin air, but are dependent on the social milieu: 'the social possibles are lived as schematic determinations of the individual future. And the most individual possible is only the internalisation and enrichment of a social possible' (p. 95). This has important implications for the biographer who wants to define the subject's project. For now it is not enough simply to refer to an ontology – it has become essential to portray the subject's entire social and historical milieu. Indeed, a survey of the 'material conditions' within which individuals' projects are formed and upon which they make history is required. We shall see Sartre performing this task in *The Family Idiot*. He has deepened the idea of the project in order to marry it to Marx's historical materialism, and in order to rescue that materialism from the crudity perpetrated by Marxists. This is the move Sartre makes beyond the existential psychoanalysis of *Being and Nothingness*, and which makes it unwise to treat both methods as though they were the same, as do Scriven (1984), Howells (1988) and Poster (1979).

This, then, is the 'progressive–regressive' method. The *regressive* moment is intended to recover 'the historical process on the basis of the shifting and contradictory relations of the formations in question' (Sartre, 1968, p. 68). However, the regressive analysis can reveal to us 'no more than the static conditions of the possibility of a totalisation, that is to say, of a history' (p. 68). To restore the dynamic we need to make a progressive investigation that will recompose the entire historical process as lived by the subject. So, while it might be considered a heresy by Marxists to affirm that the future is an essential explanatory factor in human behaviour, this is precisely the thrust of Sartre's argument. The temporal plane includes the future as well as the past: 'So long as one has not studied the structures of the future in a defined society, one necessarily runs the risk of not understanding anything about the social' (p. 97). Defining the project of the subject constitutes the *progressive* aspect of Sartre's method.

This 'existentialist approach', which Sartre also describes as the 'analytic–synthetic' method, is therefore a continuous dialectical cross-referencing between the general and the particular. In this way, 'across Madame Bovary we can and must catch sight of the movement of landowners and capitalists, the evolution of the rising classes, the slow maturation of the Proletariat' (pp. 146–8). In a footnote, Sartre admits to the genesis of this method. He refers to Henri Lefebvre, who 'has provided a simple and faultless method for integrating sociology and history in the perspective of the materialist dialectic'. He then refers to Lefebvre's desire to combine 'horizontal' and 'vertical' complexity in a manner that is similar to Sartre's and to which Sartre says he has nothing of note to add.

We have established that the 'structures of the future' are essential to Sartre's methodology, but how are we to arrive at an understanding of them? In the studies of Baudelaire and Genet, we found that the project was built into Sartre's ontology as the subject fled from doing to being and back again. The subject's particular project – i.e. to be a writer – was built on this ground. In the *Search for a Method* there is no mention of this ontological background. Sartre's inference of project is firmly based on his conception of the human being as a forward-looking, and thus a signifying, being: 'Man is, for himself and for others, a signifying being, since one can never understand the slightest of his gestures without going beyond the pure present and explaining it by the future' (p. 152).

On this basis, we must use what Sartre calls 'comprehension' to reveal the basis of the individual's project: 'To grasp the meaning of any human conduct, it is necessary to have at our disposal what German psychiatrists and historians have called "comprehension".' Sartre describes this form of understanding as 'neither a particular talent nor a special faculty of intuition; this knowing is simply the dialectical movement which explains the act by its terminal signification in terms of its starting conditions' (p. 152). Despite Sartre's claim to the contrary, some critics have contended that his 'comprehension' does indeed refer to a form of intuition, (for example, Aron, 1973, p. 6 and Collins, 1980, p. 155) and there are certainly echoes of the 'intuitive certainty' mentioned in connection with the proof of the dialectic (*CDR I*, p. 61 fn). In either case, we must admit that the results of the method of comprehension are open to question.

Sartre himself gives the example of two people in a room one of whom suddenly gets up and 'starts towards the window'. I understand this movement, says Sartre, in the context of a warm room – my companion is going towards the window so as to let in some fresh air (Sartre, 1968, p. 153). The interpretation is valid, and the method used to explain the gesture may well hold firm in such a carefully chosen example. But the more complex the project, the harder it is to be confident about any explanation based on such a technique. Of course, Sartre would reply to this criticism by saying that this progressive analysis must continually have recourse to the regressive moment for substantiation. Whether this would render us capable of asserting the existence of one indisputable project is still unclear. Again, we shall have to refer to the Flaubert study for clarification.

What is beyond dispute is that comprehension is a technique applied only to the progressive arm of the investigation. In the *Critique*, Sartre tells us that, 'we shall discover multiplicities producing totalised thoughts and acts without reference to the individuals composing them, indeed without reference to the individuals composing them, indeed without their even being aware of it'. In this case, of course, comprehension is inadequate, and we shall have recourse to what Sartre call 'intellection'. This is a higher form of understanding, 'more complex' than comprehension, and capable of totalising 'all practical realities', rather than simply those 'intentionally produced by their author or authors' (*CDR I*, p. 76).

The final points to note about comprehension with regard to Sartre's method are its political implications. The notion of arriving at a significant understanding of someone else's actions would have been wholly alien in the context of our ontological separation as expressed in *Being and Nothingness*. Now we are presented with a basis for sociality. Sartre said in a lecture on Kierkegaard in 1964 that, 'To comprehend Adam is to become

Adam' (Sartre. 1974c, p. 166), and we can become Adam, or Kierkegaard, or Flaubert, because we are all singular adventures of a general truth. This constitutes a radical shift in emphasis from Sartre's earlier depressing vision of isolated subjectivities, and as such provides the basis for a theory of concerted political action. He has conserved particularity, but blended it with a gigantic human adventure which we can all understand – 'comprehend' – because we are all dialectically a part of it, related by bonds of interiority. We are now in a position to see what kind of understanding he brings to bear on Gustave Flaubert.

# 13    The case of Flaubert

> The *Flaubert* is not a classical philosophical work with organised chapters, starting from precise principles and moving towards a precise end. I wanted to do something else: I wanted to try to reconstitute the life of a man – of a *dead* man.
>
> (Sartre, 1976a, p. 99)

Sartre's interest in Flaubert was perhaps the most enduring element of his life. He had read Flaubert since childhood (Sartre, 1978c, p. 110), and as early as *Being and Nothingness* he announced his intention to study him using the methods of existential psychoanalysis: 'We hope to be able to attempt elsewhere two examples in relation to Flaubert and Dostoevsky' (*BN*, p. 575). For 10 years, the fulfilment of this promise was held in abeyance, until Sartre was issued with a challenge: 'Around 1954, during the period when I was close to the CP, Roger Garaudy suggested to me, "Let's take someone and try to explain him – I will do it by Marxist methods and you by existentialist methods"' (Sartre, 1978c, p. 110).

The chosen subject was Flaubert, and within 3 months Sartre had filled 12 notebooks with an unsystematic study of the novelist. Pontalis suggested that he write a book from these notes, and Sartre duly completed 1000 pages before abandoning the project in 1955. However, he began to despair of his apparent inability to finish anything, and so returned to the task, determined to complete it: 'after I finished *The Condemned of Altona*, I worked on nothing else' (p. 110). This is not strictly correct, but it is true that the *Flaubert* went through many tortuous revisions and several manuscripts before being published in 1971 and 1972.

The book derives its inspiration from two principal sources. First, the *Flaubert*, 'represents a sequel to *L'Imaginaire* ... In *L'Imaginaire* I tried to prove that my imaginary objects – images – are an absence. In my book on Flaubert, I am studying imaginary persons – people who like Flaubert act out roles' (Sartre, 1974b, p. 46). Beauvoir makes the same point: 'What attracted Sartre to Flaubert was the importance granted to the imagination' (de Beauvoir, 1981, p. 18). To this extent, Sartre is interested in charting Flaubert's escape from an unliveable reality via its imaginative negation. But this does not exhaust the importance granted to the imagination in the book, because Sartre makes taxing use of his own imagination in reconstructing Flaubert's life for us.

The second source is described in the very first sentence of *The Idiot*: '*L'Idiot de la famille* is the continuation of *Search for a Method*. Its subject: what can we know of a man today?' (*IF I*, p. 7). More explicitly, *Search for a Method* involved an amalgam of approaches, such as Marxism, psychoanalysis, and sociology, and 'The idea of the book on Flaubert was to abandon these theoretical disquisitions, because they were ultimately getting us nowhere, and to try to give a concrete example of how it might be done' (Sartre, 1974b, pp. 42–3). When asked by Michel Sicard why *The Idiot* contains very little reference to the methodology used, Sartre replied, 'because it is all in *Search for a Method*. The only difference lies in that the dialectic in the *Search for a Method* is that of groups, while *The Idiot* deals with an individual' (Sartre, 1976a, p. 95). This difference may go some way towards explaining why the influence of *Search for a Method* is greater than that of the *Critique* – especially in the first two volumes of the *Flaubert* – as the *Critique* is more concerned with the genesis and behaviour of groups rather than individuals.

Beyond this, however, it is clear that the techniques developed in *Search for a Method* are better suited for the aims of volumes one and two than are those of the *Critique*. In these volumes, Sartre is concerned with reconstructing Flaubert's subjective experience and the character of his neurosis. How is he to do this? Sartre gives his own answer: 'The attitude necessary for understanding a man is empathy' (Sartre, 1978c, p. 113), and Beauvoir corroborates it: 'He adopted an attitude of empathy towards Flaubert' (Beauvoir, 1981, pp. 18–19). This empathetic technique evidently has close links with the notion of comprehension developed in *Search for a Method*, and this is the crucial reason why that essay is so important to an understanding of the methodology of *The Idiot*. However, to say that *L'Imaginaire* and *Search for a Method* constitute two distinct sources would be to give a false impression. To the extent that Sartre's aim is to reconstruct a life, the technique of empathy will inevitably involve an element of imagination on his part. It is precisely this issue which bridges the 17-year gap between *L'Imaginaire* and the *Search for a Method*, and which helps to generate important questions about Sartre's history-writing.

In his interview with Sicard, Sartre observed that *The Idiot* is not a work of philosophy at all, but rather brings many techniques together in order to reconstitute a (dead) life. We know from the developments in *Search for a Method* that Sartre will not be happy with a mere chronological reconstruction of Flaubert's life, but will want to adopt his progressive-regressive method in order to weave the individual life with the history of society and the social conditions pertaining: 'My aim is to try to demonstrate the encounter between the development of the person, as psychoanalysis has shown it to us, and the development of history' (Sartre, 1974b, p. 44). The gargantuan task involved in revealing these myriad connections prompted an interviewer to ask, 'Isn't this desire to read Flaubert like an open book – in just the way that the Creator reads his creatures – the project of a demiurge, a way of trying to become God?' In a crucial reply to which we shall have cause to refer at a later date, Sartre says:

Not at all. The most important project in the *Flaubert* is to show that fundamentally everything can be communicated, that without being God, but simply as a man like any other, one can manage to understand another man perfectly, if one has access to all the necessary elements. I can deal with Flaubert, I know him; and that is my goal, to prove that every man is perfectly knowable as long as one uses the appropriate method and as long as the necessary documents are available. I do not claim that my method is the definitive one. There could be quite a few methods different from mine, though close in spirit. (Sartre, 1978c, p. 123)

Sartre has set out his stall.

He begins Flaubert's story by placing him in his familial context; suggesting that his mother, Caroline, wanted to bear a daughter. After the birth of a son, Gustave's older brother Achille, Sartre infers that this desire would have increased – to be followed by further disappointment when a second son, Gustave, is born. As a reaction, Caroline cares for the young Gustave, but out of duty rather than love, and the boy has his first taste of rejection and alienation. To a certain extent, then, Gustave's early life was mapped out for him before he was born – all he had to do was to be born a boy. This early rejection has a critical bearing on the rest of Gustave's life. Indeed, Sartre suggests that if his relationship with his mother had been different, then so would the rest of his life:

And yet if Flaubert during his pre-history had been loved by Caroline Flaubert, if he had profoundly and physically loved his mother, this jealous love might have developed his aggressiveness ... But as we have seen, by depriving him of love, his mother denied him the means to love. At the same time he lost any chance of being aggressive – we know that the thread of his experience is *passivity*. (Sartre, 1981, p. 384)

The second factor in Gustave's 'pre-history' is that he was born in between children who died young and so was overprotected. This nurturing engendered in him a passivity from which he never recovered, and which was to be the guiding principle of all his actions. Right at the beginning, his passivity encourages him to believe that whatever adults tell him must be the truth. He is not involved in creating the world, either through word or deed: 'Gustave does not produce meaning' (*IF I*, p. 25). The word is a command that comes to him from outside. It is a thing which causes him to receive meaning and truth. He has no active relationship with the word because it is other: 'the speech of the other is a *given speech*, in every sense of the phrase' (*IF I*, p. 24). There are distinct echoes of the active/passive dichotomy which Sartre used to such effect in the *Genet* and *Baudelaire*, and which derives ultimately from the active *pour-soi* and passive *en-soi* of *Being and Nothingness*. Like the voyeur at the keyhole, and Genet with his hand in the kitchen drawer, Flaubert is pinned beneath the gaze of the Other. Indeed, his relationship with his father is described in precisely this way (*IF I*, p. 665).

This passivity means that Flaubert has difficulty in discovering the signifying nature of words, and so cannot learn to speak or read. His problem worsens as he grows closer to his father. Sartre surmises that at about the age of three, Gustave transfers his affections to his father, Achille-Cleophas, and indeed gets some return. After those unpleasant years with his mother, this 'new personage clamorously introduced into his life' (*IF I*, p. 384) lends him some solace. But Gustave's increasing problems derive from his father's attitude to the role of the individual within the family. For Achille-Cleophas individuals are subordinate tools of the family, and their only justification is to contribute to the family's search for fame and fortune. To fulfil this role, Gustave must be active and ambitious – yet he cannot be so, because he has been constituted in passivity. Frustrated at his son's inability to read, Achille-Cleophas says to Gustave: 'You will be the idiot of the family' (*IF I*, p. 383), and so Flaubert, like Genet the thief, dutifully receives his dose of Sartrean objectification. Alienated and outcast, what is Flaubert to do? His passive constitution renders him incapable of crime – Genet's road to freedom – or suicide. Certainly he will not fulfil his father's dreams, hounded as he is by the circumstances of his birth and the events of his early life.

It is worth noting that Sartre spends more time on Flaubert's early childhood than he does on any of his other biographical subjects. I have already indicated how his views on the importance of childhood varied over the years. In this study he says that the early years are more important for some than for others. For some people their history is more important than their pre-history because they are not 'completely singular', but rather find themselves 'at the crossroads of individuality and universality' (*IF I*, p. 55). Yet Gustave is a singular experience whose infancy follows him around: 'Gustave's behaviour, attitudes and dreams are rigorously conditioned by his Flaubert-being ... that is to say by the supposed sentence of his father who finds him to be an insufficient Flaubert, and so determines him to be a second-class one' (*IF I*, p. 1061).

This, then, is Gustave's constitution. I remarked in my comments on

*Saint Genet* that Sartre spends a number of pages at the beginning explaining the roots of Genet's alienation and his powerlessness in the face of the other, before going on to affirm the activity which is a feature of the human condition and therefore a part of Genet's too. In similar vein, Sartre refers us to Flaubert's conditioning and then says that, 'Passivity is his lot, but he is a child of man, not an idiot, not even a wild child, like all men, he is a surpassing, a project; he can act' (*IF I*, p. 34). In this context, Flaubert lives his bewilderment as a scheme. It is given to him but he lives it to its fullest extent, thus 'carrying out the sentence passed on him', as Sartre might have said using the language of the *Critique* (see, for example, *CDR I*, p. 247). Sartre refers to this state as one of 'passive activity' (*IF I*, p. 48). In living his passivity, Flaubert eventually succumbs to martyrdom: 'led systematically to his destruction by the force of circumstance, and the will of his father, he wants to be a *martyr*, such is his profound vocation' (*IF II*, p. 1695).

In his previous biographies, Sartre has been content simply to state this notion of living a constituted life. In *The Idiot*, in keeping with the vastly more detailed and ambitious nature of the book, he attempts to give an account of the mechanics of active passivity. He begins by stating the familiar case:

The structures of this family are interiorised in attitudes and re exteriorised in practices by which the child makes himself that which he has been made. Inversely, we will not find in him any form of conduct, as complex and elaborate as it may appear, which is not originally the going-beyond of an interiorised determination. (*IF I*, p. 653)

But just what is involved in this 'going-beyond'? Sartre presents us with a situation in which the constituted life, the given, thinks of itself as a totality – a passive 'thing', not subject to change. However, the totality is never allowed to settle, because a life is always being lived and so is never wholly constituted. Consequently, the 'totality' finds itself confronted at every moment by threats to its 'wholeness', and it is the clash between these two elements which provides the 'going-beyond' of active passivity. In the face of the threat from without that seeks to detotalise the thing which tries to be a totality, 'the perpetual totalisation rises up like a defence against our permanent detotalisation', and so is an 'intentional enterprise, orientated towards unification' (*IF I*, p. 653; see also Sartre's comments on the relationship between totality and totalisation in *CDR I*, pp. 45–6).

There are two ways in which the 'permanent totalisation' can seek to render the 'permanent detotalisation' harmless, and so preserve itself. First, it can fall into bad faith by making an imaginary assimilation which maintains the contradiction while providing the illusion that it has been absorbed. In this case, 'the unification in progress will have a structure of unreality in it', and the totality will be imaginary (*IF I*, p. 655). Second, and this is what happens 'most often', a furious battle takes place at the heart of the 'permanent totalisation' which leaves both elements changed but genuinely assimilated in a new transcendence (*dépassement*). Sartre describes it in the following way:

the inassimilable element, by its mere presence, provokes the birth of real, antagonistic elements which are thrown at it, attack it, and try to reduce it to powerlessness – which cannot happen without causing a profound alteration to the totalisation in progress. It would be worth comparing these reducing agents – whose effects are worse than the thing being fought – to antibodies that are hurled at a transplanted heart and cause the death of the very organism that they are supposed to defend. (p. 655)

This toing and froing between the detotalised and the retotalising is called 'personalisation', and amounts to an attempt by Sartre to give an account of the dialectical processes involved at the heart of Marx's historical materialism: 'In any case, personalisation in the individual is nothing more than the going-beyond and preservation (intimate assumption and negation), at the heart of the totalising project, of that which the world has made – and continues to make – of him' (*IF I*, p. 657). Having given an account of the theoretical mechanics of Gustave's 'active passivity', Sartre is now in a position to describe how he went beyond the constituted Flaubert which his father and mother had made of him.

To begin with, Flaubert lives his conditioning in much the same way as Genet did. We remember that Genet wrote a poem in prison so that his fellow-prisoners would laugh at him, thus making Genet the source of his own misfortune. Similarly, Flaubert's early ambition is to be a comic actor, so that he could be the source of the laughter aimed at him. Sartre suggests that his parents' indifference to such a profession was probably the main reason why this ambition was never fulfilled. Instead, Flaubert reverts to writing – learning that through literature he could abolish the world: 'to write is to take possession of the world' (*IF I*, p. 958). Sartre is not entirely complimentary about this strategy, aware that it constitutes a false assimilation of the vagaries of the world by the person:

for a long time he was in the habit of escaping the incommodities of the real 'on the wings of the imagination'. We have seen himself avenging himself of his family, his friends, and his masters by dreaming that he was Nero or Tamburlane – or else he took himself off to the Orient or to the Indies to escape the bedroom or the study room where he was imprisoned. (*IF II*, p. 1934)

Gustave's strategy of imaginative derealisation takes another shape when he finds himself at the Collège Royal de Rouen at the age of ten. He detects his schoolmates laughing at his attempts to emulate the success of his elder brother, Achille, who came top of the class in every subject. Flaubert realises that the intellectual task is beyond him and decides, instead, to turn his tormentors against themselves. To this end, he invents the character of *Le Garçon*, thus directing his schoolmates' mockery against himself, and fulfilling the 'primal choice' (Collins, 1980, p. 131) engendered in his early childhood. After a series of upheavals in the college, to which I shall refer in the next chapter, Flaubert passed his *baccalauréat* in August 1840, and his father decided on a career in law for him. Despite reservations, Flaubert provisionally agreed to this, although he still believed that he was a literary genius and wanted to prove it. For a number of years he engaged himself in producing the book which would justify his claims. It did not appear. In 1842, he failed his first-year examinations at Law School, but passed at the second attempt. The following year, he failed the second-year examinations and did no work for the February 1844 re-takes. He knew that he would fail again. What was he to do? He was in an impossible position. He had not produced the book which would have proved him a literary genius, and he could not pass the examination which would have taken him towards a law career. Even if he could have, it would have placed him firmly in the arms of the bourgeoisie – a class which he felt to be beneath him. Flaubert's solution to this impasse, according to Sartre, was as radical as it was ultimately ineffective:

In Flaubert's case, everything happened as if a unique moment was enough to secure the passage from a normal state to a pathological one. The morbid creation and the Fiat (i.e. the neurotic assimilation of the neurosis) were gathered together in a single moment on a moonless night in January 1844. (*IF II*, pp. 1784–5)

In this 'single moment' at Pont-L'Evêque, Gustave drops the reins of his carriage and falls at his brother's feet, apparently in the throes of an epileptic fit.

Sartre identifies two methods of avoiding the future which Gustave had employed up to that point. First, he used the technique of the 'over-flying consciousness' in his literature in order to 'install himself in the Eternal'; and second, he would plunge into a pure present hedonism – 'the future is black, so let's drink'. The first strategy fails because eternity is not accessible to him as a finite being, and the second fails because 'he can forget the Future but not suppress it'. In that case, 'One method remains open to him: that which he chose at Pont-L'Evêque. To kill a boy with a future, and, by the same token, to give birth to a man without a future' (*IF II*, p. 1868). Here we can see the roots of Sartre's opposition to any interpretation of Flaubert's 'crisis' as having an 'accidental' nature – the fit at Pont-L'Evêque was most definitely purposive. Moreover, it can be accounted for in terms of necessity and has meaning:

The most commonly held thesis...is that it is a matter of *accidents*. In short, originally the facts were non-significant like a cold in the head or a purulent pleurisy – and that it is Gustave himself who gave them meaning *a posteriori*, by utilising these unfortunate accidents of chance as a means of reorientating his life. (*IF II*, p. 1786)

Sartre states his opposition to this:

In the previous pages, we have tried to establish the contrary thesis: *le mal* was organised as the function of an original intention. His overwhelming structuration, at Pont-L'Evêque, is not an accidental fact, but a necessity provided with meaning. (*IF II*, p. 1786)

Thus there are two crucial elements to Sartre's analysis of Flaubert's collapse. First, that it was intentional and purposive; and second, that this purpose was derived from Gustave's childhood: 'constituted since Flaubert's protohistory' (*IF II*, p. 1654). This was no mere accidental collusion of events, but rather a well-defined and dialectically bonded set of circumstances and intentions. Sartre says that between 1838 and the attack at Pont-L'Evêque,

Gustave was subject...to ill-defined problems which worried his family, who only recognised discontinuous manifestations in them, separated from one another by 'normal years'. We are going to try to establish that there is just one inflexible process involved, which never ceases to organise itself, and to be enriched and deepened until the explosion of January 1844 was made inevitable...I also propose to show that this malaise...far from being simply undergone, is the object of a passive option and that Flaubert makes himself to the same extent that he is made by the situation and by events. (*IF II*, p. 1467)

Clearly, Gustave is being held intimately responsible for his life, in much the same way as Sartre's early existentialism attempted to foster a sense of responsibility. There is no hiding behind social or personal history for the existential human being, and no hiding, either, behind an unhappy childhood for Flaubert. We are still what we make ourselves. But what sense does it make to talk of responsibility in a situation which Sartre describes as 'inevitable' and 'a necessity'? The dialectical process has to be *lived*, to be sure, but if it is impossible to live the process any way other than that 'undergone' by Flaubert (to say 'chosen' would also be accurate, but saying too much in this context), then both freedom and responsibility need to be interpreted in unaccustomed ways. The best that can be done would seem to be to revive the categories of good and bad faith developed in *Being and Nothingness*. Bad faith would now accompany the attitude suggested by 'it happened to me', and good faith would accompany the attitude suggested by 'I did it' (for example, Flaubert's epileptic attack). But even in the second case, in the context of dialectical necessity, the thought in parentheses would be, 'but I couldn't have done anything else'. Sartre may have persuaded us that we carry out our own sentence, but it is a sentence nevertheless.

So Flaubert's epilepsy (if that is what it was) was part of a life-plan, self-conceived and intentionally enacted. Sartre concludes volume two with the observation that as well as being personal, Flaubert's neurosis was 'historical and social: it constitutes a dated and objective fact where the characteristics of a certain society – the French bourgeoisie under Louis-Philippe – come together and are totalised' (*IF II*, p. 2135). It is to this objective neurosis to which we now turn.

Volume three of *The Family Idiot* deals with the objective conditions of Flaubert's life, and these are held to comprise the institutional world – a 'product and expression of the infrastructure' – and the historical situation. Both of these react with the 'familial intersubjectivity' of the Flauberts and so contribute towards the 'concrete history of an irreducible micro-organism which cannot escape the historical situation, but which suffers it and totalises it in its own way' (*IF III*, p. 10). The institutional world and the historical situation together combine to define what Sartre calls the 'Objective Spirit', or 'Objective Mind'. As Hazel Barnes observes, this notion comes close to being equivalent to a cultural heritage (Barnes, 1981, p. 248). But Sartre's innovation consists in analysing in detail the relationship between an individual and the Objective Spirit. Sartre variously defines the Objective Spirit, 'in a definite society at a given time', as 'none other than culture as the practico-inert' (*IF III*, p. 44), or as a 'system of values and ideologies', which, when verbalised, becomes 'material'. 'Written words are stones', he says, and, 'These irreducible passivities taken as a whole, I call the Objective Spirit' (*IF III*, p. 47). In relation to Flaubert the literary figure, Sartre is more concerned with the cultural aspects of the Objective Spirit than anything else, and the most concise definition he gives in this context is that, 'The Objective Spirit of an epoch, is at once the sum of published works considered at that time, and the multiplicity of totalisations made by contemporary readers' (*IF III*, p. 57).

What, then, was the heritage that Flaubert encountered? On the whole, Sartre asserts, nineteenth-century writers looked towards the eighteenth century for their lead, and he observes two characteristics of that epoch which had become common currency by the time Flaubert began writing. First, there was a tendency to see humanity in a molecular fashion. Ever since the post-war period, Sartre had been quick to condemn anybody who defined human beings as a dispersal – chiefly because of the negative political and epistemological ramifications this involves. Sartre posits the dialectical–synthetic against the molecular view – a position born of the notion that there is a dialectical unity in human reality. The corresponding modes of knowledge are dialectical and analytical reason, and Sartre says that although 'dialectical reason was in the air', the writers of the eighteenth and nineteenth centuries 'had not perceived its appearance' (*IF III*, p. 118). In the eighteenth century, Sartre observes,

bourgeois prudence, we know, invented the hybrid concept of nature in which the apparent unity could be referred back to the Creator. But at the same time, this hid their own exteriority to natural events, as well as their mechanistic materialism which is the ultimate conclusion of analysis. The idea of Nature had exploded, and that of mechanicism had triumphed. (*IF III*, p. 118)

The likelihood of Flaubert's own internalisation of mechanicism was boosted by his father's scientific profession – for Achille-Cleophas, the cosmos was no more than a giant Newtonian machine.

The second factor that Flaubert encountered was the view that held the writer to be beyond social affiliation – even, in a sense, beyond humanity. Coupled with the mechanistic science referred to above in which scientists believe they can stand outside the thing they are studying, this results in what Sartre calls the writer's 'over-flying consciousness', detached from the world. He notes that,

during the second half of the nineteenth century, the enlightened elite practised the over-flying consciousness and refused to think on its own historicity. It revealed that vices and virtues, and works of art as well, are historical *products*. But not for a moment did they ask themselves if pure theory – or its pretence – is not itself a product. (*IF III*, p. 264)

Consequently, writers are placed 'above humanity, whose needs and ends they envisage *from outside*', and the result is that, 'They understand that *praxis* remains impossible. A dream, if you like. A nightmare. In any case, an illusion' (*IF III*, pp. 264–5). The message is clear – we cannot act in good faith unless we dirty our hands in the real world.

In keeping with the negative implications of the Objective Spirit, Flaubert developed a hatred of humanity and so did not want any readers for his books. A substantial readership would have indicated failure. Nevertheless, he acquired a public. How did this come about? Now Sartre reveals Flaubert's intimate relationship with the spirit of his epoch.

After the 1789 revolution, Sartre surmises that the call went out for everyone to own property and to join the ranks of the bourgeoisie. Slowly, it became apparent that this property-owning democracy was not available to everyone, and the bourgeoisie realised that their comfort was based on peasant and proletarian impoverishment. How was the bourgeois to explain this failure? Sartre suggests that the bourgeoisie responded by mobilising class hatred. The result was that the wrath of the landless bore down on the property owners, who internalised it and translated it into self-contempt. Sartre sees this situation wholly reflected in Flaubert's books – filled as they are with hatred of self and humanity. In other words, Flaubert acquired his readership because he was saying exactly what the bourgeoisie wanted to hear. Sartre describes the pessimistic tenor of the age as follows:

between 1850 and 1870 the time had not yet come – despite certain individual attempts – for defining man as a practical agent who makes history on the basis of previous circumstances. Christianity had been cut adrift and had left a legacy of 'Christian ideas gone mad' which resulted in the founding of a pessimistic humanism based on failure, useless and passively suffered sacrifice, incommunicability, alienation from work ... effort without success, and fundamentally, hatred of self. (*IF III*, p. 297)

In sum, 'Gustave and his reader were united in their pessimistic vision of history' (*IF III*, p. 430).

The next question bears on why Flaubert rather than anyone else was particularly suited to incarnate his class. We recall from his *Search for a Method* that Sartre wants to show that Napoleon the individual was necessary, and that no other individual could have filled his place. Now we are about to learn why no one other than Flaubert could have fulfilled the demands of his time – it has to do with the precise relationship between this individual and his epoch. We also learn that some historical individuals are more important than others because of the synchronicity between their history and the history of their society. Why, for instance, did not Leconte de Lisle attain the readership that Flaubert enjoyed (or despised)? The answer lies in Sartre rejecting the simple Marxist notion that men and women merely reflect their epoch. The picture is more complex in the sense that, 'History is not and does not answer to any concept; what exists is an infinite series whose law is that of recurrence, defined precisely in these terms: man is the son of man' (*IF III*, pp. 436–7).

In this sense, psychological and individual factors come into play in deciding whether one particular 'son of man' will represent his epoch rather than another. The crucial difference between Leconte de Lisle and Flaubert is that the former's hatred was perceived by the bourgeoisie to be inauthentic. Gustave, on the other hand, had sustained a personal rejection and a feeling of failure with respect to his father which Leconte de Lisle had not. Consequently, the latter's revolt was seen to be a fake. For this reason, de Lisle's life up until the collapse of the Second Empire in 1870 is merely 'rhetorically' rather than 'really' symbolic of French society (*IF III*, p. 431). All of this made Flaubert the ideal candidate to reflect the situation of the bourgeoisie – indeed, he was the only person who could have done it in the way he did.

But Flaubert's identification with his class does not end with his books. In a very precise way, his crisis at Pont-L'Evêque in 1844 actually anticipated the 1848 crisis of the bourgeoisie. We might wonder why the crises were not synchronous, but Sartre says: 'In fact, there is no reason for the catastrophe of the microcosm and that of the social macrocosm to take place at the same time' (*IF III*, p. 440). Flaubert's demise represents the collapse of his class, and, 'at the heart of the macrocosmic temporalisation; microtemporalisation, as the retotalised totalisation of the historical totalisation only differed from the latter in its speed' (*IF III*, p. 430). Sartre seems to be saying that individuals are not always congruent with their epoch; they may be in step, or behind it, or in front of it. Hazel Barnes observes that:

Sartre's view is that Flaubert's 'life programme' was synchronic in only one of its three periods; that is, during the years of the Second Empire. In the last part of the reign of Louis Philippe he was 'ahead of his life'; after the fall of Napoleon III, he 'outlived himself'. (Barnes, 1981, p. 292)

Sartre describes the general situation picturesquely:

There are some lives which burn like nylon, and others like candles, still others like a piece of coal which is slowly extinguished beneath the ashes...The consequence is that the period can be completed in an individual well in advance of its reaching its end socially. For this reason, even short lives may be oracular; in them the age has chosen to reveal in reality its meaning and the circumstances of its future abolition. (*IF I*, pp. 442–3)

Thus Flaubert prefigured the demise of the Second Empire in that his 1844, and the bourgeoisie's 1848, both involved a plunge towards illusion: Flaubert's attack removed him from the world of *praxis* while the bourgeoisie abdicated in favour of a military aristocracy. It is important to note that Flaubert's life is not merely symbolic of his class in a literary sense, but rather is dialectically related. We cannot say that the crisis was 'like' that of the bourgeoisie in 1848, but that it *was* the crisis of 1848, as lived by an individual, and connected dialectically and diachronically with it in a very precise way.

Thus it is not enough to say that, 'Flaubert's literature...is a totally *representative* critical mirror of the class practices of the 1848–1871 bourgeoisie' (Scriven, 1984, p. 113; my emphasis). It actually *is* these class practices – and not just for the obvious reason that Flaubert is a member of that class, but because *Madame Bovary* is a singularised dialectical totalisation of an epoch. Similarly, to say that *Madame Bovary* 'distils' the 'alienation and neurosis of an entire generation' (p. 113) is to deprive the dialectical relationships between *Madame Bovary*, Flaubert, a class and an epoch, of their heuristic value. Totalisations are not distillations but (provisional) culminations. A distilled product is one in which not everything that was present at the beginning of the process is there at the end. The totalisation both preserves everything and contains something more – so *Madame Bovary* needs to be seen as a totalising incorporation in which nothing is left behind. If anything this is not a process of purification or evaporation (as in distillation), but of *sedimentation*.

Similarly it is not enough to say (with Christina Howells) that Sartre's 1844 neurosis '*reflects* and *symbolises*' the abortive 1848 revolution (1988, p. 177; my emphases), or that (with Joseph Halpern) the methodology of *The Idiot* requires a mere 'extension' from the case of Flaubert to the society in which he lived (1976, p. 150). Rather the neurosis is an anticipation and incarnation of the events of 1848, rigorously and dialectically related to them by bonds of internal necessity. And if it is objected that an event in the future cannot be related to an event in the past in this way, then the lessons of the *Critique* have not been learnt. For there, Sartre is explicit that 'the inert totality of worked matter' (*CDR I*, p. 122) can, for *praxis*, constitute, as demand or 'exigency', '*a future which cannot be transcended*' (p. 235). Thus, 'passivising *annulment* modifies it [*praxis*] from the future towards the past within the petrified framework of exigency' (p. 235). In other words in 1844, the bourgeoisie's 1848 was a future which was inscribed in the present in untranscendable fashion, and Flaubert's 1844 was demanded by that future.

This very tight, singular, and dialectical relationship between an individual or an individual event and his/her/its history is most clearly expressed in volume two of the *Critique*, as I explained in chapter 7. It is to our disadvantage that this text has been unavailable until recently because it is an invaluable guide to understanding volume three of *The Idiot* – and particularly the issue of Flaubert's relationship to his epoch.

In demonstrating this, Sartre hopes to have fulfilled his promise of describing the dialectical relationship between individuals and their epoch, and having done so he reverts to something approaching a straight biography. He describes how Flaubert was at his most contented during the years of the Second Empire, in that it reflected his views on the political world. His hatred for humanity had led him to believe that the vast majority of people was incapable of sharing power, and Napoleon III enacted the principles of that belief. During these years his life was entirely synchronic with that of his society. Then defeat at the hands of the Prussians in 1870 brought about the demise of the Empire, and Napoleon was deposed on the 4th of September. With the installation of the new republic, Flaubert found himself returned to the ranks of the bourgeoisie from which he thought he had escaped. Financial ruin followed, and his flight into illusion, as well as that of the Second Empire, was seen to have failed.

*The Family Idiot* has been called many things – a biography, a disguised autobiography, a novel, a work of philosophy, and a piece of literary criticism. Aronson, indeed, is at a loss to describe it, and is led to assert that, 'Sartre is self-consciously creating a new genre' (Aronson, 1974, p. 94). At the very least we are dealing with a *history* book, and since we are concerned with Sartre's theory of history, an assessment of the nature of *The Family Idiot* is essential. Our recurring theme has been that of method, and one of the most provocative elements of the method which was developed in the *Search for a Method* and utilised in *The Family Idiot* is that of comprehension. Christina Howells notes that this programme closely parallels the Lacanian psychoanalytic approach for the comprehension of an individual, in that the original neurosis is not *directly* identifiable, but that the life-style, memories and so on give a hint of it (Howells, 1979, p. 102).

In this connection Sartre was once asked why he had stopped writing novels and he replied:

Writing on Flaubert is enough for me by way of fiction – it might indeed be called a novel. Only I would like people to say it was a true novel. I try to achieve a certain level of comprehension of Flaubert by means of hypotheses. Thus I use fiction – guided and controlled, but nonetheless fiction – to explore why, let us say, Flaubert wrote one thing on March 15 and the exact opposite on March 21, to the same correspondent, without worrying about the contradiction. My hypotheses are in this sense a sort of invention of the character. (Sartre, 1974b, p. 49)

In a 1971 interview in which Sartre is perhaps at his most optimistic as to how far he has told the 'truth' of Flaubert, he again stresses the veracity behind his reconstruction:

I would like it to be read with the idea in mind that it is true, that it is a true novel. Throughout the book, Flaubert is presented the way I imagine him to have been, but since I used what I think were rigorous methods, this should also be Flaubert as he really is, as he really was. At each moment in this study, I had to use my imagination. (Sartre, 1978c, p. 112)

It is precisely this tension between using his imagination and telling us about Flaubert 'as he really was' through the use of 'rigorous methods' that has worried many commentators – an issue with which I shall be dealing in the last chapter. For now, we must note that Sartre evidently realised the confusion that this tension caused, and in 1976 he partially retracted the reference to the novel:

Perhaps I have exaggerated a little in calling it a novel. I didn't see it as such while I was writing it and the part played by the imagination ... is all the same stitched up by a truth which is there in the imaginary. (Sartre, 1976a, p. 97)

In the same interview, he also appears to have reassessed another goal in *The Family Idiot*. We remember that in 1971 he said he wanted to show that everything is communicable, and that every man is 'perfectly knowable', given the correct techniques and sufficient documentation (Sartre, 1978a, p. 123). These intentions led Sicard to ask how stable the assessment of a human being can be – are we not involved, rather, in an infinitely large task? Sartre replies:

At the level on which I work, no. The totality does not involve the infinite: the questions I ask are precise, they confirm each other precisely, and one is on the way to a totality which is not infinite. At the reader's level, one is indeed moving from question to question, towards the infinite. (p. 95)

So Sartre recognises that there may be a progression towards an infinitely large task, but that if one asks the right questions of the subject, then infinitude can be avoided. At this level, 'one can arrive at a totality', but it is different for the reader: 'There is an infinite number of possible questions about Flaubert; and I don't ask these questions. But a reader is led by reading to ask some of them and they constitute an order of questioning which leads towards the infinite' (p. 95). This humility is reflected in his belief, stated in the same interview, that the method in *Search for a Method* cannot, after all, tell the whole truth: 'A person is never reducible to the reflections of the *Question of Method*. I think that a personality is also a totality, but that the details and questions of detail are infinite in number' (p. 95).

I dwell on these two interviews because they admirably express Sartre's own ambivalence about just what he was trying to do in *The Family Idiot*. He is at odds with himself both about the extent of his goal and the methods used. Because the aim of the work becomes unclear, its success also becomes equivocal. In terms of his original desire to reconstitute a life, critics have varied as to the merits of the book. Hazel Barnes, for instance, thinks that it *does* succeed: 'My own experience has been that when I return to Flaubert either his literary work or his correspondence – I find everywhere new details to support Sartre and, perhaps more important, the feeling that they are intimate parts of a person I have come to know. For me, the biography is not a novel in the pejorative sense. Its truth is *le sens* of Flaubert' (Barnes, 1981, p. 413).

Aronson, on the other hand, finds himself crushed beneath a wall of words and surmise: 'All of that psychic information and speculation about Flaubert simply cannot be kept in any one mind long enough to form a coherent picture', and concludes that, 'It should not be read, and, except for Sartre's friends, a few Sartre or Flaubert scholars, or Ph.D. candidates in search of a new field to explore, it won't be' (Aronson, 1974, p. 101).

Certainly the pact of freedom between writer and reader – so central in
*What is Literature?* and apparently so abused in *Saint Genet* – seems again
to have been abandoned. The speculation of which Aronson complains is,
of course, necessitated by gaps in the documentation of Flaubert's life
which Sartre has to fill. As Sartre stresses, the speculation is not pulled out
of thin air, but is based on letters and observations by Flaubert's
contemporaries. He well realises that it is impossible to reconstruct an
individual from a single cell, as it were, and the extent of documentation is
one of the reasons why he chose Flaubert as his subject: 'he is one of the
very rare historical or literary personages who have left behind so much
information about themselves. There are no less than 13 volumes of
correspondence, each of 600 pages or so' (Sartre, 1974b, p. 44). This,
together with the testimonies of witnesses and remarks by his family,
contribute to a 'circumstantial' reason (but one 'of great importance')
why Flaubert is such a suitable subject to study.

Despite this voluminous evidence, though, there remain periods in
Flaubert's life where scant information is available. For instance, Sartre
spends several pages near the beginning of the work talking about the lack
of documentation on the first few years of Flaubert's life. In fact, this is true
of anyone of his epoch:

we don't *know* anyone we love among the dead of former times. Gide, yes – but that
was yesterday. The day before yesterday, there is nothing. The nursing, the
digestive and excretory functions of the infant, the earliest efforts at toilet training,
the relationships with the mother – about these fundamental givens, nothing... The
mothers accomplished their tasks sleepwalking; diligent, often loving, more from
habit than awareness. They have said nothing. (*IF I*, p. 41)

Sartre goes on to say that, 'This ignorance is fairly serious' (*IF I*, p. 45) in
Flaubert's case because, as we have already seen, his prehistory was more
important for the rest of his life than it is for most people. In view of this
'conspiracy of silence', says Sartre, 'a choice must be made to abandon the
search, or to glean clues from everything, examine documents from
another perspective, see them in another light and wrest from them another
kind of data'. Then, 'Of the two alternatives, I choose the second. I know
the harvest will be meagre' (p. 45). He says that, 'The truth of the
reconstruction cannot be proved', but that, 'If our reconstruction is not
rigorous, you can be sure that it will be instantly ridiculed', because, 'from
his thirteenth year, the cards were on the table; Gustave wrote books and
letters, he had permanent witnesses' (p. 46). In other words, Sartre intends
to measure his invention against the corroborating evidence of Flaubert's
contemporary witnesses, thereby conferring a status of truth on that
evidence as well as his own invention.

This technique – although it may be the only one open to him – is questionable on three counts. To begin with, there is no reason to assume that contemporary accounts are at all accurate. Certainly, to measure a mother's reflections against her son's youthful writings and call it proof is dubious at best: 'We have proof: Flaubert's adolescent writings entirely corroborate his mother's memories, they allow us to catch a glimpse of the early experience as it was lived from within' (*IF I*, p. 29). A little later, Sartre himself outlines the problem with this approach:

His correspondence and his rare autobiographical attempts must be consulted with circumspection – if he is telling the truth, he does not know it; what is not said and what is missing are much more revealing than the public confessions or the private confidences. (p. 167)

The second problem is that on a number of occasions there is simply no documentation to which to refer. To pick an instance at random, there is the episode of *Le Garçon*, which is vital to Sartre's analysis of Flaubert making himself what others have made of him. In a letter dated 24 March 1837, Flaubert announces that he has taken on the role of *Le Garçon*, but how this came about we cannot tell because there is an 18-month gap in correspondence previous to the March letter. Thus the date of the character's appearance can only be determined 'very approximately by re-reading the previous letters' (*IF II*, p. 1214). In view of this, one is led to wonder how many other 'approximations' there are in *The Family Idiot*.

On the face of it, this is not a particularly trenchant criticism, but in the context of Sartre's claim to have written a 'true novel', to have shown Flaubert 'as he really was', and to have demonstrated that 'everything is perfectly knowable', the question of approximations derived from dubious evidence becomes rather more crucial. It must be said also that these criticisms may seem gratuitous in the face of the vast edifice of documentation, interpretation, and verification that Sartre provides in *The Idiot*. Measured against the text, this chapter cannot hope to convey the richness and depth provided by his exhaustive use of the progressive–regressive method.

The third criticism concerning corroborating various sources of evidence gets to the heart of Sartre's progressive–regressive method. Besides checking the evidence of one of Flaubert's contemporaries against another, Sartre also plays off his present lived experience against his future – indeed, this is the essence of the progressive moment of the investigation. He writes that, 'it is a methodological principle to begin the enquiry at the ultimate stage of the experience being studied', and that this amounts to, 'a systematic interpretation of the present in the light of the achieved future' (*IF I*, p. 174). Evidently, there is a danger in this technique of looking back from the 'achieved future' and interpreting the present in such a manner as to 'fit in' with that future. Inevitably, there will be accusations of Sartre leaning towards coherence rather than correspondence truth – not the kind of certainty normally associated with biographies. This, rather, is what Michael Scriven correctly refers to as 'a form of internal and circular self-verification' (1984, p. 107).

In sum, we see Sartre prevaricating – both in *The Family Idiot* and in his remarks about it. On the one hand, he claims to want to explain everything about Flaubert. Moreover, he claims that he has the method to do it, and that he has succeeded. On the other hand, he says that he can only provide explanations within carefully conceived guidelines, that his method is not entirely secure, and that other interpretations of Flaubert are possible. In the final chapter I shall discuss the reasons for this prevarication.

# 14    Conclusion

The universe lay spread at my feet and each thing was humbly begging for a name, and giving it one was both like creating it and taking it. Without this fundamental illusion, I should never have written.

(Sartre, 1964b, p. 43)

I have argued that Sartre's political trajectory brought him into contact with Marxism, and thereby with a complex theory of history. I have suggested that the progressive refinement of that theory of history is best regarded as a political project, carried out at the service of Marxism, as are the biographies that Sartre wrote as a result of it. Both the biographies and the more general theory of history, then, are intended to persuade us of Marxism's continuing relevance to an understanding of the historical process and the part that individuals play in it. The conflicting demands of this project produce a tension, with Sartre torn between claiming that, as a historian, he is able to 'communicate everything', and also that he is involved in a 'perfectly hopeless attempt ... to master everything' (Sartre, 1974d, p. 19).

Sartre was an aggressive thinker who pushed the techniques he developed to their very limits. Consequently his work brings dilemmas of this sort into the kind of relief not achieved by more timid minds. What we witness in this case is the desire for total communication encountering its predictable – but continually postponed – impossibility. In this sense Sartre provides us with a particularly dramatic exhibition of the tension between the speculative philosopher of history, seeking a description of the grand sweep of forces that make human history, and the historian, struggling to marshal scanty and resistant evidence into some sort of order. The former tends towards totalising confidence, while the latter deals in resignation. I want to conclude this book by saying something about how Sartre's work contributes to this debate, particularly in respect of the issue of the truth status of the historical account, and then to refer to its political implications. In the process I shall take the opportunity to place Sartre in respect of recent trends in French intellectual life.

In standard terms, Sartre's claims 'to communicate everything' and to have an untranscendable historical method at his disposal seem extremely ill-advised. Philosophers of history never tire of pointing out the problems associated with the first type of claim; that the uncertainties of memory, testimony, and evidence will always cast doubt on the veracity of histories; that objectivity is unattainable; and that the historian will always select facts for interpretation. At the same time it has been pointed out *ad nauseam* that history has not finished anyway, and that no fully truthful account will even in principle be possible until it has. This criticism calls into question Sartre's second claim to have a fully worked-out and watertight method at his disposal. As Christina Howells rightly points out: 'the reflexivity of knowledge implied by the totalizing dialectic must make a finished "totality" theoretically as well as practically impossible – knowledge of the totality will always intervene to modify that totality' (Howells, 1988, p. 111).

Yet Sartre believes that at least two of the conditions for 'communicating everything' are in place: a unitary history rather than several unrelated histories, and an unsurpassable method for writing it. As far as the issue of a unitary history is concerned, and beyond the remarks made about this in chapter 4 (pp. 65–6), Sartre asks himself: 'under what conditions is consciousness of a single history possible?', and Raymond Aron notes that this concern with a single history involves, 'not just the consciousness of any kind of history, not just the consciousness of a fragment of the human past, but of a *single* History or, in other words, of the unity of History' (Aron, 1973, p. 3). Sartre felt that the *Critique* takes us to 'the threshold of history' (*CDR I*, p. 87), and it is there that he is clearest about the existence of History as opposed to histories. At one point in the first volume, Sartre is discussing the role of intellection in the study of history:

critical investigation will reveal actions without an agent, productions without a producer, totalisations without a totaliser, counter-finalities and eternal circularities ... In such cases, and in many others which will turn up in due course, either the Truth of History *is not unified*, or totalising intellection must be possible. Vagabond and authorless, these free actions ... must be totalisable, cannot remain foreign bodies within developing History; consequently, they must be intelligible. (*CDR I*, p. 76)

Here Sartre explicitly rejects the possibility of 'foreign bodies', for 'foreign bodies' would threaten the notion of a 'single History', and intellection must be shown to be able to appropriate them into that history. At the same time, the expressive use of capital letters for the 'Truth of History' comprises circumstantial evidence for the far-reaching nature of Sartre's aims and aspirations. In similar vein he claims that 'we are not trying to reconstruct the real history of the human race; we are trying to establish the *Truth of History*' (*CDR I*, p. 51); and he makes clear the reason for capitalisation when he overtly distinguishes between the 'Truth of History' and 'several truths':

If there is to be any such thing as the Truth of History (rather than *several* truths, even if they are organised into a system), our investigation must show that the kind of dialectical intelligibility which we have described above also applies to the process of human history as a whole, or, in other words, that there is a totalising temporalisation of a practical multiplicity and that it is intelligible, even though this totalisation does not involve a grand totaliser. (p. 64)

Quite apart from the use of capital letters, this quotation is crucial. In it, Sartre explicitly comes out against the notion of 'several truths' in favour of one 'Truth'; and he also claims that his method – the 'dialectical method' which provides for History's intelligibility – is singular and unsurpassable in that it 'applies to the process of human history as a whole'. Indeed the dialectical unity of history is simultaneously revealed by the method and makes the method possible and unsurpassable.

Adding all these remarks to the ones made in chapters 4 and 7 concerning the implications of the dialectic for the nature of history, it is clear that Sartre believes history to be unified (in a special dialectical sense) rather than fragmented. The further contention that Sartre reckoned himself to be in possession of a method that can tell the Truth of History is underscored by his reference to historical materialism (as method) as 'the only truth of history'. However, he says that this has been, 'contaminated by the historical relativism which it has always opposed, it has not exhibited the truth of History as it defines itself' (*CDR I*, p. 19). This denial of relativism is reiterated elsewhere when Sartre writes that Marxism, 'as dialectic must reject the relativism of the positivists. And it must be understood that relativism rejects not only vast historical syntheses, but also the most modest assertions of Dialectical Reason (*CDR I*, p. 23). Here Sartre castigates relativism for not allowing for syntheses – and it is not just *any* synthesis that Sartre is recommending, but a synthesis which is the dialectical unity of history with all its bonds of interiority. We remember from the *Flaubert* that a world without access to dialectical reason is unhappy indeed, founded on 'failure', 'useless sacrifice', 'alienation from work', 'incommunicability', and 'the hatred of self' (Sartre, *IF III*, p. 297).

In these senses, Sartre's work amounts to a full-scale exhibition of two kinds of history-writing: that which *discovers* the past and that which *constructs* it according to methodological rules. In the first case research is driven by the accumulation of 'facts', and in the second, by the deployment of method. Of course 'discoverers' employ methods and 'constructionists' cannot do without facts, but greater or lesser importance is attached to method or fact in either case.

If, as I suggest, Sartre's biographies are viewed as an integral contribution to his developing theory of history, and if, as I also suggest, his development of a theory of history is all of a piece with his demonstrating the truth of Marxism, then his biographies bear a considerable burden. On their success depends (at least partly) the success of his campaign on behalf of Marxist method. But how is one to measure the success of a biography? A reasonable criterion (and one to which Sartre himself subscribes) would be to see how far the biographer had captured the 'truth' of the subject, and I have suggested in chapters 10, 11 and 13 that Sartre's claims to have told the truth of his subjects are vitiated by the deployment of methods that depend for their success on the 'disappearance' of the subject, and by the use of imaginative reconstructions that sometimes fall foul of subsequent evidence.

Arguably, though, such a view confuses the two forms of history-writing outlined above, and confounds the different criteria for truth at work in them. For discoverers, the standard criteria for truth-telling are those I mentioned earlier: degree of objectivity, status of evidence, and so on. For constructionists, arguably, greater attention should be paid to the adequacy of the methodological rules than to the facts deployed. Now, if we accept this distinction, and if we characterise Sartre as a constructionist rather than a discoverer, is it fair to apply discoverer-type tests to his history-writing?

This is a tempting proposition, not least because it responds to the complexity of this aspect of the philosophy of history. Indeed, I have taken account of this complexity by discussing at some length (in chapters 4 and 12), Sartre's treatment of the dialectic and the method he derives from it. However, I do not think he can be absolved so easily from submitting to the truth-tests usually applied to fact-gathering and interpretative historical writing – and this for four reasons.

First, while we might argue in Sartre's case that truth has more to do with the truth of his speculative system than with the histories derived from it, there is still a sense in which, if the system is right, then so should the descriptions generated by it be right. In other words, his system is not only about the process of history, but also about how to write history, and in the second sense his explanations must be able to be checked against criteria for verification. It must be stressed that this is particularly important for Sartre, because the success of his biographies is bound up with his demonstrating the superiority of his historical method and, thereby, of Marxism itself.

Second, I have already pointed out that the distinction between 'discovery' and 'construction' is hazy. Even the most committed constructionist will produce historical examples which can, and ought to, be subjected to standard scrutiny. Third, Sartre himself is a cardinal example of the haziness of such a distinction. It would be hard to deny his constructionist credentials given the self-conscious way in which he develops and then deploys a historical method. But at the same time his history-writing, and particularly his biographical studies, are replete with the type of historical evidence (letters, documents) usually associated with studies not ostensibly driven by a particular methodology.

Fourth, and most important, Sartre himself claims not only to have generated an unsurpassable method for constructing history, but also to have discovered the truth of his biographical subjects. In this sense Sartre's biographies are very traditional. As I have remarked on several occasions, he sought to tell the truth of Baudelaire, Genet, and Flaubert, and the intention was for their lives to emerge fully fledged from the deployment of method. In his own words he neatly encapsulates his own bridging of the gap between construction and discovery, and the subsequent simultaneous reliance on both method and documentation: 'every human being is perfectly capable of being understood if the appropriate methods are used and the necessary documents are available' (Sartre, 1978c, p. 123).

Sartre, then, is both a discoverer *and* a constructionist, and the success of his project must be judged by criteria appropriate to each. As a discoverer he depends on facts, and as a constructionist he relies on method, and the differing demands of these approaches pull him in conflicting directions. When he is in the throes of exemplifying the method derived from Marx and Hegel he believes that there is a Truth to be told, against other more humble (and, in his later life, clearly subordinate) inclinations. In a sense, the method is tyrannous. Sartre allows it to dominate to the point where his claim to tell the Truth of History is simultaneously based on, and vitiated by, the deployment of the method itself. His method leaves him, on occasion, fulfilling the function of the arrogant artificer, rather than that of the humble historian. This project reaches its apogee with his monumental biography of Flaubert and its tendency towards an attempt at total communication – a project in stark contrast, for instance, to Roland Barthes' technique of the 'deconstructed biography': 'Purged of the "one grand principle', deconstructed biography is innocent of power, taking pleasure in its unwisdom and its refusal to conclude or in any other way to radiate an assurance of mastery' (Collins, 1980, p. 23).

Nothing could be further from Sartre's later intentions than this, and the entire burden of his theory of history makes attempts to link Sartre to various themes in postmodern philosophy hard to sustain for long. In my view he stands firmly opposed to the post-structuralist tendencies that were emerging as he entered the final phases of his productive life. In this sense his work is instructive of the deep divisions that were emerging within French intellectualism from the mid-1970s onwards, and it is misleading to try to demonstrate a continuity between Sartre and later post-structuralists. For one thing post-structuralism is bound up with post-Marxism, and we have seen Sartre profess the belief that Marxism is fundamentally unsurpassable: he is firmly located within the Marxist canon, and he expressly felt it impossible to occupy a position beyond it. Nevertheless Christina Howells has made an ingenious attempt to draw parallels between Sartrean and post-structuralist thought, and by way of a conclusion I would like to address her views in some detail.

The themes to which she refers are: 'The decentred subject, the "death of man", the paradoxes of *qui perd gagne* [loser wins] and of "difference", the rejection of Hegelian dialectics and the recognition of the impossibility of ultimate synthesis' (Howells, 1988, p. 194). Without addressing all of these, enough can be said to show that it is going too far to refer to Sartre as 'a precursor and indeed a founder of certain [i.e. those enumerated above] contemporary philosophical tenets' (p. 194; my parenthesis).

As far as the 'death of man' is concerned, Howells refers twice to Sartre's aphorism in the *Critique* that 'Man does not exist' (pp. 113 and 194; her translation) as evidence for her point of view. But the passage from which this quotation is selected (a passage that Howells herself goes on to quote in full) runs as follows: 'it must be understood that there is no such thing as man; there are people, wholly defined by their society and by the historical movement which carries them along' (*CDR I*, p. 36). Howells argues that Sartre anticipates 'Foucault and the Structuralists' with this remark (Howells, 1988, p. 113), and it is true that Sartre once remarked that, 'I am not at all hostile to structuralism as long as structuralists remain clear as to the limits of their method' (Sartre, 1990, p. 88). But here Sartre's point is not to oppose 'man' to structures, but to oppose some hyper-organism called 'man' to billions of individual 'men'. Sartre glosses the previous passage with another that makes this clear: 'if we do not wish the dialectic to become a divine law again, a metaphysical fate, it must proceed *from individuals* and not from some kind of supra-individual ensemble' (*CDR I*, p. 36).

The point of Sartre's 'there is no such thing as man', then, is not to stress structures, but to dramatise his own methodological individualism. For the same reason, Sartre's heroic attempt to show how the dialectic is 'woven out of millions of individual actions' (p. 36) is distorted and made trivial by attempts to rescue him from bourgeois individualism. He does not need rescuing. Stronger still: it is precisely his individualism that marks him off from 'crude Marxists', and founds the specificity that he was so keen to reintroduce to Marxism. Depriving him of his methodological individualism amounts to depriving him of his political project.

Next, while it may be true that Sartre recognises 'the impossibility of an ultimate synthesis' (Howells, 1988, p. 194) – although, as I have shown, he appears not always to believe himself – this is not enough to call him a precursor of postmodern concerns. While it might be postmodern to refuse to entertain ultimate syntheses because knowing changes the known (and this is Sartre's position), he also believes that totalising praxis is subject to an intelligibility that is singular and beyond appeal, and this is certainly not a postmodern position. Furthermore, it is clearly his plan strategically to work on the assumption that apparently plural syntheses are reducible to a single grand totalisation-without-a-totaliser. No postmodern writer would make that strategic assumption – Sartre is as far from 'gazing in wonderment at the diversity of discursive species' (Lyotard, 1984, p. 26) as Lyotard is from underwriting the notion of 'universal consensus' (p. 65).

Sartre is the purveyor both of one of the major versions of the narrative of legitimation to which Lyotard refers and to which he is opposed: 'humanity as the hero of liberty' (p. 31), and of the vehicle, Marxism, which wavers between this version and the 'hero of knowledge' version (pp. 31 and 36–7). Sartre felt both that humanity was the author of its own history, and that Marxism gave it its best chance of taking control of the historical process. To the extent that Sartre's project can be summed up in the following way, it amounts in fact to about as explicit a combination of Lyotard's two legitimating narratives as is possible: 'At its most immediate level, dialectical investigation (*l'expérience dialectique*) has emerged as *praxis* elucidating itself in order to control its own development' (*CDR I*, p. 220). Of course it would be invidious to take Lyotard as representative of postmodern concerns, and the differences between various types of postmodernism have themselves been amply catalogued (see, for example, Boyne and Rattansi, 1990, pp. 25–36). Nevertheless it is significant that Sartre can be so firmly located in opposition to Lyotard, and this should at least give us pause for thought in the face of claims for Sartre's anticipating postmodern or post-structuralist themes.

Finally, Howells sees in Sartre a Derridean gloss on the '*qui perd gagne*', or loser wins, principle. The inauthentic version of this principle (best represented by the Hegelian dialectic) has it that every apparent failure is really 'success in another dimension, i.e. in the future or on a different level of attainment' (Howells, 1988, p. 199). According to Howells, both Sartre and Derrida agree that this is unsustainable. She writes that Sartre's version 'sees the possibility of failure as proof of the freedom of human consciousness from the deterministic process' (p. 199). In other words, losers win because their freedom is affirmed by failure.

Sartre's position can indeed be read as one in which failure breeds success in that the experience of failure is a condition for reaching historical understanding, but I do not want to pursue the point here. Nor is that Sartre's critique of Hegel's dialectic cannot be seen in Derridean terms, but rather that 'loser wins' is itself an incomplete and stylised version of Sartre's position. In the first place, as I pointed out in chapter 7, in the context of the dialectic the whole notion of 'failure' is problematised (cf. p. 108). Second, *qui gagne perd* (winner loses) or even *qui perd perd* (loser loses) are better characterisations than *qui perd gagne* of the overwhelming bulk of Sartre's political anthropology. From the woman in the Dop shampoo factory carrying out the sentence of abortion passed by the dialectic, to the Chinese peasants flooded out of their homes by deforestation, to the Russian peasantry forced to collectivise by the exigencies of the Revolution, losers lose more often than they win in Sartre's universe. Even when losers do win, the trophy simply guarantees them further trouble: 'In so far as, having achieved our own goal, we understand that we have actually done *something else* and why our action has been altered outside us, we get our first dialectical experience of necessity' (*CDR I*, p. 222). The two senses of 'own goal' are neatly instructive.

Sartre cannot realistically be viewed as anticipating postmodern themes. He is better described as inhabiting the Marxist branch of a bifurcated modernity – opposing capitalist pluralist solutions to the redemption of modernity's promise. If I have presented him as pessimistic as to the fulfilling of that promise, this is not because he is opposed to modernity's strategies and assumptions, but because his theses on alienation make rational control of our circumstance (an abiding modern theme) seem unlikely. But, while he may be pessimistic in this respect, he is full of the 'totalising confidence' that we can take as a mark of the modern consciousness. As Sartre himself writes, 'the scientist must adopt, in every case and at every level, a totalising attitude towards his subject matter' (p. 16). This is his animus, and it is not postmodern.

So, despite his exhortations to 'let this life develop before our eyes' (*IF I*, p. 29), and to let the truth 'emerge' without privileging any moment of it, it seems clear that Sartre's truth emerges within well-defined limits – i.e. those dictated by the progressive–regressive method derived from dialectical reason. The result is a monumental system embracing the Truth of History, compromising the freedom granted to the individual by the existentialist project. The irony is clear. Sartre was led to the theories of Marx and Hegel by his desire for useful action in the radical stream of French politics. He saw in 'crude Marxism' an unsatisfactory method – 'Its sole purpose is to force the events, the persons or the acts considered into prefabricated moulds' (Sartre, 1968, p. 37) – and he sought to humanise it. But these words could constitute the postscript to his own biographies of Baudelaire, Genet, and Flaubert. He began with a theory of the human condition based on choice and free action – both crucial ingredients of any purposive political project. Then the desire to fulfil a progressive and leftist political project led him to an encounter with Marxism. But Marxism provided him with a theory of history whose deployment in the context of writing history compromised the themes that had led him to it in the first place. Sartre's great achievement lies in underwriting, for good or ill, the human origin of the whole of the historical universe, but his project of creating a humanist Marxism was ultimately compromised by dialectical necessity. Always remembering, of course, that, 'What I have just written is false. True. Neither true nor false, like all that is written about madmen or about men' (Sartre, 1964b, p. 48).

# Bibliography

PRIMARY SOURCES

Sartre, Jean-Paul (1943), *L'être et le néant: essai d'ontologie phénomenologique* (Paris: Gallimard).

(1944), 'A more precise characterisation of existentialism', from *Action*, 17 December; translated in Contat and Rybalka (1974) II (page references are to this translation).

(1946), *Materialism and Revolution* (translated in A. Michelson, 1968; page references are to this translation).

(1948), *Psychology of the Imagination* (New York: Philosophical Library).

(1949a), David Rousset and Gérard Rosenthal, *Entretiens sur la Politique* (Paris: Gallimard).

(1949b), *Situations III* (Paris: Gallimard).

(1950), 'Faux savants ou faux lièvres?', preface to Louis Dalmas, *Le communisme yougoslavie depuis la rupture avec Moscou* (Paris).

(1955), *Situations I* and *III*. Selections translated as *Literary and Philosophical Essays* (London: Hutchinson).

(1957), 'Jean-Paul Sartre on his autobiography', an interview with Olivier Todd, *The Listener*, 6 June.

(1962), *Sketch for a Theory of the Emotions* (London: Methuen).

(1963), *Saint Genet: Actor and Martyr* (London: W. H. Allen).

(1964a), *Baudelaire* (London: Hamish Hamilton).

(1964b), *Words* (London: Hamish Hamilton).

(1965a), *Anti-Semite and Jew* (New York: Schocken).

(1965b), *Situations* (London: Hamish Hamilton). First published as *Situations IV* (Paris: Gallimard, 1964).

(1966), *Nausea* (Harmondsworth: Penguin).

(1968), *Search for a Method* (New York: Vintage).

(1969a), *The Communists and Peace* (London: Hamish Hamilton).

(1969b), *The Spectre of Stalin* (London: Hamish Hamilton).

(1971), *L'Idiot de la famille*, I and II (*IF I* and *II*) (Paris: Gallimard).

(1972a), *L'Idiot de la famille*, III (*IF III*) (Paris: Gallimard).

(1972b), 'Justice and the state', in Sartre, 1978b.

(1974a), *Between Existentialism and Marxism* (London: New Left Books). Selections from *Situations VIII* and *IX* (Paris: Gallimard, 1972).

(1974b), 'The itinerary of a thought', in *Between Existentialism and Marxism*.

(1974c), 'Kierkegaard: the singular universal', in *Between Existentialism and Marxism*.

(1974d), 'The purposes of writing', in *Between Existentialism and Marxism*.

(1976a), 'Sartre parle de Flaubert', *Magazine Littéraire*, November. An interview with Michel Sicard.

(1976b), 'Socialism in one country', *New Left Review*, 100, November.

(1977), *Being and Nothingness* (London: Methuen).

(1978a), *Critique of Dialectical Reason Volume 1: Theory of Practical Ensembles* (CDR I) (London: New Left Books).

(1978b), *Sartre in the Seventies* (London: André Deutsch). First published as *Situations X* (Paris: Gallimard, 1976).

(1978c), 'On the *Idiot of the Family*', in *Sartre in the Seventies*.

(1978d), 'Self-portrait at seventy' in *Sartre in the Seventies*.

(1978e), *What is Literature?* (London: Methuen).

(1978f), 'Justice and the state', in *Sartre in the Seventies*.

(1980a), *Existentialism and Humanism* (London: Methuen).

(1980b), *Sartre by Himself* (New York: Urizen).

(1981), *The Family Idiot* (Chicago: University of Chicago Press). Translation by Carol Cosman of first part of volume one of *L'Idiot de la famille*.

(1983), *Cahiers pour une morale* (Paris: Gallimard).

(1984), *War Diaries: Notebooks from a Phoney War, November 1939–March 1940* (London: Verso).

(1985a), *Critique de la raison dialectique, tome II (inachevé): l'intelligibilité de l'histoire* (Paris: Gallimard).

(1985b) with J-B Pontalis, '*Freud*' *Scenario* (London: Verso).

(1990), 'Jean-Paul Sartre répond', in Cordier.

(1991), *Critique of Dialectical Reason Volume 2 (unfinished): The Intelligibility of History* (*CDR II*) (London: Verso).

SECONDARY SOURCES

Archard, David (1980), *Existentialism and Marxism* (Belfast: Blackfast Press).

Aron, Raymond (1973), *History and the Dialectic of Violence* (Oxford: Blackwell).

Aronson, Ronald (1974), 'The ultimate Sartre?', *Telos*, 20, Summer.

(1980), *Jean-Paul Sartre – Philosophy in the World* (Verso: London).

(1987), *Sartre's Second Critique* (Chicago and London: University of Chicago Press).

(1990), 'Sartre sur Staline', in Geneviève Idt (ed.), *Etudes Sartriennes* (Paris: Université de Paris X).

Atkinson, Ronald (1978), *Knowledge and Explanation in History* (London: Macmillan).

Barnes, Hazel (1974), *Sartre* (London: Quartet Books).

(1981), *Sartre and Flaubert* (Chicago and London: University of Chicago Press).

Beauvoir, Simone de (1965), *Prime of Life* (London: Penguin).

(1978), *Force of Circumstance* (London: Penguin).

(1981), *La cérémonie des adieux* (Paris, Gallimard).

(1985), *Adieux: a Farewell to Sartre* (London: Penguin).

Blakeley, Thomas (1968), 'Sartre's *Critique of Dialectical Reason* and the opacity of Marxism–Leninism', *Studies in Soviet Thought*, 8.

Boyne, Roy and Rattansi, Ali (eds) (1990), *Postmodernism and Society* (London: Macmillan).

Catalano, Joseph S. (1974), *A Commentary on Jean-Paul Sartre's 'Being and Nothingness'* (New York and London: Harper and Row).

    (1986), *A Commentary on Jean-Paul Sartre's Critique of Dialectical Reason, Volume 1, a Theory of Practical Ensembles* (Chicago and London: The University of Chicago Press).

Caute, David (1964), *Communism and the French Intellectuals* (London: André Deutsch).

Caws, Peter (1979), *Sartre* (London: Routledge and Kegan Paul).

Charlesworth, Max (1975), *The Existentialists and Jean-Paul Sartre* (London: George Prior).

Chiodi, Pietro (1978), *Sartre and Marxism* (Brighton: Harvester).

Coe, Richard (1968), *The Vision of Jean Genet* (London: Peter Owen).

Cohen, Mitchell (1988), 'Looking at Sartre: engaged life, ambiguous afterlife', *Dissent*, 35, Summer.

Cohen-Solal, Annie (1987), *Sartre: a life* (London: Heinemann).

Collins, Douglas (1980), *Sartre as Biographer* (Harvard: Harvard University Press).

Contat, Michel and Rybalka, Michel (1974), *The Writings of Jean-Paul Sartre, Volumes 1 and 2* (Evanston: Northwestern University Press).

Cooper, David (1964), 'Sartre on Genet', *New Left Review*, May–June.

    (1965), 'Two types of rationality', *New Left Review* January–February.

Cordier, Stephane (1990), *Jean-Paul Sartre* (Paris: Libraire Duponchelle).

Desan, Wilfrid (1974), *The Marxism of Jean-Paul Sartre* (Massachussetts: Peter Smith).

Dray, William H. (1964), *Philosophy of History* (Englewood Cliffs: Prentice-Hall).

Fauvet, Jacques and Duhamel, Alain (1977), *Histoire du Parti Communiste Française* (Paris: Fayard).

Flynn, T. (1986), *Sartre and Marxist Existentialism* (Chicago: University of Chicago Press).

Garaudy, Roger (1970), *Marxism in the Twentieth Century* (London: Collins).

Gardiner, Patrick (ed.) (1959), *Theories of History* (The Free Press of Glencoe).

Gerassi, John (1989), *Jean-Paul Sartre – Hated Conscience of his Century* I (Chicago: Chicago University Press).

Halpern, Joseph (1976), *Critical Fictions: the Literary Criticism of Jean-Paul Sartre* (New Haven and London: Yale University Press).

Hayman, Ronald (1986), *Writing Against: a Biography of Sartre* (London: Weidenfeld and Nicholson).

Hodard, P. (1979), *Sartre entre Marx et Freud* (Paris).

Hook, Sidney (1949), 'Reflections on the Jewish question', *Partisan Review*, 16, May.

Howells, Christina (1979), *Sartre's Theory of Literature* (London: Modern Humanities Research Association).

    (1988), *Sartre: the Necessity of Freedom* (Cambridge: Cambridge University Press).

Hyppolite, Jean (1971), 'La Phénomenologie de Hegel et la pensée française contemporaine', in *Figures de la pensée philosophique* (Paris: Presses Universitaires de France).

Idt, Geneviève (ed.) (1990), *Etudes Sartriennes* (Paris: Université de Paris X).

Jameson, Fredric (1971), *Marxism and Form* (Princeton: Princeton University Press).

(ed.) (1985), *Sartre after Sartre* (Yale: Yale University Press).

Kaelin, E. F. (1965), 'Three stages on Sartre's way', in G. L. Kline (ed.), *European Philosophy Today* (Chicago: Quadrangle Books).

Kanapa, Jean (1952), 'Sartre, the communists and peace', *Masses and Mainstream*, 5, December.

Kerner, George (1990), *Three Philosophical Moralists: Mill, Kant and Sartre* (Oxford: Oxford University Press).

LaCapra, Dominic (1978), *A Preface to Sartre* (New York).

Laing, Ronald and Cooper, David (1971), *Reason and Violence* (Norwich: Tavistock).

Lecarme, J. (1973), *Les critiques de notre temps et Sartre* (Paris).

Lévi-Strauss, Claude (1972), *The Savage Mind* (London: Wiedenfeld and Nicholson).

Lichtheim, George (1963), 'Sartre, Marxism and history', *History and Theory*, 3, 2.

(1966), *Marxism in Modern France* (New York and London: Columbia University Press).

Littlejohn, D. (1970), 'Sartre's Genet', *Interruptions* (New York: Grossman).

Lukács, Georg (1961), *Existentialisme ou Marxisme* (Paris: Nagel).

Lyotard, Jean-François (1984), *The Postmodern Condition: A Report on Knowledge* (Manchester: Manchester University Press).

Manser, Antony (1966), *Sartre, A Philosophic Study* (Connecticut: Greenwood Press).

(1971), 'Praxis and dialectic in Sartre's *Critique*', in Mary Warnock (ed.), *Sartre – A Collection of Critical Essays* (New York: Doubleday Anchor).

Marcuse, Herbert (1948), 'Existentialism: remarks on Jean-Paul Sartre's *L'Etre et le néant*', *Philosophy and Phenomenological Research*, 8, 3.

McBride, William (1989), 'The case of Sartre', *Social Research*, 56, Winter.

Mészáros, István (1979), *The Works of Sartre, Volume 1* (Brighton: Harvester Press).

Michelson, A. (1968), *Literary and Philosophical Essays* (London: Hutchinson).

Munford, Clarence (1968), 'Sartrean existentialism and the philosophy of history', *Journal of World History* 11, 3.

Nizan, Paul (1968), *Aden-Arabie* (New York: Monthly Review Press).

Poster, Mark (1975), *Existential Marxism in Postwar France* (New Jersey: Princeton University Press).

(1979). *Sartre's Marxism* (London: Pluto Press).

Rabil Jr., Albert (1967), *Merleau-Ponty: Existentialist of the Social World* (New York and London: Columbia University Press).

Rossanda, Rossana (1975), 'Sartre's political practice', in R. Miliband and J. Seville (eds.), *Socialist Register* (London: Merlin Press).

Savage, Catherine (1989), *Malraux, Sartre and Aragon as Political Novelists* (Florida: University of Florida Press).

Schrader, George (1959), 'Existential psychoanalysis and metaphysics', *Review of Metaphysics* 13.

Scriven, Michael (1984), *Sartre's Existential Biographies* (London and Basingstoke: Macmillan).

Sontag, Susan (1967), *Against Interpretation and Other Essays* (London: Eyre and Spottiswoode).

Stack, George (1971), Sartre's dialectic of social relations', *Philosophy and Phenomenological Research*, 30, 3, March.

Stern, Alfred (1968), *Sartre* (London: Vision Press).

Thompson, Kenneth and Margaret (1985), *Sartre: His Life and Works* (New York and Bicester: Facts on File).

Trotsky, Leon (1975), *My Life: An Attempt at an Autobiography* (Harmondsworth: Penguin).

Turnell, Martin (1948), 'Mr. Sartre's Baudelaire', *Changing World*, 1, 4, May–July.

Verstraeten, Pierre (1990), 'Y a-t-il une morale dans "Critique de la Raison Dialectique"?' in Geneviève Idt (ed.), *Etudes Sartriennes* (Paris: Université de Paris X).

Warnock, Mary (1965), *The Philosophy of Sartre* (London: Hutchinson).

(ed.) (1971), *Sartre – A Collection of Critical Essays* (New York: Doubleday Anchor).

Zévaès, Alexandre (1947), *De l'introduction du Marxisme en France* (Paris).

# Index